Welcome into the life of
Philip Despard Pemberton Holmes, universally known as Pip.

Pemberton Holmes Ltd. had been founded by his great-grandfather and grandfather and, as its fourth president for more than forty years, Pip immersed himself in family, business and community commitments.

While world president of the International Real Estate Federation, usually known by its original acronym FIABCI, he intensified his travels in dozens of its member countries to encourage essential training and education, protection of the right to hold title to property and, above all, the need to be guardians of the land.

Designing your life and living by what you believe is admirable, but as this memoir outlines it, Pip Holmes designed and lived his life with high energy, intelligence, ample wealth, a great partner, considerable style and a strong sense of fun.

Order this book online at www.trafford.com/07-1629
or email orders@trafford.com

Most Trafford titles are also available at major online book retailers.

Note for Librarians: A cataloguing record for this book is available from Library
and Archives Canada at www.collectionscanada.ca/amicus/index-e.html

Printed in Victoria, BC, Canada.

ISBN: 978-1-4251-4006-9

*We at Trafford believe that it is the responsibility of us all, as both individuals and corporations,
to make choices that are environmentally and socially sound. You, in turn, are supporting this
responsible conduct each time you purchase a Trafford book, or make use of our publishing services.
To find out how you are helping, please visit www.trafford.com/responsiblepublishing.html*

*Our mission is to efficiently provide the world's finest, most comprehensive book publishing
service, enabling every author to experience success. To find out how to publish your book, your
way, and have it available worldwide, visit us online at www.trafford.com/10510*

 www.trafford.com

North America & international
toll-free: 1 888 232 4444 (USA & Canada)
phone: 250 383 6864 ♦ fax: 250 383 6804 ♦ email: info@trafford.com

The United Kingdom & Europe
phone: +44 (0)1865 722 113 ♦ local rate: 0845 230 9601
facsimile: +44 (0)1865 722 868 ♦ email: info.uk@trafford.com

10 9 8 7 6 5 4

Pip

The Story of
PHILIP DESPARD PEMBERTON HOLMES

CAMILLA TURNER

Pip dedicated his story
to his children
Diana, Susan, Jennifer and Craig

and all his family

and extended family

CHAPTER SUMMARIES

A NOTE TO READERS   13

CHAPTER ONE: CANADIAN BY BIRTH   15
Pip decides to tell his life story. Being actively Canadian. Father's background. Vancouver Island connection. Swellendam to Windlesham. Rocklands. Cuthbert's start. Versailles. Pemberton & Son-in-law. Mother's background. Men of the HBC. Rushden Hall. Mountjoy Square. J.D. and the Isthmus. Island colony's legislators. Gonzales. Brothers and sisters.

CHAPTER TWO: BOY IN MOTION   23
A life-long affliction. Becoming self-propelled. Caleb Pike homestead. Holmes Hill and Squally Reach. Town life. Mother returns. Solarium. Grandfather Pem. Mountjoy's gardens. With Goggy to Vernon. First job. Douglas Lake Cattle Company. Joe Coutlee. St. Christopher School. BBs from the attic. Horses to the summer house. Finnerty Bay farm.

CHAPTER THREE: THE COWICHAN VALLEY   33

Pemberlea at Cowichan Station. Clydesdales and Ayreshires. Tickling trout. Mixed farming. Barn cats. Harnessing and threshing. Learning from the seasons. Crash of '29. Major Holmes at Pemberton's. A time for practical measures. Brentwood College School. Cowichan River flats. Rocky's end. The Lake.

CHAPTER FOUR: BRITISH COLUMBIA BY BIKE   43

Two-wheels mobile. By bike to Lake Cowichan, Parksville, Comox, Alberni. The forest fires after Elk Falls. M.V. *Uchuck*. Long Beach. Visiting Dr. Lovekin. Canada declares war. Biking to Douglas Lake Ranch. The Silk Train. Merritt mosquitoes. Steveston ferry. By Packard to Kingston. Des at RMC. Victoria College at Craigdarroch. That motorcycle.

CHAPTER FIVE: HORIZONS LEVEL   55

Recruits. BCATP. Manning Depot. Fort Macleod. New moustaches. No. 4 ITS. A dinner at the MacDonald. High River. Tiger Moths. Currie Barracks. Streetcar stove. LACs and NCOs. Nav and night flights. Wings won. Nav over water.

CHAPTER SIX: CANADIANS OVERSEAS   65

Not New York. RMS *Queen Elizabeth*. Quarantine flag. The Guinness nurse. Last from the Loch. Real Nawton. Leaflets over Rennes. Diversionary decoys. Don McKay. Wombleton on the dales. Canadians in Bomber Command. Gaggles and gardening. Briefings. Pinky. Turning twenty-one. Meeting the Me262s. Atomic bombs. Telegram: the DFC.

CHAPTER SEVEN: DESIGNING A LIFE   79

Club debut. Air Force officers. Road trip U.S.A. The company's sixtieth. Circular driving routes. BCS fire. Government Street address. Mortgage training. Seen as a vocation. Designing his life. Tugs for the Air Force. To serve the Crown in Canada. Welcoming the princess. FIABCI emerges. Paternal blessings.

CHAPTER EIGHT: INDUSTRY RESTRUCTURED   93

Real estate licensing essential. Industry under scrutiny. Herbert Fullerton. The Norris report. McPhee and McKenzie at UBC. Tom Cantell and B.C.'s legislation. Real Estate Council. Dermot Murphy. Institute of Real Estate Agents. Funding it all. Philip White. Exploring Vancouver Island. Sophie gone. Brentwood reopens. UBC open house. Catherine into his life.

CHAPTER NINE: PROGRESS ON ALL FRONTS 107

Cuthbert to Pip. Head of CAREB. Electronic future. Finding FIABCI. Training and licence law. Land as an asset to be guarded. Joining FIABCI Canada. Family celebrates a fiftieth. Commemorating Cuthbert with parkland. Deciding to go international. Victoria Chamber of Commerce. Bikeathon. Victorian Days community festival. B.C. Chamber of Commerce. Asia Pacific Real Estate Federation. Honorary citizenship. His Council of the Western Isles.

CHAPTER TEN: BLUEPRINTS AND GREENPRINTS 123

Chambers of the Island. Blueprints or greenprints? Australia on New Towns. Good progress with training. Michael Page. Monitoring APREF. New name is CREA. The FIABCI Medal of Honour. That dinner in Madrid. John Tysen predicts. A pace of tremendous rapidity. How to invigorate an economy. Status report on 1975. Core work of the congresses.

CHAPTER ELEVEN: TOP OF THE WORLD 133

FIABCI's world president. Responses to his election. Communications base for training and education. Alert on Zambia. Booking a world workload. Listening to real estate realities. Through Israel with Blumberg. Irish Auctioneers and Valuers. Artisanship. *Financial Post* profile. Canberra speech: local-level liaison, community-based world voice. Professional Exchange Program. Victoria office carries on. Itinerary through South America.

CHAPTER TWELVE: FIABCI AND THE ASIA PACIFIC 145

Chicago telex. San Francisco World Congress. Enter laughing. Serious resolution. Chapter presidents sign on. The Habitat conference and after. By ferry and car through B.C. Diplomacy in New Zealand. FIABCI and APREF on the move. Moustachio'd in Japan. Tokyo koi. Korean monks and new-found friends. Thai coup. Houston to Brussels and on.

CHAPTER THIRTEEN: FOR THE HUMAN SETTLEMENT 159

Order of St. Lazarus. Second of February. Battle of the Oak Bay Pumping Station. Relaxing and breezing in Finland. Herring in Sweden. Amsterdam '77 and new starts. Truths and techniques for the human settlement. Perspectives and actions. An honour for Ciputra. Research for ideas. "A great experience."

CHAPTER FOURTEEN: CYCLES OF CIVILIZATION 173

Impact of energy considerations on human settlements. Christopher Alexander. Sukhum Thirawat. Elephants in the teak forests. World Scene Division and communications reach. Of oil and computers. BCREA after Habitat. The civilization cycle: conception to oblivion. Homegrown B.C. ideals. Hamburg IBMs and the Alster. Stockholm and the uses of land. Aide-de-camp once again. Conference centre airings. Jakarta housing.

CHAPTER FIFTEEN: PHILOSOPHY CONSOLIDATED 185

Global Housing Foundation. Summing up the vocation for Tokyo '79. Governments, property owners, agricultural lands. To plan and project. To improve the profession. Energies and decompression. Provincial Capital Commission projects. FIABCI's documentation conduit. Cold Christmas in Crete. University of Victoria's governors. Real Estate Amendment Act.

CHAPTER SIXTEEN: RECESSION VERSUS DREAMLAND 195

Recession pinches the province. Chairing Toronto. The Commissionaires. South Pender picnic hike. Indonesia's new middle class. Building Dreamland. A visit to Borobudur. Refusing the buyouts. Three local offices. Praise after long tenure.

CHAPTER SEVENTEEN: HEART OF THE DRAGON 205

Medical warnings. Workload redesign. Rome without stress. Forty years at the company. "Judgement is born of experience." Taiwan's dynamism. Heart of the Dragon speech. Time with the cadets. Recovering from a stroke.

CHAPTER EIGHTEEN: THIS PACIFIC ISLAND 215

Company centenary. A legacy of greenspace. Pip on cable and in print. Hundred-year goals. Vancouver Island another Switzerland. Speeches and the Hon. Grace. Boaties and the Bardol B. His heart. Starting the succession. Plan for the Island. Government House Foundation. Pip's sixty-fifth. One day in Vienna. Transitions and continuations.

CHAPTER NINETEEN: NEW SPACES FROM OLD 227

Fundraising finesse for the Royal. From Kenya to South Africa. In and above Montreux. Chairing the plenary session: real estate and world security. Moving house. Gordie Esdon. Awards and a treasure. RCAF's St. Clement Danes. Yorkshire revisited.

CHAPTER TWENTY: ASIA, AFRICA, EUROPE, HOME   239

Bombay carpet shop. Dinner in Phuket. Bareboat heat. CJVI advisory board. Ashton Armoury and its museum. Tanda Tula and Londolozi. The Welsh and the Zulus. Dumbleton reunion. Rorke's Drift dinner. Governor General Adrienne Clarkson and John Ralston Saul. Photographing polar bears. Summer sessions at the Legislature. Pemberton Memorial Chapel at RJH. Honouring Dr. Inazo Nitobe. Lord Lister and the Pemberton Operating Room.

CHAPTER TWENTY-ONE: DUTY AND AFFECTION   251

Big dog in Bermuda. On the way to Konya. Dinner delivers a tribute surprise. Of regattas and Carrs. The Pip Holmes Bursary Trust. Levée duty 2007. Affectionate visits. Christ Church Cathedral. "Much more that is unknown."

CHAPTER TWENTY-TWO: FOR LOVE OF THE FUTURE   263

Book of condolences. Letters arrive. Catherine. Into the future: Pip's photo album.

NOTES TO THE TEXT   273

IDENTIFICATIONS AND CORRECTIONS   299

ON THE COVER   299

A NOTE TO READERS

MANY PEOPLE KNOW one aspect or another of Pip's life, but few know the whole sequence or how many aspects there were in all. This book is meant to do what he himself intended: to tell his family, friends, colleagues and others about his life.

This is not a formal biography but a report from one person's personal and business memorabilia of what was aimed for and what was accomplished. Pip's voluminous files of speeches, research notes, letters and clippings shaped the chronological structure. His letters and speeches are often directly quoted but, when paraphrased, have been kept as true as possible to his turn of phrase. He wrote quite a number of short retrospective essays in his later years, and the views expressed and events highlighted in those have been incorporated. The plaques, medals, framed award certificates and labelled photographs that marked Pip's successes provided me with dates and names I couldn't find elsewhere. The text was drafted from a wide variety of materials provided for the project, all of it set out on long trestle tables upstairs in the Holmes house, and I did further research of my own. To within a few days of his death, Pip provided additional perspectives and details.

A number of people had talked with Pip at various times about his life story, including Joyce Haller, who taped and transcribed hours of his boyhood memories, and John Eggenberger, who urged his friend Pip to work on a memoir and wrote and talked with him with an emphasis on wartime RCAF adventures. William Rodney, retired from Royal Roads Military College, contributed additional notes on the sequence of aircrew training, and Buzz Bourdon of Ottawa also read the two wartime chapters when considering an article on Pip. Colin McCullough went through the whole manuscript from his long-time vantage point as newspaper publisher in Victoria, and Michael Page did the same, clarifying a number of points pertaining to Pemberton Holmes Ltd. Dermot Murphy, long-time friend and colleague of Pip's, aligned for me the complex early sequences in British Columbia real estate legislation, training and education. Catherine Holmes, with her precise memory and volumes of photo albums from their shared lives at the ready, was a welcoming and affectionate resource person all the way through.

Nic Hume and Gary Webster each contributed their photographs as a professional and personal tribute to Pip, and Adrian Raeside's mischievous cartoon of Pip in heaven, done for Catherine, is also included here as a donation with his best wishes.

I'll dedicate my part in this project to my father, because he taught his children a most valuable perspective—a pilot's-eye view of earth and sky—and wrote his own life story for us to know him by, both of which are wonderful gifts for a father to give.

Camilla Turner
15 December 2007

CHAPTER ONE
CANADIAN BY BIRTH

"MY LIFE SPANNED some significant events, and I would like my family to know my story," Pip wrote as he made a start on his autobiography. "I realized with regret I had absolutely nothing that had been written about the childhood memories and early life of my mother, father or grandparents. One can always learn about the achievements that have been publicly recorded, especially in these days of computers, but their personal recollections can be learned only from their own written words. Each generation has a different upbringing, with some more religious, some more affluent, some more relaxed, and so on, and only in later life can one look back on childhood, youth and early mature life with perspective and in a rational way. Now at that stage, I've decided to write my story for my family."

Pip very much wanted to tell his story to his children, but his health declined before he could do it. He had kept files and made many notes about events in his life, however, and had analyzed various sequences of events in retrospect. His account didn't dwell on his first two marriages, both of which, as he put it, started happily but ended unhappily. He said that his third marriage, to Catherine, was completely happy and utterly compatible. "Working as a team," he wrote, "we proved to be true soul-mates who worked hard, met many challenges and were rewarded with great fun and excitement."

That he was adamantly, actively Canadian by heritage, legacy, vocation and effort was central to what he was made of, and he knew and loved the land. "We are always talking about what a Canadian is," he said, "but it's not complicated. We are all from different backgrounds, different cultures, different nationalities, and we come together in our commitment to Canada."

The spirit and experience of forebears can sometimes affect individual lives deeply, and since heritage was important to Pip and he knew his own so well, a brief retelling of his family background can give context to his story and insight into how he decided to live his life.

His father's story emerged from two Anglo-Irish families in the Old World and the New, including some notables in the lineage. Among them, for instance, was Admiral Sir Charles Holmes, the admiral who before the Battle of the Plains of Abraham in 1759, led a flotilla of naval boats up the St. Lawrence River carrying troops for British commander General James Wolfe.

Another notable was Admiral Sir Robert Holmes, who at one point captured New Amsterdam and, in honour of the Duke of York, renamed it New York. Arriving back in London expecting praise, he was instead punished for initiating a state of war before war had been officially declared and was flung, though briefly, into the Tower. Sir Robert later commandeered a Dutch galleon off the coast of New Guinea and shipped the gold in its cargo back to England, where it was minted into certain coins first made for the Africa trade. Worth twenty-one old shillings, the coin became known as the guinea.

The admiral retired to the Isle of Wight as its governor, where his statue depicts him in a French uniform. It seems he captured a ship that was carrying an unfinished statue of a certain French admiral, all but the head, because the work was due to be completed only after the subject sat again for the sculptor in the studio. Sir Robert claimed it from the captured ship, promptly had his own image added and placed the finished statute in a Yarmouth church.

Pip's father's mother, whose family name was Norris, was much superior to Sir Robert in her behaviours and bloodline. Her grandfather had owned a large estate named Hughenden Manor in High Wycombe,[1] Buckinghamshire, which was later bought by Benjamin Disraeli as a country residence during Queen Victoria's reign. When Pip and Catherine went to visit the property, which had by then been owned for many years by the National Trust and opened to the public, they found to their chagrin that the place was awash in references to the memory of the British Prime Minister and that all the Norris history had been relegated to a small room at the back of the chapel.

The line of connection to Vancouver Island is through John Norris's eldest daughter Ellen, who married wealthy landowner Henry Dumbleton of Thornhill Park, Hampshire. He had spent some years in South Africa, where he bought a huge tract of land for farming and built a house. Ellen never did go to South Africa while he was hunting big game and acquiring land but stayed in England, where she eventually inherited Hughenden. At that point, Henry Dumbleton sold the farm in Africa to his younger brother Bertram and headed back to England, settling down with Ellen in Hughenden Manor. Bertram built a large colonial-style home on the South African land he'd bought and named it Oakhurst Farm. A number of his descendents are still living there.

Ellen and Henry Dumbleton's eldest son, referred to in the family as Henry the Second, also went to South Africa to visit his uncle and, while there, fell in love and married a young Spanish woman, Clara Marion Garcia. They stayed for a while in South Africa, living in Swellendam, but in due course returned to England.[2] When the young Dumbleton pair realized the Windlesham winters at Hall Grove were making Clara ill, they acted on the recommendation that for her health, they should move to Vancouver Island.

They built a house on Belcher Street in Victoria they named Rocklands and settled in to raise their family.[3] Their youngest daughter, Clara Eveline, later travelled to India to visit her sister Alice Beatrice, who was married to Maj. Halford Dumeresque Gerrard, an officer in the Indian Army. While Clara Eveline was in India, she met a young fellow—William Cuthbert Holmes—who'd read law at Trinity College, Dublin, and had become a judge in the Indian Civil Service. They married and had three sons and a daughter.

Clara Eveline's father Henry Dumbleton needed someone he trusted to help him with monetary matters, mainly because his sons were being spendthrift with the family fortunes. He asked his daughter's husband William Cuthbert to take early retirement and move his young family from India to Vancouver Island to help him with the finances, which he did soon after.

The eldest son of William Cuthbert and Clara Eveline, Henry Cuthbert Holmes, had been born in India in 1890 and educated in France, Switzerland and Germany.[4] Moving to Victoria as a boy with his parents, he continued his early schooling, attended the second year of Victoria College, which was then part of McGill University, and went on to Balliol College, Oxford. By the time he was grown, he was fluent in Hindi, French, German and English. He read law and later was called to the Inner Temple, becoming a barrister. He never did carry on to practise law, because the First World War broke out and he was commissioned in the cavalry, joining the Irish Guards.

Wounded in France, he was sent home to Victoria and, while recuperating, became reacquainted with Philippa Despard Pemberton, second daughter of Mary Ann and Frederick Bernard Pemberton. Cuthbert proposed, and before his return to the Irish Guards in France, he and Philippa married on 12 October 1917. Being entirely comfortable in the subtleties of French and German and well suited to the assignment, he was appointed Secretary to the Peace Commission and spent two years working in Versailles.

He joined his father-in-law's Victoria real estate company on 2 May 1920, and he and Philippa and their children became part of the community. In 1933, Cuthbert Holmes became third president of Pemberton & Son, and in 1943, the company name was changed to Pemberton, Holmes Ltd.[5]

———————

Pip's mother's side of the family is rooted in Western Canadian and Hudson's Bay Company history, since a number of his mother's forebears were from Scotland and were HBC explorers, traders and factors. Her mother was descended from Peter Warren Dease, surveyor of Canada's northwest and Arctic coastlines and Chief Factor for the HBC—"of a strong robust habit of body, possessing such firmness of mind joined to a great sauvity of manners"—whose real life reads like a boy's adventure story.[6] He learned the land by experiencing it, travelling all over it. Within British Columbia, a lake, a river, a mountain, a town and three reserves have been named after him.[7] To his great-great-great grandson Pip, he was an inspiring combination of skilled explorer and senior company leader.

Peter Warren Dease and his wife Elizabeth Chouinard were married for forty years, and it was a strong and affectionate bond. Elizabeth, who was Métis, taught him much and found him the best possible guides and translators for his exploration trips. Their daughter Nancy married HBC chief trader and explorer John Bell, who had been transferred to the company's Mackenzie River District in 1824.[8] One of Nancy and John's sons, Peter Warren Bell,[9] became an HBC chief factor like his grandfather and married Ellen Sarah Dupont, daughter of an aristocratic French family from Montreal, and it was their daughter, Mary Ann Ahern Bell, who married Frederick Bernard Pemberton, dear grandfather to Pip.

The Pembertons were originally from the midlands region of England, and one of the old family homes, Rushden Hall, still stands in Northamptonshire. They were in mining, hence the three black buckets in their coat of arms, and John Pemberton was equerry to Queen Elizabeth I for thirty years. In Rushden Church, the effigies of John and Mary Pemberton and their eight children ("for her fower daughters, for me fower boyes") have been restored to proud state. It isn't clear when or why these Pembertons moved to Ireland, but the political situation was likely a factor during the period they left England.

Rushden Hall remained in private hands until the 1930s but during the Great Depression was sold for tax reasons. The county's city council bought it and still use it for their offices. Its elegant reception rooms have been restored fully and are rented out for events such as weddings and corporate functions. The grounds around the hall, well-tended and with massive old trees, are open for people to walk in and enjoy.

Pip's mother's great-grandfather was Lord Mayor of Dublin and had his house in Mountjoy Square. It was her grandfather, the Lord Mayor's son Joseph Despard Pemberton, who arrived in the Colony of Vancouver Island from Ireland in 1851. A professor of mathematics and engineering, he designed three railroads in Britain and travelled through the Suez Canal to witness what was considered a marvel of new engineering design. He'd just won third prize for the design of the Crystal Palace in London.

The year he was thirty, J.D. walked across the Isthmus of Panama to see for himself where the best route might be for a Caribbean-to-Pacific railway, and for his troubles, contracted yellow fever. To speed his recovery, he took to swimming around the hull of the ship that would later carry him northward to San Francisco and to Astoria on the Columbia River.

His destination was Vancouver Island, so he was obliged to walk north from Astoria to a point near present-day Bellingham, Washington, where he arranged with an Indian paddler to cross the straits through the islands by canoe. He was dropped off at Cattle Point a distance east of Fort Victoria and walked the rest of the way to the gates of the fort.

As first HBC surveyor-general on the island and one of the legislators for the colony, J.D. Pemberton was involved in decisions about the engineering and location of the first naval lighthouses on the coast, Fisgard Light[10] and Race Rocks, and he explored and mapped widely on Vancouver Island and the mainland. Keeping the usual journals and professional records, he found an alternate route to the 1858 Gold Rush region and was commemorated in the naming of Pemberton, B.C.

He served in the first Legislative Assembly of the island colony and pushed for Victoria to become the capital when the island colony and mainland colony joined in 1866.[11] Thriving in Victoria, he asked his childhood sweetheart Theresa Jane Grautoff in London to marry him and built for her the gardens and mansion they named Gonzales.

Theresa Jane and J.D. Pemberton's eldest son was Frederick Bernard Pemberton.[12] F.B. took his degree in engineering at Trinity College, Dublin, and in 1887 went into business in Victoria with his father under the company name Pemberton & Son, Engineering and Surveying. He married Mary Ann Ahern Bell, and their second daughter Philippa Despard Pemberton married Henry Cuthbert Holmes.

Philippa and Cuthbert Holmes had two daughters and three sons: Cicely, Desmond, Philip, Elizabeth and Vincent. Their middle child, second son, born 2 February 1924, was Philip Despard Pemberton Holmes, universally known as Pip.

J.D. Pemberton was a member of the colonial legislature of Vancouver Island (top). Back, l-r: J.W. McKay, J.D. Pemberton, The Clerk (Joseph Porter). Front, l-r: T.J. Skinner, Dr. J.S. Helmcken, James Yates.
PHOTO CREDIT: CITY OF VICTORIA
ARCHIVES, CVA#PR252-7160

Gonzales (right) replaced a simpler farmhouse on the 1,200 acres.

Mrs. J.D. Pemberton (Theresa Jane Pemberton) photographed in her rose arbour (bottom).

F.B.'s 1913 Cadillac could manage the Malahat road for Cowichan Valley visits (top).

Frederick Bernard Pemberton (far left), often referred to as F.B. and called Grandfather Pem by Pip, was never without a boutonnière, often a rose, in his lapel.

F.B.'s sister Sophie Pemberton (left) in the sun at Priory Walk.

Between F.B.'s 1930 Chrysler and Cuthbert's Model A Ford (bottom), a brief rest.

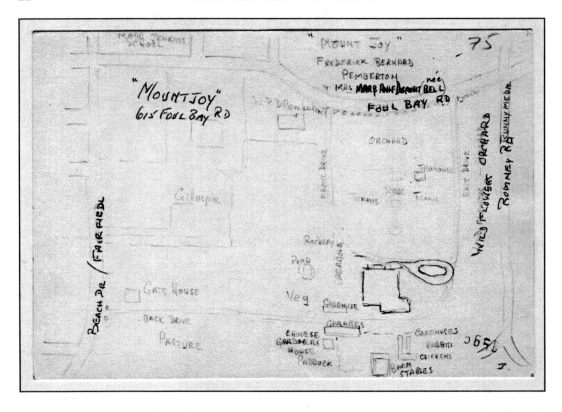

Map sketched on the back of the photo of the house (top). "Grandfather Pem had been given twelve acres of land…by his father, and he named his house Mountjoy after the Dublin city square."

Mountjoy on Foul Bay Road (right), where F.B. Pemberton and Mary Ann Dupont Pemberton lived, was a place a boy could explore season after season. It provided ponds, orchards, a playhouse, animals, household and garden staff, family, friends, books, sports, and a variety of very fine cars.

Rose garden between the tennis courts (bottom), Some Garry oak meadows were undisturbed.

CHAPTER TWO
BOY IN MOTION

A PART OF Pip's life story rarely mentioned is his asthma, troublesome especially as a boy. "Coping with this affliction may have influenced whatever I did," he said. "My parents were certainly concerned and supportive but seemed to know that for me to live a full life, I'd have to learn to live with the asthma and just get on with it." Even after months at a treatment centre when he was seven, his parents didn't forbid him to do things that might bring on the attacks. He learned to judge for himself.

Medical treatment for asthma recommended by medical authorities of the day centred around enforced inactivity. The general thinking was that the onset of attacks correlated with activity, but in Pip's case, this wasn't so. He continued to be highly active and, without apparent medical repercussions, took pleasure in activities deliberately involving great exertion.

Recalling that time, he said: "It seems to me I knew very early I could do all the things anybody else could do—and to my mind, sometimes better." This knowledge was a comfort to him, and he never let on about his asthma or used it to deflect responsibility—or amusement, or adventure.

One of his earliest recollections was of a little red wagon, "a real beauty, a marvel." He'd been given it when he was four and pulled it, pushed it, put stuff in it and sat in it. Eventually realizing he could seldom recruit anyone to pull him around in it, he crossed the magic threshold into being self-propelled. Newport hill ran down beside 336 Newport, and he clambered up and launched from the top. "I can still remember viscerally the first sensations of speed, excitement and not a little old-fashioned fear," he said. "I couldn't stop or slow the wagon, and I knew I was in an adventure more than a little over my head."

Between swerves and sporadic take-offs, the front wheels developed high-speed wobbles and over he went face first into a gravel pathway, badly scraping his cheek and cutting through his upper lip with his teeth. His mother cleaned up the cuts and alternately soothed and chastised him for "intemperate behaviour." He healed well and never forgot the rush of that wild ride in the speedwagon.

"When I look at the picture of me and my sister standing on a log when we were about four or five," Pip said, "I'm struck by the look of supreme confidence thrusting out of the picture. The world was my oyster, and I was *launched*."

A real treat for the children was to head out for the annual Easter picnic where Grandfather Holmes lived, northwest of the city in the Millstream Highlands. They considered Caleb Pike homestead to be absolutely perfect in its natural state and the yearly jaunt "exactly the way picnics are supposed to be." They loved it.

From their point of view, nature pure and unspoiled involved extended games of hide and seek, tag, foot races and other energetic pursuits. For small boys, it also involved new explorations and much adventure, which mattered greatly. They crawled under logs or other shelters for refuge from the rain and discussed at length how ants knew about picnics. Talking was considered important entertainment. "The adults' discussions were always of interest to me," Pip said, "and I often sat and listened. It's not that I always grasped what their conversations were about, but I liked listening."

An annual ritual involved climbing to the hilltop, as they called Holmes Hill.[13] Like nearby Lone Tree Hill, it was wild, rocky and almost barren of trees. They loved that spot, and the grassy slope near its summit was a great place to play a game somewhat akin to baseball. The great chase after the ball, when it headed over the ledge, was a major part of the game.

A strenuous hike would get them to the top of a cliff overlooking Finlayson Arm and Squally Reach, where they could visit the shaft of the old copper mine and roll boulders down the long slope to the water below. "How our parents permitted these explorations seems a little cavalier nowadays, but that was the tenor of the times," Pip said. "We were given great latitude and were expected to behave responsibly and ethically. And we did."

Town life was instructive in a different way. Gonzales was the home Pip's great-grandfather J.D. Pemberton built for his family in 1886 at the corner of Rockland and St. Charles.[14] The California redwoods J.D. planted in the 1880s, knowing they would carry on for centuries, were perfect shelters for family children even by the 1930s. "It was at Gonzales I started to understand that my family was influential in the life of Victoria," said Pip, "and I knew this incurred an associated family responsibility to the city."

His mother had fallen ill after her youngest son Vincent was born and was unable to look after her whole flock when they were all together in the household. When it became clear she needed to travel to England for specialized treatment, Cuthbert had no choice but to parcel out his children to the care of other members of the family. It was decided that Pip should move with his father and elder brother Desmond to live with Grandfather Holmes at 11 Cook Street.

One of the household chores assigned to him during the six months he was there was to tend to the mountain sheep. This did not entail shepherding. It was a matter of cleaning and mothproofing the hunting trophies that were taken down from the walls each year to preserve them and keep them looking presentable.

His asthma became troublesome enough that doctors decided he must go to the Solarium Hospital for Sick Children for treatment, and Pip remembered his father taking him to Mill Bay and having to leave him there at the Solarium. It was a very unhappy circumstance that left them both in tears, he said, but their many visits together were upbeat: "His love and support for me were obvious, and I have been and always will be truly grateful. Mum was often in our conversations and our thoughts, and I knew that just because she was away in body didn't mean she was away in spirit."

His mother was in England for about a year and a half and was still very weak when she returned. Careful not to leave the impression that having his mother fall ill, being under treatment himself or moving from one part of the family to another was considered hardship, Pip said: "I don't recall these times as being tough at all, other than missing my mother when she was away. Life was one great big adventure, and having to pack up and go elsewhere to live wasn't a problem. This was the way things were, and I was happy within it."

A tricycle appeared on the scene unexpectedly: "I think it was given to me because I made a fuss about being in the Solarium for so long. The trike might have been a bribe to settle me down." Once back at 11 Cook Street again, he started heading out on long jaunts "all by myself" along the Dallas Road paths edging the sea cliffs. He found great satisfaction in being among family again, able to resume his usual vigorous activity and breathe the clean wind off the Strait of Juan de Fuca. He loved watching the tides ebb and flow and the clouds making patterns on the mountains along the far shore, and he particularly loved chatting with the people he met along the way.

About a month after Pip returned from his stay in the solarium, his Grandfather Holmes passed away, so he was moved again to live with his Pemberton grandparents. Grandfather Pem had been given twelve acres of land at Foul Bay Road and Gonzales Road by his father, and he named his house Mountjoy after the Dublin city square. With business picking up all through the 1920s, the company continued to thrive satisfactorily under its second president,[15] though F.B. was noticeably less interested in real estate than in horticulture.

F.B.'s was a big household, a happy one, and Pip was pretty much free to do as he pleased. He still wasn't far from the ocean, but whenever possible, he padded around after his grandfather. A botanist and keen horticulturalist, Grandfather Pem was a rich source of new information for the lad who was always tagging along.

"He knew the Latin name for every flower, tree and shrub," Pip said, "and many other things. F.B. and an American horticultural entrepreneur crossed something with something else and got a better grapefruit. They did the same with cantaloupes and then other crops. Grandfather Pem never threw away an old shaving brush, because he used them like this—*fttt, fttt*—to do the cross-pollination." F.B. was also justifiably proud of his understanding of landforms. As his grandson said: "He knew his land."[16]

The gardens that F.B. designed at Mountjoy were known across the continent. Five Chinese gardeners, whose accommodations were built on the grounds, were kept busy maintaining a flourishing conservatory off the drawing room, five greenhouses, a vegetable garden, a large fruit orchard, a classic Italian garden with benches and sculptures, a Japanese garden with treasured rocks and shallow pools, two tennis courts flanking elaborate rose gardens, and at the foot of the long lawns, a tea house. When F.B. opened the gardens on the sports days of certain private junior schools, tea and fruit drinks were served from the tea house.

Apart from playhouses specifically for the children, the whole property became an extraordinary place for them to explore. A stream much frequented by ducks cut across the main track between Gonzales and Mountjoy and ran westward through the property on its way to the Inner Harbour. Leading off from the kitchens was an endlessly busy laundry, and Pip was drawn to the repair shed and to the big tool shop—"always a big fascination for me." Grandfather Pem was very handy with his hands, Pip said, and taught his grandson as much as he could absorb.

Children in the family were always assigned chores to do. One of Pip's was to lift the young squabs off their nests, fending off the flapping of the mother pigeons, and put them into fattening pens. "I must admit they were delicious roasted," he said, "best atop a piece of toast." Mountjoy's rabbit pen was fenced in with wire netting sunk four feet into the ground so the rabbits couldn't dig themselves out and escape. Pip, scrutinizing the situation, noted that whenever the gate opened, the buck rabbits would give the others a take-cover warning signal with a thump-thump kick of their hind legs.

There were chickens in chicken houses to tend to, plus three cows, plus the riding horses in the barns and pasture. The carriage house became the garage for Grandfather Pem's first car—"a chain-drive, one-cylinder, crank-start De Dion-Bouton, an open two-seater that never went up hills without a push."[17] Grandfather Pem loved cars.

The first summer he was living at Mountjoy, Pip left Vancouver Island for the first time to go travelling with his grandmother to the B.C. interior. Grandmother Pemberton, always called "Goggy," decided to visit her sister Jessie Ricardo at the Coldstream Ranch near Vernon. Jessie and her husband managed the ranch, which ran a small herd of cattle and produced prodigious amounts of apples, according to Pip. He was allowed to help by feeding the chickens, which was familiar work, and packing apples, which was new. "A blissful interlude," he said.

The interlude was short-lived, though, cut off by an epidemic of chicken pox in Vernon. Goggy was nervous that Pip might catch it and therefore took him and herself out of harm's reach to the sixty-room Sicamous Hotel on Shushwap Lake. "It was one of those lovely large old CPR hotels," Pip said, "and this one was built on pilings out into the lake." Near there was where he landed his first paid job.

One of the ways train drivers got their instructions, and this is familiar to many Canadians, was by grabbing a pouch containing a message from the station master, an accurate grab made more feasible by connecting the pouch to a large metal hoop hung at reachable distance beside the tracks. When the train slowed but was still moving at a good clip, the trainman caught the ring, removed the pouch and threw the ring back out along the tracks farther along. Pip's job was to run out to fetch the hoops back for the station master, and this earned him fifteen cents a day. "I was ecstatic!"

Goggy and Pip decamped from the hotel not long after and made their way to Douglas Lake Ranch near Merritt. The largest cattle ranch in Canada, it spreads over half a million acres of dry rolling hills and bunch grass[18]. That Nicola Valley ranch owned by friends of Pip's grandparents, who until 1886 had owned a share of it, was full of wonders for a little boy. "It opened up a whole new world," he said.

It was also full of potential harm. "One particular occasion highlights itself in my memory," Pip said, "and that's the afternoon I walked down to the little lake to watch the cowboys coming back after a day's work. They came riding in to the edge of the lake and slid out of the saddles just as the horses stepped into the water to drink. The day was perfectly still, like a painting, then one whinnied. All of a sudden, a number of horses that were still half-wild burst out of their corral and headed toward the others at the lake at full gallop." Pip was walking directly in their path.

"Head cowboy Joe Coutlee knew instantly there was a stampede in the making and a boy in danger," Pip said. "A powerful man, 'Roaring Joe' was still in the saddle, and he wheeled around and grabbed me up by the collar of my shirt as he swept by me. At full speed, he headed straight toward a manure wagon a bit away from the fracas and flung me on top of the smelly pile. 'STAY THERE, KID!' he bellowed back over his shoulder, and I did."

Pip had attended grades one and two at St. Christopher School at Currie and Newport, Miss Ashworth presiding, and for grades three to six, he went on to Monterey School. The brick building built in 1914 on Monterey Avenue "was about a ten-minute walk from the ocean," and other than that, he said, he doesn't have many recollections about elementary school. His life was less bounded by school than by family, friends and his endless explorations.

He got used to riding his scooter everywhere, preferably over as much distance as possible. He'd stop by Moulton Combe, his Aunt Susie's home on Newport Avenue, to see if he could "snaffle up a cookie or two" from the Chinese cook Wong, "who was very easy to deal with, but my aunt not so easy." Only later did bicycles become his main means of transportation, and his distances then expanded exponentially.

After he was given a BB gun on his tenth birthday, one of his diversions became target practice. The Daisy BB gun was one of the first on the market, but Pip didn't remember any particular name brand. He did remember posting himself at his bedroom window high up in Mountjoy's attic and taking a good many potshots at the sundial in the garden. What gave him away and ended the sharpshooting from the sky was the "nice little pinging sound" when the pellet hit the sundial's metal base.

The crows in a park near Newport were next best after sundials, but they had disadvantages. They were speedy on the wing, and they fought back. The very best enemies to play with, though not shoot at, were pals who were good at storming through thick brush and trails on the rough terrain the boys called Blueberry Hill. The whole area was owned by Dr. Jones, who lived there in his old stone house, but after his death, his daughter Ruth found the taxes onerous and donated several acres of it to the city for a park. The rest was developed as residential, but the boys were long gone by then.

Another diversion, which was technically a chore, was to ride the horses from Mountjoy to Finnerty Bay.[19] It was an annual event to move the horses from the house in town to Grandfather Pem's summer house about seven or eight miles northward, where they were stabled and ridden during the summer. The route the youngsters followed started along Foul Bay Road. Running north-south, it was still a country road, since no houses had been built on the east side of it. They then trotted up Cadboro Bay Road until they reached the summer house.

Two or three horses always had to be moved—"two quite spirited ones and a very calm work horse"—by riding each of them bareback to the destination and then walking back to get another one. Pip could usually manage to do two horses in a day, which the household considered pretty good going.

The horses apparently discussed in a language of their own a method of ridding themselves of riders. This allowed them time for grazing. About three-quarters of the way to the farm, the road went through Garry oak meadows in an area of grassy uplands, and the oaks' lowest branches could scrape off anyone who wasn't paying attention or didn't know the game. "I'd catch the reins and climb back on and carry on well enough," said Pip, "until they got huffy and scraped me off again." Same route, same routine, no matter which horse. He was convinced the horses discussed it in the barns.

The Finnerty Bay property was where F.B. had planted forty acres of commercial holly, an enterprise he brought to Vancouver Island to encourage its cultivation, since almost everywhere else in Canada was too cold in winter for the holly to thrive. Cutting and shipping tons of holly sprigs to buyers before Christmas every year became a regular occurrence at the farm.

One of F.B.'s edicts, said Pip, was that all the grandchildren should turn up en masse at Mountjoy just before Easter. The object was to pick twenty-five gross of daffodils—twelve dozen daffs being a gross—to decorate the local churches. "He lined us all up on the lawn, twenty-five steps back, ready to go. It was very well organized, but it was a great push to get it done and all the flowers delivered."[20]

Grandfather Pemberton also harvested a great crop of figs every year. Pip remembered the old fig trees "between the front garden and the upper front garden, each spreading twenty feet by twenty feet," and when the figs were ripe, picking the best of them to be sold through a specialty fruit store in Victoria.

Pip and his sister Elizabeth (left).

Baby "Pippy" had his studio portrait done (below), and in the boy is seen the man.

Four of the five siblings visiting Caleb Pike homestead (bottom, l-r): Pip curious about something; Desmond; Cicely in charge; and Elizabeth. Vincent was born later.

The trophy heads needed annual cleaning (top left).

The rocks behind 336 Newport were a favourite vantage point (top right).

Oaks and firs where the children played ball atop Holmes Peak (above), and familiar horses working at Millstream (bottom left).

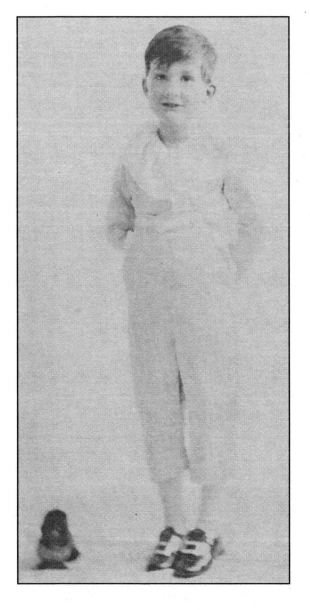

The scooter gave him quick access to more of Oak Bay (top left).

After months at the Solarium for athsma, Pip was back at 11 Cook Street with family and mollified by his new tricycle (above).

Life in town, he said, gradually taught him his family's role in the community (left).

CHAPTER THREE
THE COWICHAN VALLEY

SUSTENANCE CAME FROM the land in most direct fashion. Vegetable gardens and henhouses at Mountjoy and Finnerty Bay supplied family tables week after week, and F.B.'s farm in the Cowichan Valley was highly productive. Good results at the farm weren't optional but essential if everyone was to be fed, and every fall at harvest time, everyone who could be there helped out with threshing machine, tractor, horses and hay wagons.

Grandfather Pem had a thousand acres of prime land between the Koksilah River and Kelvin Creek near Duncan, and he named it Pemberlea. He bought the land before World War I for his two eldest boys, Despard and Warren, both of whom volunteered for duty in the First World War and transferred from the 88th Infantry Battalion to the Royal Flying Corps. Both were killed in action.[21]

John Brown, an Ayreshire Scot, was hired to manage the farm. Mrs. Brown cooked endlessly for everyone and put up preserves for winter, and three of her brothers worked with John on the farm and on generally keeping the property in good order. "They all lived and worked there," said Pip. "All Scots." The four men had served overseas during WWI in the Canadian Army and had come out of it still able to work.

Old Bill Reid, the head horseman who "chewed tobacco and had a great sense of humour" and whose sister was farm manager John Brown's wife, took care of the twelve great Clydesdale horses that were the main suppliers of farming power. One of the other men looked after more than a dozen Ayreshire milk cows and their calves and supervised the sheep and lambs. The pigs seemed largely his responsibility as well.[22]

These skilled people and others at the farm were the guiding hands who kept Pip, his brothers and their cousin Peter Duke busy, safe and learning. One skill Old Bill had mastered was how to tickle a trout, and on a Sunday, his day off work at the farm, he showed Pip the trick of it. On an overhanging bank of Kelvin Creek where it flows northeast into the Koksilah River, they lay flat on their bellies so Bill could reach an arm into the water in the shadow of the bank. Pip had been warned to stay still and keep quiet.

Slowly moving his hand up behind and underneath a resting trout, Bill tickled it ever so gently until his fingers were right behind the gills. Quick as lightning, he slid his fingers forward into the gills and at the same instant flung the fish upward and backward onto the streambank. Pip didn't believe this could be done, even after seeing it. After two rainbow trout lay flopping on the grass, he had to admit it was possible, but he could never duplicate the feat. The fish were carried on a willow twig from the creek to Mrs. Brown's copper frying pan.

Family farms around the region in the 1920s and 1930s were mostly holdings of fifty to a hundred acres. Mixed farming was hard work, and there was lots of it all year round: making sure the animals were tended, gardens and grain fields were coming along and preserves were put up when the season was right. Whatever was produced from one activity, even the waste, was put to useful purpose for something else.

The boys were expected to pull their weight and enjoyed doing so, in fact, often working along with the farmhands or garden-and-grounds people on whatever chores needed doing. They had free run of the farm and took great pains not to wander within range of the bulls, which they knew were often mean and in a miserable mood.

The farmyard at Pemberlea was busy underfoot with ducks, turkeys, quail, pigeons and, always and everywhere, chickens. The grain and hay for the animals was grown there, harvested and stored. Cattle produced the beef, milk and butter the family needed, and the rest of the milk was sold to the local dairy. At first light in summer and before daylight in winter, the chicken house was searched for fresh eggs and the Ayreshires had their first milking of the day.

One of the farm's mysteries for the boys, and there were many to be mulled, was how each cow coming into the barn for milking knew her own stall and would have no other. Each cow also had her own basin of special grain and a crib of hay from the hayloft above. Once, a cow that was generally good-tempered took it on herself to pin young Pip flat against the wall of her stall so that he absolutely couldn't move or breathe, but Bill arrived in time to push the cow aside and haul Pip out of there.

At milking time, the calves were separated out from the mothers and the younger calves were issued a half-bucket of milk each. Though the boys were expected to help pitch hay into the cows' cribs, only those in the milking crew were allowed to do the hygienic washing of udders and scalding of milk pails. After the first starter pails were done, the milkers settled themselves on their three-legged stools, put foreheads against flanks and started the rhythmic zing-zing of milk into pails.

Cats in the barn, always around as mousers and ratters, were quick to pick up whatever benefits they could during milking. As Pip explained, "a great thing was to take aim with a cow teat and let fly toward a cat twenty feet away with a squirt of warm milk—*zowie*—square in the mouth. The cats absolutely loved it and would purr and wash their fur endlessly, but the Scots thought it was a damned waste of milk and tried to stop us doing it."[23]

Horses were the mainstay of all the hauling that needed to be done, and the Clydesdales were bred for it. Docile and quiet in nature, they'd been bred near Clyde in Scotland especially for farm work. A matched pair of Clydesdales could haul a fully laden hay wagon up from the fields to the barn—"Gee! Haw! Whoa there!"—with a farmer riding atop the load with the reins. With any luck, the boys would be up there as well.

Hitching up the horses was too much for youngsters to do, but Pip said he loved to watch the complicated process of assembling the team in the right positions and getting their harnesses in place. The workmen, with head horseman Bill in charge, pulled the harnessed horses into the wagon traces and hooked them up. "There was a lot of grunting and pulling, and sometimes things were said that I didn't know the meaning of until some time later," he said.

"What fascinated me no end was the threshing machine," Pip continued, "especially the way the tractor ran it using a long flapping belt looped from a pulley on the tractor to a pulley on the thresher. The whole arrangement shimmied and shook and made a highly satisfying racket." The sheaves of grain, already cut and stooked in the fields, were hauled to the thresher by wagons pulled by the Clydesdales and were flung by workers with pitchforks onto the conveyor belt to be drawn into the machine. "I never did figure out what went on with the innards of that machine."

Further joy ensued when Bill Reid was given the job of firing up the trusty Fordson tractor, in all ways a colourful event. After the thing was finally running with great amounts of smoke and noise, he'd pop the clutch that goosed the tractor into great spasmodic leaps forward, with Bill roaring above it all: "Buck, you bugger! Buck!"

Pip's main job in support of the threshing crew was, by comparison, quieter. He carried pails of ice-cold water from the spring to the workmen, farm manager and head horseman. It was clearly an important contribution to the effort, and he loved doing it. The evidence was immediate: when he appeared with the water, the men stopped what they were doing and drank long from the lip of the pail. He was often enough thanked kindly, which he appreciated.

The onset of asthma attacks was likely around the threshing machine, but they didn't stop Pip from participating. He also found that an attack often coincided with a bout of hayfever, and he gradually learned to deal with each as a separate event. The asthma was a serious matter, and at the onset of an attack, he'd take himself out of circulation by sliding off the hay wagon or away from the machinery and finding a cool dark place in the farmhouse. He said he "usually headed for a big, cold leather sofa" and, while sipping liquid honey, did battle with the problem privately.

It was a battle that those with asthma recognize. The effort of drawing another breath, said Pip, called for concentration that was almost beyond belief just to focus on getting breath into his lungs: "The prospect of death was never very far from my mind during the worst of those traumatic times, but I fought through and sooner or later was able to gain control. I felt then that my very survival was at stake—but as soon as possible afterward, I was out and about again, hopefully in time to catch the same wagon on its way from unloading its load of hay and heading back out into the field for another load."

As his life progressed, medical advances provided more options for handling the effects of the disease, and he was also much better able to anticipate and nearly control the attacks. "I didn't want any special treatment because of it. I have always taken pains to make sure my affliction remained unknown to others, and I think I've been successful in doing so." If ever there existed a concentration of factors pushing the onset of an asthma attack, threshing time at Pemberlea might have been it, but he contended that being immersed in farm life strengthened body and spirit in equal measure. The farm at Cowichan Station and what he learned there were deeply important to him in ways he realized later on, many times over.

Pip said he adored the place and spent as much time there as he could arrange. It was at Pemberlea, for instance, that he first really understood by osmosis the rhythm of the seasons and the run of natural cycles—spring planting, summer cultivation, autumn harvest, winter preparations for spring—and took it in thoroughly that good planning, good manpower and good timing fit together in a repetitive cyclical process toward a goal. He also understood how various related processes can be made to dovetail. The experiences and people at Pemberlea, he said, influenced him permanently and taught him criteria by which a person was judged to have done well.

Pemberlea and the large gardens on the Finnerty Bay land provided them with food, because F.B. supplied a large sack of vegetables every week for the households of each of the local family branches. This regular supply of fresh produce, always welcome, became much more important after the collapse of the stock market in 1929 and in the years of economic depression that followed. Real estate, insurance and property management, like other segments of the economy, were flattened, and the family company was hit hard.

After F.B.'s bankruptcy and retirement from the presidency in 1929, Cuthbert had taken on the job of rescuing Pemberton & Son and then somehow keeping it solvent.[24] One business analyst commented on what he decided to do: "Through friends, relatives and associates, he mobilized mortgage capital and enough money to buy out the non-family investors."[25]

Another writer analyzing that era credited Cuthbert with survival decisions in a tough context: "Major Holmes brought the company through the tough times of the Depression very largely through support achieved in mortgage work, which led eventually to major involvement in private mortgages. The big mortgage corporations were panic-stricken at the time because of the horrendous financial situation. On a local basis, Pemberton's not only could provide the funds people needed but could manage them and see that they were paid. Many British Columbia firms requiring capital secured it from underwritings of Pemberton's in its capacity of supplying a complete and integrated financial service."[26]

Philippa wasn't well, so Cuthbert was sustaining his family and giving his children the best schooling available under adverse personal and financial circumstances. As Pip put it later, the family in the 1930s "didn't have the residue of financial support that others in our circle may have had." The economy started to gather strength in the late 1930s, a context that helped the firm's recovery, but there were many difficult days and nights. "How he did all that," Pip said later, "is a continuing wonder to me. I take my hat off to my father for his tenacity, courage and stamina."

Cuthbert took Pip along on driving tours to properties that were of interest to him and often shared his thoughts with his son. Pip as a youngster was proud to be riding along in what he called the jalopy, listening to his father talk to him about the properties in certain parts of the city or surrounding areas, the houses and outbuildings already built on the properties, the mortgages that were held on them, the situations of the people holding the mortgages and all sorts of other details. The driving tours and business talks continued as Pip matured. "It was during these rides with my father that I assimilated the fundamentals of the real estate business," he said.

Cuthbert needed to increase his cash flow in 1933, when Pip was nine, so he made an expedient decision and rented out the family house on Newport to a wealthy American woman. That meant its property taxes could always be paid. The house could be well-maintained to keep it intact, and they were able to retain ownership without depleting their resources. For the time being, he and Philippa and the children moved into a rented duplex on Fort Street. And was this arrangement taken as a blow to social status? All things considered, apparently not. It was a good arrangement in context, one of a number of practical changes that had to be made.

From age twelve to seventeen, Pip attended grades seven through twelve in Brentwood Bay on the Saanich peninsula. He has fond memories of Brentwood College School, "enjoyed every minute" of it and kept up a lifelong connection. The boys, and it was just boys until decades later, lived in residence during the week. Some of them went home for weekends, though not always. They learned to live reasonably amiably in a group under rules that were expected to be obeyed by all, and enforcement of the rules was fair but firm.

Mathematics, physics, chemistry, history and literature were the focus of much of the curriculum. Their academic program was also strong in fundamentals of language and expression—writing proper sentences, paragraphs and essays—and good penmanship was much admired and was expected to be developed and maintained. Etiquette and social graces were taught and practiced so that the students could be counted on to act appropriately and be comfortable in any circumstance.

Sports in great variety were encouraged, if not mandatory, and everyone participated. Pip involved himself in rugby, rowing and racquet sports but never warmed to cricket. The boys all joined a naval cadet corps and practiced target-shooting with rifles. They were taught to shoot by Maj. Fred Richardson, who was such an excellent shot himself he was chosen to shoot for Canada on the Bisley team.[27] "Six times at Bisley," Pip remembered being told. Elder brother Des was a keen shot and headed up the Brentwood rifle shooting team.

Major Richardson took them several times to Heal's rifle range to get the feel of .303 bolt-action rifles at ranges up to eight hundred yards. "For the first time, we felt the kick of a heavy gun," Pip said. No more sundials. During the 1930s, they usually used the .22 range underneath the school gymnasium, where they lay flat and shot at Dominion Marksman paper targets on a pulley system.

The training plus his past experience shooting from the bedroom window seemed to serve Pip well, because he earned the Dominion Marksman Gold Ring and was wildly proud of it—even years after it slipped off his finger, bounced off the end of the dock into ten feet of water and sank forever into the soft mud bottom of Maltby Lake. He tried but never did find it among the waterlily roots under the silt. "Gold, at a specific gravity of nineteen, is heavy," he said ruefully.[28]

Des and Pip sometimes went after blue grouse in the hills above Cowichan Lake but more often went duck and pheasant shooting together on the Cowichan River flats or at Mainguy Farm, also known as Swallowfield, near the mouth of the Chemainus River. Pip built a plywood dinghy and painted it in camouflage colours. As they drove home after a shoot one night, the dinghy flew off the car's roof and landed on the highway behind them.

Though it wasn't much damaged, it certainly needed repairs, so next day they looked for a canoe to rent. They found an Indian dugout canoe that looked fast, had admirable lines and was very, very expertly balanced. Keeping the tippy thing upright in the river current became a major exercise in boat-handling, but the craft itself was memorable. As Pip put it: "There are canoes, and then there are *canoes*."

After Des left for Royal Military College in 1938, Pip continued to hunt and fish with his godmother Mae's husband, Harry Seale, who ran the big Layritz Nurseries. Harry had grown up in England, was an all-round athlete and always ready to share his great fund of knowledge. He'd driven early motorbikes and racing cars and was a long-distance runner and figure skater. He was also an excellent shot and a great sports fisherman who taught Pip everything he possibly could about fly-casting. He had his own car, and in the fall when the shooting season opened, the two would start out together at 4:30 in the morning, have breakfast at an all-night restaurant called the Poodle Dog and pick up the rowboat from Mrs. Beryl Stewart's marina in Cowichan Bay.

Harry taught Pip the lore of duck-blind positioning ("not stuck on a mudbank but preferably on a turn of the riverbank"), of camouflage netting, hip waders, ammunition, decoys and keeping the lunch bags dry. "The big challenge after rowing back to the marina dock at sunset," they agreed, "was to stay awake during the slow drive over the Malahat on the steep and dark way home."

Pip and a friend were in the Sooke Hills going after blue grouse one day, and as usual, Pip's Labrador spaniel Rocky was with them to flush out the birds and retrieve them. Rocky came down in a big jump after a bird he'd flushed and the other man fired. He got the bird all right, but a good deal of shot got Rocky in the eyes and head.

Pip ran to him where he fell and knew when he'd had a close look that Rocky was blinded and dying and that he had to shoot him. Devastated, he buried his dog on the hilltop under a cairn of stones.

———————————

During the summers, from 1936 onward, Pip's parents continued to rent out the Newport Avenue house and stay at the cottage at Maltby Lake, which they called Highland Lake or often just The Lake. The cottage had been built in the early 1900s by two of the Dumbleton sons who'd purchased the shooting rights around the lake and, afterward, the small area of land around the cottage. Cuthbert and Philippa bought it in the 1930s from "the aunts."

Around the same time, Col. A.W.R. Wilby made an agreement with Cuthbert that he'd build another cottage on the north shore of the lake but not hold title and, for this arrangement, would pay half the taxes. Wilby's cottage was later sold to another old friend of Cuthbert's and Philippa's, Frank Ward, who when he died left it to his friend Dickie Francis, and she used it until the 1960s.[29]

Various people were still farming roughly half the property around the lake, but in the late 1940s, Cuthbert decided he'd buy out those farmers if they were willing to sell. They proved willing, and thus he came to own the land surrounding the whole lake. The children kept a pony there, clambered around in wildflowers and forests and swam like otters. They memorized all its best places to hide, plant things, read and daydream.

Later, an old barn was converted into a house by Pip's younger brother Vincent. When Vincent and Maureen were first married, they lived in the converted barn, but by the early 1960s, Maureen was finding it a difficult place with a young family. They bought Pip's parents' home on Newport and resettled themselves in town after Pip's parents moved into a house on Beach Drive facing the sea. John Thomson, eldest son of Pip's older sister Cicely, moved into what the family always called "The Barn" and lived there with Pru, his first wife, then with Carmel, his second wife. At first, he paid rent to Vincent, but it was later decided he should contribute toward the taxes. Vincent decided to buy the cottage from Dickie Francis, since she wanted to sell.

Pip eventually built an A-frame cabin on the high rock above the south shore and kept it *au naturelle* without the mod cons of the three other cottages on the lake. From the start, the A-frame, its deck and its dock served for many years as a welcoming place for family and guests.

With cousin Peter Duke, supposedly feeding the lambs but becoming cowboys (top left).

The great barn at Pemberlea, Cowichan Station, and hay wagons (centre left).

Jack Brown, farm manager at Pemberlea (top right, in light shirt), just behind head horseman Bill Reid (in cap), with a farmhand running the thresher.

Clydesdales at the farmyard gate (right).

Frederick Pemberton's summer house in Victoria, Finnerty Bay farm (above), in August 1907. He introduced commercial holly on forty acres to ship to buyers early every winter and planted highly productive vegetable gardens. Pip and the other boys rode the horses up from Foul Bay Road to stable them here for the summer months.

On Finnerty Bay's front porch in the early 1930s (left, l-r): Desmond, Philippa Holmes, Elizabeth on Philippa's lap, Cuthbert Holmes, Cicely, and Pip down in front. The house burned down in 1935.

CHAPTER FOUR
BRITISH COLUMBIA BY BIKE

PIP IN 1935 began a series of long bicycle trips to explore Vancouver Island and the B.C. mainland. Always in love with freedom of movement and the vehicles that gave him that, he graduated from wagon, scooter and tricycle to a real two-wheeler at about age ten. "From very early on, before age five or six," Pip said, "I was an inveterate traveller. I wanted to be *mobile!*"

He bought his first bike by saving up money earned from chores, some from the farm and some from "waiting table for my Pemberton grandparents." That in particular was fun, and he found it lucrative. "I sometimes got twenty-five cents in wages for one sitting. Very good wages." His first significant purchase was a heavy CCM bicycle, with a large flat carrier-basket over the front wheel and a double-duty kickstand under the back one.

He delivered papers, sold magazines and kept saving his pocket money, and all of it went into the travel pot. With a carefully calculated budget of thirty-three cents a day, all inclusive, he planned the first of his biking holidays. With bread being ten cents a loaf and butter twenty-five cents a quarter-pound, that seemed a reasonable daily allowance. Pedal-power transportation was already paid for, and he calculated in the cost of buying a new tire in case a punctured one couldn't be patched. A sleeping bag, pup tent and matches for a campfire were packed on the bike.

The first and rather experimental trip in 1935 went north up the road from Victoria over the daunting Malahat summit to the Cowichan Valley, where food and shelter awaited at Pemberlea Farm. Another eleven-year-old, Brentwood school friend Ken Logan, met him there, and the two explored all over the valley from saltwater at the mouth of the Cowichan River to nearly the top of the valley.

With that a success, the 1936 expedition was planned around an invitation extended to Pip and his brother Des from Tim Stanley Clarke to visit his log house on Cowichan Lake. "The House on the Point" became the second biking destination and a good base for more explorations of the region.

The third trip the following summer involved three friends on a much longer trip north to Parksville, a trip of about a hundred miles each way. They camped beside the Englishman River below the bridge at the two-lane highway and cooked and swam and hiked the river valley. When breaking camp, they charitably left several spare tins of pork and beans on the bridge for the next campers but found the cans next morning tipped into the river, out of reach of everyone, and were annoyed at the waste of them.

The Parksville trip didn't work out as well as the earlier jaunts because one or another of the three participants tended to feel left out at one time or another during their discussions and decisions. They were learning first-hand about the third-man-out dynamic, Pip explained, but their working relationship was maintained well enough that the expedition was considered suitably successful.

The fourth bike trip, a month-long trek the summer Pip was fourteen, was with friend Mark Wilby to Comox, 140 miles from home up the east coast of Vancouver Island.[30] A favourite Brentwood teacher, Ken Ostler, lived in Comox where his parents owned the waterfront hotel, and he said they were welcome to stay. The boys did the distance northward in two days, arriving late on the second evening, and since it was too late to knock on the door, they set up camp in a nearby field.

Thoroughly worn out, they slept until a cow at first light grazed her way into their tent and slurped a lick on the side of Mark's face. He let out a bellow and frightened the cow. She reared back, popped the tent pegs and headed fast across the field with the tent on her back. They got their tent back and decided on early breakfast at the hotel.

In year five, 1939, Pip and Mark planned an ambitious two-month trip. First destination was Campbell River, and again they found a good spot to camp beside the river below an old bridge. While dinner was cooking over the fire, they heard rustling in the woods and out emerged "an entirely naked and rather hairy logger" heading for his evening bath. After very quick but polite nods, the fellow lined up a good run toward the fast river and hit it hard in a shallow dive, bobbed to the surface a hundred feet downstream and let loose with a loud Scandinavian folk song. He scrubbed and sang until he floated aground on a sandbar farther down where he'd left his towel and clothes, then disappeared back to wherever he'd come from. The fellows got on with their dinner.

A helpful garage attendant down along the highway, when they mentioned they smelled smoke, reassured them that the fire was way back in the hills and wouldn't be a worry where they were going. The boys camped for two nights just above Elk Falls, which hadn't yet been dammed and was still in full flow, and for two days explored the falls and the shores of the lake. On the third morning, smoke was filling the sky. They bicycled out in a rush, and the garage attendant this time was saying the authorities were looking for firefighters because the fire was out of control. That information was a clear signal to start biking in earnest.

The fire was burning parallel to the highway all sixty miles and more to Courtenay. South of Courtenay, the flames were leaping the road across the treetops, and Comox harbour was filled with naval vessels ready to evacuate the town's population. In the end, the boys weren't harmed or recruited to join the firefighters, but they certainly didn't pause very much en route back to Parksville and considered the whole event a very close call.

They set off westward to puff their way up the infamous Alberni summit and race downhill coasting at high speed all the way into Port Alberni. They biked to Stamp River Falls and then onward to Uncle Will Pemberton's cabin on the south shore of Sproat Lake. It was sheer luxury for tired boys on bikes and a terrific place to stay for a while, especially with a rowboat at the dock for their use.

At Lake Cowichan, Pip had already learned the family's highly practical Rules of the Lake: (1) learn to swim properly; (2) boat or no boat, never go to the centre of the lake or beyond so that you're always able to get back; (3) a punctured foot or toe necessitates antiseptic soaking until healed. Since Sproat Lake has a nasty habit of brewing up sudden furious storms that mean danger, the Cowichan rules applied. They never needed Rule 3, since nobody's foot was hurt, but it happened that Rule 2 was essential when they had to row like mad and pull the boat up and out of reach of wind and waves. As for Rule 1 about learning to swim, they were already strong swimmers and enjoyed the water.

They spent their last day there, Pip said, "cleaning and polishing the cabin to within an inch of its life" and chopped and bucked up "enough firewood to last a year." When they eventually got home, however, an angry uncle was saying he'd heard from the cabin caretaker that the boys had left a terrible mess. "What defence have couple of youngsters against the word of someone who obviously resented our showing up and enjoying ourselves, probably disturbing his peace?" said Pip. "I'll never forget that caretaker or his dirty trick, or how we should have protected ourselves from such a rascal."

They wouldn't be facing the uncle quite yet, though, because after their housecleaning at Sproat Lake, they biked west to the outer coast. No road existed from Port Alberni along the inlet that almost bisects the Island, so at the Alberni dock, they walked their bikes onto the deck of the original M.V. *Uchuck* and settled down in between freight and other passengers going to Bamfield. The boys were disappointed to have no time to visit the terminus of the Trans-Pacific Cable where it came ashore in Canada, so they left the grand old buildings behind for another time. As the *Uchuck* set off again through the Broken Group islands toward Ucluelet, stopping wherever necessary at floating logging camps and fish camps, they noticed that their bikes were already being eaten by the Pacific's salt fog.

From the Ucluelet dock, they bicycled three or four miles along a narrow dirt road until it opened out onto the sea. They had reached the southernmost bays of Long Beach when the tide was out, leaving the damp sand hard enough to support their bicycle tires. Oh, wondrous new road! Accumulations of enormous logs high on the beach above the softer sand hid a few green glass Japanese fishing floats that had gone adrift on Pacific currents and grounded here—treasures to be protected in backpacks.

Before heading homeward, there was one more person to see, and he was only about ten miles up the beach. Dr. Lovekin had ingeniously solved the problem of providing himself with a good house to live in on a coast not yet connected by land routes to the east side of the Island or the mainland. On a barge in Vancouver, he assembled the house he wanted, had it towed into position off Long Beach and during a particularly high tide, had the whole affair winched well up the beach onto his land. All his supplies, in fact, still reached him by barge.

Pip and Mark found their host to be a delightful and world-travelled pioneer, born on an Ontario farm and one of the early ones to follow and exploit the development of oil as it was being discovered in various parts of the world. He had done well, and when in his travels he saw a piece of property he loved, he usually bought it. This mile and a half section of Long Beach he loved well enough to live on, perhaps for the rest of his life. Before heading off, they were asked to sign their host's guest book and found they were his first visitors. Many years later, Dr. Lovekin showed Pip the guest book with "P. Holmes" at the start of it.

"We saw some of the most beautiful places imaginable during that trip in the summer of '39," said Pip. "Absolutely striking. I've often wondered at the influence all this magnificence has on us. There's so much beauty in terrains the world over, but British Columbia is blessed with the best."

On 3 September 1939, Prime Minister Mackenzie King and Minister of Justice Ernest Lapointe arranged a broadcast over the CBC Radio network in English and French. German tanks and bombers had invaded Polish territory, and that morning, the British government demanded the withdrawal of German forces within two hours.

Prime Minister of the United Kingdom Neville Chamberlain had already been on the BBC: "I am speaking to you [from] the Cabinet Room at 10 Downing Street. This morning, the British ambassador in Berlin handed the German government a final note stating that unless we heard from them by eleven o'clock, that they were prepared at once to withdraw their troops from Poland, a state of war would exist between us. I have to tell you now, that no such undertaking has been received and that consequently, this country is at war with Germany."[31]

Canadian Members of Parliament were recalled to Ottawa. In Parliament, Mackenzie King summed up the situation for them on 7 September, and on 10 September 1939, war was declared. On the sixteenth of the month, the first Canadian convoy of merchant ships sailed for Britain, and by 17 December, Canadian troops were in Scotland ready for the fight in Europe.[32]

Pip was impatient to finish school and be part of the war effort. "It was really impossible to imagine accurately the feelings of my parents," he said later, referring to that time. His mother's two brothers had been shot down. His father had lost his brother, a highly decorated and gallant fellow soldier in the First World War, and Cuthbert had himself been severely wounded.

But family stories from an earlier war intensified his drive to join up. Restless, he continued the duck-hunting trips to the Chemainus and Cowichan rivers but without the companionship of his older brother. Des had left for Royal Military College in Kingston, where he was enrolled in RMC's two-year intensive "wartime short course."

During the summer of 1940, Pip put his energies into getting into fighting trim the best way he knew how. He and his friend Mark planned one last trip, this one about four hundred miles' worth of bike riding from Victoria to the B.C. interior and back.

The destination after the spring school term ended was the Douglas Lake Ranch between Merritt and Kamloops. He'd loved his stay there when he was a boy and wanted to see it again. The start of it involved crossing from Vancouver Island on the Canadian Pacific boat to Steveston and biking across the flat Fraser delta farmland to Chilliwack. The young men found a welcome there with the Field family, whose son was also a Brentwood boy.

With only fifty miles accomplished the next day because of a leisurely breakfast with the Fields that carried on late into the morning, they got through the first low hills of the Fraser Canyon and made camp on the banks of Silver Creek between the noisy highway and the loud river rushing over boulders. Next day they biked through to Hope and then into the canyon proper.

Either the long uphill climb wasn't as tough as they'd anticipated or they were fitter than they knew. Although they did a lot of hill-walking and bike-pushing in the heat and against a headwind, they made good time. The highway they were on was at a certain point only twenty feet above the transcontinental CPR railway line, and their camp that night, on the banks of a stream south of Lytton, was in a spot specifically chosen for its proximity to where the famous Silk Train Express would roar through.

Perishable bales of high-value silk had been shipped from Asian to North American ports starting in the 1870s, and connecting trains out of those ports usually had highest priority on the transcontinental rail system. Though quantities of the special cargo dwindled during the 1930s, speed records set by the trains were legendary. Both fellows wanted to see one blast by at full speed, so they finished their campfire meal, set the alarm clock for 11:15 p.m. and dozed a bit. When the alarm woke them, they drank mugs of hot cocoa and walked in the dark the short distance to where the road was closest to the railway.

From a great way off, they could hear the great steam locomotive even above the roar of the Fraser River. The canyon walls reverberated with the sound of the howling whistle that ricocheted off the rockface and was magnified by it. Then the single enormous headlight flashed around the bend straight into their faces—and their eyes snapped shut. With a powerful rush of air and noise, the great train flew past them. And for all their exertions to get there, what did they see? "Nothing, really," said Pip, "but our hearts were thumping, the ground was vibrating, and it was altogether a whopping sensation!" Was it worth the trouble? "Of course it was! I can *see* it to this day."

On the road nearing Spence's Bridge, they stopped to chat with a man who'd lost his family, his business and any desire to get them back. He had become one of many tramps living outside conventional society after the Depression years, and he gave them some local advice: "Around these parts, never, never, sleep on a haystack. All the rattlesnakes will discover your nice warm body on a chilly night, and you'll wake up with a good dozen rattlers snuggled up to you. Cold-blooded, y'know, and poisonous. Give you a mean bite." Vancouver Island has no rattlers, and this had never crossed their minds.

They peddled their way almost to Merritt in a complete sweat. It had been 114° F. all afternoon on the bicyclists' gravel road, so they picked a breezy spot near the river to camp, just emptied their pockets and sat down in the shallows fully clothed. After a very long time, they perked up enough to make supper, clean up the cookpots, set up the tents and mosquito nets and tuck in at sunset. The breeze faded to nothing, and to their dismay, mosquitoes came out "in the billions." The netting either did nothing or made a bad situation worse, and they knew they couldn't stay.

Trudging into the village, they found a restaurant open and blew the budget on coffee and pie—thirty-five cents, a whole day's allowance. When the place closed, they found a spot to snooze in between the double front doors of the main hotel but were soon booted out. Pip's parents had always said that if he found himself in trouble, he should go to the police, and the police station was their last resort. They found the duty constable fast asleep in one of the two jail cells, so they crept into the empty one and fell asleep on the cots. They were out of there at dawn before the constable woke up, and thus ended Pip's only night in jail.

After breakfast at their camp, with all mosquitoes gone in the morning chill, they found a phonebox to call Frank Ward, owner-manager of the Douglas Lake Ranch. Frank sent a truck to fetch them, which was a warm welcome considering it was twenty-five miles into town. The ranch, vast and beautiful, was a marvellous place to explore for a week. Though J.D. had sold his share more than fifty years before, his great-grandson recognized immediately the quality of the ranchland. A conception of the sheer extent of it took longer to sink in.

Frank Ward lent them .22 rifles and an old pickup truck and challenged them to see how many gophers they could dispatch. Gopher holes are dangerous to cows and horses because a misstep into one of the holes can break an animal's leg, so ranchers generally declared open season on "the varmints." The rules of the challenge said the first shot didn't count if you missed. You got a free turn and tried again.

The unexpected presence of lady guests, Diana and Sheila Francis, improved the sociability situation for Pip and Mark and prompted a few good chatty picnics during days of riding the open range. After the week, they were off the horses and back on their bikes—back on the dusty road to Merritt, back along the Nicola River, with one night's camping on the stream running into Hedley, then back on the long hot stretch to Spence's Bridge and the Fraser Canyon. They found to their chagrin that the brisk hot winds were now blowing consistently northward, full in their faces. It was a long, long ride to the Steveston ferry dock, and the first place they went after they got back to the Saanich Peninsula was into Maltby Lake for a swim.

The bike journeys had been increasing in distance and challenge as Pip grew, but the longest trip was not by bicycle but by car from B.C. to Ontario and Quebec in the late spring of 1941, just after he graduated from Brentwood. Des was graduating from Royal Military College that spring, and the family wanted to be there. They appointed Pip the man in charge of organization, and his experience in planning bike trips became very useful to the effort. He had learned to drive long before he was legally old enough, which was not uncommon, and the car he learned in was a 1928 Packard. "It was a big and powerful machine, a beauty," he said, "and I loved driving it."

Pip was anticipating the trek because he loved driving, but he was upset that the departure date meant he would miss the photographer's visit to record the grandly victorious Brentwood 1st XV—"first fifteen"—rugger team. He had a good laugh when he heard later that his teammates perpetrated a slight ruse for the photo record of the triumph. They devised a life-size head-and-shoulders image of him and managed the situation so that "he" was represented in the group photo. It was well enough done that it passed muster, so his face was recorded among his teammates' faces forevermore.

Desmond Holmes was senior cadet in the spring of 1941—the Battalion Sergeant Major, or as the family blithely called a BSM, "the one in front who held the sword." The Commandant of RMC and his wife had invited Philippa and Major Holmes and family to stay with them for the graduation ceremony and June Ball, an invitation they'd accepted with pleasure, so General and Mrs. Hertzberg and family welcomed Cuthbert, Philippa, Pip, Des and his girlfriend Muriel Uhthoff.

Driving across the country meant logistical planning. Maps were spread on tables. Routes were evaluated and selected. Daily mileages were calculated, and stopping places and overnight stays discussed. Based on information that roads were better in the northern states than across the western provinces, they realized an all-Canadian route would be a tough go and opted for a U.S. route. Two cars had to be tuned up and spares and supplies put in the trunk. A budget was devised, and for five people's luggage, what to pack for the trip and for the graduation ceremonies had to be discussed.

Pip was in the lead car with his mother and Muriel, and his father followed in a back-up car. Their route followed U.S. Highway 20, which called for crossing Lake Michigan by ferry. For a young driver—Pip was seventeen—it was great experience, entirely without mishaps. When they reached Kingston, they briefly settled into a hotel, then met up with Desmond, who provided a detailed calendar of events for them.

Then through the Hertzbergs' hospitality, they proceeded to enjoy themselves. The evening event of the program, the June Ball in 1941, was the first time Pip wore white tie and tails. "One of my comely dancing partners got her lipstick well and truly all over my stiff white collar," he said, making a face. "I took a royal ribbing over *that*!"

RMC graduation parades are generally impressive affairs, but this one, with Des leading the cadets, was also very emotional. He and most of the others were leaving shortly for war service in the U.K. and Europe.

After Kingston, the family drove to visit Charlie and Jean Dupont in Montreal and at Balsam Lake, where they had a family place. Cousin Charlie was already an engineer officer in the RCAF, largely involved in its marine division. At the start of World War II, Ottawa had decided Canadians would not be eligible for permanent commissions, so Des joined the British Army sappers, the combat engineers, as a commissioned officer. It was "one of the country's more asinine decisions," as one fellow put it, "because Canada lost the services of an outstanding regular force career soldier."

The U.S. was not yet in the war when the family made the long drive back along the same route they'd followed earlier, but there was still a minor hitch when they were crossing back into Canada: questioning about Muriel's surname, Uhthoff. Though Muriel's mother was "as Scottish as a bagpipe," the surname was obviously not from the Lowlands or Highlands. All was in order, however, and across the border they came.

In the fall of 1941, Pip was due to begin courses in Craigdarroch Castle, the enormous stone structure in Victoria's Rockland district that was the former home of the Robert Dunsmuir family. Since 1921, it had been the location of Victoria College, affiliated with McGill University, and Pip enrolled in a university program toward an economics degree.

He very much wanted a motorbike to get back and forth to classes. He knew that having his own car was out of the question, but he broached the subject of this much-desired motorbike at every opportunity.

Pip's father was a staunch supporter of the Gyro Club, and that year the club was staging a variety of competitions to raise money, including a hole-in-one contest. In a cavalier moment, Cuthbert said to Pip that if he could get a hole-in-one at the golf competition, he would buy him the motorbike. Pip practiced and practiced his drive, and when the moment came, Pip drove the ball long and straight. He said he wasn't sure which or who got there first—the golf ball, his father or himself—but it most certainly was in.

Knowing that in those lean times the financial outlay was considerable, he told his father the promise didn't need to be kept, but Cuthbert replied that a promise is a promise and he'd certainly buy the bike. Pip was so elated he had the golf ball mounted on the front mudguard.

The "wondrous new road" of Long Beach (left).

A racing start in a fit life, at Brentwood (centre left).

Saltwater and freshwater beaches were nearby (bottom left).

With bicycle packed (below), Pip was ready for a trek from Victoria over the Malahat to the Cowichan Valley.

The gate of the Douglas Lake Cattle Company Ltd. (top). Pip had gone to the ranch with his grandmother as a boy and returned by bicycle in the summer of '40.

Great-grandfather J.D. had sold his share of the immense cattle range (centre right) at Douglas Lake Ranch more than fifty years before.

The B.C. interior can be tough terrain for bicyclists (centre left) or serenely perfect (above). Pip explored mainland B.C. by bike first and repeated his routes by car many times on working trips and family holidays. He knew the regions of the province well.

Des graduated from Royal Military College in June 1941 (left), and Pip at seventeen drove the family from the west coast to Kingston, Montreal, Balsam Lake and back to Victoria.

With a hole-in-one, he won a Harley-Davidson (above left), which was of course ridden sedately to Victoria College (above right).

CHAPTER FIVE
HORIZONS LEVEL

PEOPLE IN BRITISH Columbia were hearing report after report about increases in Nazi power and successive invasions: Austria, Poland, Czechoslovakia, Belgium, France, Denmark, Holland, Norway. Pip had no doubt he'd soon be in the services. Exactly which branch he wasn't sure about at first, but his eagerness to join up was unswerving. He and the family decided that the Royal Canadian Air Force fit his adventurous spirit, so in March 1942, away to the RCAF Vancouver recruiting centre he went.[33]

Because he thoroughly believed it was important to do his part, Pip was unshakeable about his role in the conflict. As he saw the situation, nation was at war against nation, and what was at stake was human civilization itself. It was not until late in the war and afterward that information emerged on prisoner-of-war camps, concentration camps and extermination campaigns. What became known later served to reinforce the recruits' early sense that what they were training to do was important for humanitarian as well as political and military victories.

Pip explained his point of view on the bombing raids. Until the Allies were in a position to land an invasion force in Europe, the raids were the only way the war could be delivered back into Germany itself. The raids were directed to destroy its industrial infrastructure, which meant the Nazis had to shift critical resources from other fronts, and that in turn gave Canada's allies more capacity to deploy and manoeuvre.

In December 1939, following a model used successfully during World War I, Britain, Australia, New Zealand and Canada reached agreement about the training of pilots and aircraft crew. Canada had about four thousand personnel in the RCAF at the outbreak of war, but by 1944, under the British Commonwealth Air Training Plan, there were s said that one pilot and one plane needed ten ground crew: the instrument ╱ehicle mechanics; engine mechanics, or fitters; air frame mechanics, or riggers; drivers, cooks, service police, administrative personnel.

Pip's goal was to be one of the pilots. Nine out of ten recruits said the same thing, but severely selective evaluations throughout training were designed to place the right skills into the right jobs. The sorting was organized in steps, with specific skills identified at each step, and the scrutiny and evaluation started tough and got tougher.

Like all recruits entering the RCAF, he was posted to Manning Depot in Edmonton. Of the large group of recruits boarding the train in Vancouver, many spent the next two days playing cards and losing. Pip watched the losers, the winners and the process of the game as a whole, but he refused to participate and made a vow he kept to the end of his life that he'd never play cards for money. There were more interesting ways of losing money.

At Manning Depot, even the earliest procedures were designed to weed out anyone unsuitable for the services and get the others used to living the military life. Much of what determined success for an Aircraftsman 2 was whether or not he could fit in comfortably and be a positive contributor. The new boys underwent additional medical examinations and had their vaccinations. They were taught Air Force rules and regs, pushed to get themselves fit and to learn how to march and drill. Each one was kitted out with underwear, overcoat and everything in between from cap to shoes, plus a hussif containing essentials such as soap, towels and toothbrush, plus a large duffel bag for personal effects and clothing.

In the barracks, with each bunking room sleeping about sixty, they learned to keep their bunk, kit and personal dress up to standards. On all counts, Pip's boarding school experience stood him in good stead. He also managed with aplomb an impromptu surprise stint as a waiter in the Sergeants Mess and considered it good fun, though this time it didn't earn him any pocket money.

The recruits worked six days of the week from six in the morning straight through to early evening, though Sundays were marginally less regimented. Their training, which was handled mostly by non-commissioned officers, covered military law, medical and general hygiene and first aid but not airmanship or navigation. Recruits learned to march in disciplined flights of about sixty men, and the position of right marker, against whom the ranks and files literally aligned themselves, often enough went to Pip, who'd had previous experience in the cadet corps while at Brentwood.

They were granted leave from time to time during training to visit home or other places, and civilian families in Edmonton also welcomed the young recruits into their homes during these hard first weeks. Pip and many others say they'll never forget the Edmontonians' kindness and hospitable generosity.

After this introductory phase, aircrew recruits were posted to a flying station. Pip's was No. 7 Service Flying School at Fort Macleod, Alberta. The process of signing in at the Fort Macleod airbase produced a meal card, bed, bedding and other necessities, plus specific assignments around runways and hangars.

He and his colleagues learned to gas up the planes and push or pull them into or out of hangars without doing damage. They were taught how to do guard duty, and by watching and being sent on errands around the airbase—go here, go there, get this, get that—they learned who was working on what, plus the rudiments of engine maintenance and how airframes were maintained and made flight-ready. Their ever-present NCO enforced discipline.

Five of the men decided they'd grow moustaches, and they set a steep penalty of five dollars for shaving off any new moustache if it looked wretched. Gradually, Pip's raspy wisps grew out into a fine RAF-type moustache that he sometimes had a problem fitting into his oxygen mask in flight. The moustache became a trademark.

Dr. Kennedy of Fort Macleod, friend of a friend of the family, welcomed Pip and his pals to a day of golf and a cold beer during what little free time they had. On weekend leave, they explored Waterton Lake National Park and found it full of wonders. Less wonderful was experiencing the effects of major-league hail. One storm was so powerful and the hailstones so big the cloth covering of the Ansons on the open tarmac was completely shredded off.

After about a month of tarmac duty—the usual time for these postings ranged from three to five weeks—those selected for pilot training were despatched to an Initial Training School. In Pip's case, this was No. 4 ITS at the University of Alberta campus in Edmonton.

Pip and another man, with whom he got along well, were assigned to what had originally been the women's dorm. This roommate, with two years of medical school behind him, was killed in a flying accident soon afterward, and the eager young men so full of fight and idealism had to come to terms with the blunt realities of their new lives.

They pushed on with the rudiments of physics, chemistry, mathematics and trigonometry. They were taught navigation, meteorology and the principles of airmanship, as well as the art and science of flight controls for pitch, roll and yaw using models, diagrams and much waving-of-hands. Hours of study went toward aircraft recognition, a skill very strongly emphasized. They covered the fundamentals of military writing and law and of gasoline engine operation and repair. They had their first instruction and testing in the Link Trainer[34] and continued to do a daunting amount of marching drill. They were wildly impatient to get flying.

The tight-knit Australian contingent at No. 4 ITS didn't take lightly to anything considered unnecessary discipline. Even the merest hint of a slight wasn't tolerated. At one point, the Aussies took affront that their national flag was nowhere to be seen on campus, so they pulled down the Canadian flag one night and put up their own. Confined to barracks for a week, they chopped through the barracks wall with fire axes the first night and for good measure chopped down the flagpole. Pip wasn't sure how it finally turned out, but he remembered that on the one side, there was much sputtering and wringing of hands, and on the other, that the Aussies were thereafter pretty much left alone.

Graduation from ITS was a very big event.[35] When they knew they'd passed, eight of them who'd been selected for pilot training decided they'd celebrate at the top hotel in Edmonton, the MacDonald. Pip phoned the maitre d' and calmly booked a table for sixteen. By that time, all the fellows had local girlfriends, and the young ladies were tickled at the invitations for a big night out.

The maitre d' was appalled to see trainee airmen arriving for dinner—not officers or even NCOs but trainees—and demanded guarantees there would be "no funny stuff." He also expected firm proof up front they could pay their bill. They convinced him somehow that they were worthy of being let in, then had a first-rate meal and danced for hours to the music of a very good band. "It was magnificent," said Pip.

———————

After graduating, they were no longer nobodies. Some were assessed for navigation duties and were heading for Air Observer Schools. Those assessed for pilot training, the pilot trainees who were now authorized to wear the white flash on the fronts of their wedge caps, were going to one of the Elementary Flying Training Schools. Pip was posted to No. 5 EFTS at High River, Alberta.

He was surprised to find that the whole of No. 5 EFTS seemed to be operated by civilians—station commander, instructors, ground crew and support personnel. Seldom was a full formal RCAF uniform seen, and when one was, it had no rank badges on it. This was the Royal Canadian Flying Club way of doing things, a method almost entirely without the strict discipline for trainees at stations operated by the RCAF. This imposed on each man full responsibility for his own behaviour and proper attention to duty, and Pip said the high level of self-discipline required to avoid a "cease training" notation seemed to benefit them all. The base, at any rate, ran like clockwork.

They were mainly back in the classrooms again, except during lessons on the pre-flight inspection, the walk-around routine for their aircraft. They were also each assigned their instructors. Pip's was a bush pilot, a Mr. Hawkey, which fact may or may not have influenced his style of flying. Pip said he "loved the Tiger Moth from the first moment I saw it,"[36] and thus started his love affair with flying. "The joy of that first flight," he said, "was indescribable."

During the flight, Mr. Hawkey put the two-seater biplane into a tight spin and glanced over his shoulder to check the expression on his student's face. "I must have looked okay," said Pip. "Unbeknownst to me, I'd passed my first test." He took to flying with ease and soloed at seven hours or so, which more than anything else convinced him he'd made the right choice in joining the RCAF.

Some of the Tiger Moths they used were open-cockpit designs and some were canopied. Canadian-built Tiger Moths were modified by de Havilland "by adding wheel-brakes, a tail-wheel, a stronger undercarriage with the wheels set slightly forward, and a cockpit that could be closed by a sliding hood."[37] During Prairie winters, the canopied ones were much preferred. The planes had no radio equipment and noise levels were high in the cockpit during flight, so instructors and students shouted into Gosport speaking tubes that functioned much in the same way as stethoscopes.[38]

At first, they flew circuits-and-bumps over and over—took off, flew one circuit and landed; took off, went up, circled around again, landed. Then came aerobatics: steep turns first, then stalls and spins, then rolls and loops. Pip was in his element: "The exhilaration of it…!" Tricky winds from the Rockies made for some interesting moments in the air.

The accepted procedure for dealing with trainees' landings in strong wind was to load the fire truck with as many other trainees as it would hold and position it with engine running at the downwind end of the runway. There they'd wait for the next attempted landing. The problem wasn't fire as much as planes that would stay airborne after the engine had been cut. As the plane trying to land approached a groundspeed of zero, the fellows would swarm off the truck and leap to grab the plane's wings, holding it down at ground level by cumulative body weight until the pilot was able to taxi it into the hangar. "Some sport that was!" said Pip. "Very basic, but it worked."

They learned in class and in the air how to carry out rudimentary cross-country flights as well as the late evening flights that counted as night-flying in their logbooks. After sixty flying hours, both solo and dual, Pip was ready for the check ride. It was a big hurdle for neophytes. Conducted by a very senior instructor who hadn't flown with them before, this check ride was designed to see whether the new pilot could handle the plane under any circumstances. Take-offs, landings and circuit discipline were evaluated, and the instructor could judge how the new pilot handled loops, rolls and recovery from spins.

The plane Pip and the examiner used had its problems. Its frame had been wrenched out of kilter by one too many hard landings. "It was a miserable wretch to fly," said Pip, "but I was doing quite well until it came time to perform a roll, my favourite manoeuvre. I just didn't have enough control-stick movement to get it to roll. The instructor turned around to make sure I was doing all the right things, which apparently I was, but the machine absolutely would not roll. I respectfully invited the instructor to try, and thankfully, he couldn't do it either."[39]

———————

Pip passed and was notified he'd been assigned to No. 3 Service Flying School in Calgary. Bunk space there was at Currie Barracks on the far side of the airfield from the army base. To get back and forth, the fellows were allowed to ride free on the Calgary public transportation system—specifically, on an electric-powered streetcar that had a small stove in the back. The smart tactic in winter months was to try for a seat near the stove.

Innate skill and disciplined work weren't necessarily enough to succeed. Fifty LACs—Leading Air Craftsmen—started the course, all of them intensely proud of the LAC propeller insignia on their sleeves, but only about half got to graduate. Classwork continued to intensify, this time with thorough coverage of aircraft systems and performance under various conditions. The trainees memorized checklists and did cockpit checks while blindfolded. Under any circumstance, they had to click the appropriate switch instantly and be able to reset any circuit breaker.

The instructors, not a lot older than the students but often experienced bush pilots, were NCOs and officers of the RCAF. Admiration and carefully respectful friendship at a slight distance set the tone. They were evaluators, not buddies. A nice little trick of theirs was to tweak some part of the plane to make it temporarily unserviceable before aircraft walk-around checks and expect the student to spot the problem. It was bad news for the student if he didn't spot it. The cockpit pre-start checkup was another routine that had to be done to perfection, with testing done again and again. One by one, individual students were given a "cease training for cause" and directed into other roles.

The twin-engined Cessna Crane was a real performer as a trainer. "Starting up the Crane's two multipiston radial engines was a real high after the Tiger Moth's little in-line four-cylinder," said Pip, "a real thrill of noise and rumble through metal, of instruments coming alive, the smell of fuel and exhaust. You'd taxi out to take-off position, busy with tarmac traffic, going through the checklists, watching the RPMs, oil temperature, gas mix, fuel flow, always a magneto check. That was power and responsibility, and it was yours to handle with your own expertise."[40]

On cue, they were rolling and *up*, generally to a circuit altitude of about 1500 feet before powering back to cruise speed of about 110 knots. For landings, speed was pulled back to about 80 knots and gradually down to about 65 knots over the threshold of the runway. At exactly the right airspeed, the right distance down the runway and height from the ground, the idea was to stall and simultaneously touch down with a minimum of thumps and hops and preferably without blowing a tire or sliding off the runway.

"How the instructors let fledgling pilots proceed down perilous paths and not take the controls from us was sometimes quite incredible," Pip commented. "Those instructors have my heartfelt admiration and thanks."[41] A young pilot would soon have to trust his own judgement when he put a Halifax or Lancaster through evasive action to shake off fighters or get clear of flak, so though their progress through flight training was brisk, the process of developing skilled judgement was at the core of the lessons.

The practice was to solo as quickly as possible, regardless what they were flying. In the U.S. Air Force, training was often on multi-engine aircraft with two pilots, but the Canadians on operations would be flying British-designed bombers with one pilot, not two. Any problem with a little too much individuality — say, showing off during formation flying — was quickly fixed by one's peers.

The Cessna Cranes had no radio compass or other direction-finding equipment, so great care went into preparation for cross-country flights. On the missions in Europe, the pilots would have to reach the right waypoints, the right targets and, all the fates willing, the right way home. Training included map-reading in all conditions, marking and later finding a series of a definitely identifiable "pinpoint" towns or features of the land.

Dead-reckoning calculations reconciled the planned track and the actual, with headings corrected as needed during the flight. "No matter how good a flyer one was," Pip said, "the wind experienced during flight never seemed to match what was forecast for its direction and speed. Cross-country flying was always a challenge, and you simply could not get it wrong."[42]

No night cross-country exercises were assigned until the student was unfailingly successful in controlling his aircraft with the basic flight instruments: altimeter, airspeed indicator, turn-and-bank ball, vertical climb/descent meter, needle gauge, RPM gauge. They mastered instrument instruction in the Link Trainers, again using the irreplaceable ground-based machines that simulated actual cockpit conditions.

These simulators were mainstays of pilot training in many countries during the war and for decades afterward, because they could duplicate any kind of normal or extreme flight situation the instructor chose for the hapless student inside the machine. The ungainly thing lifted, bucked, tilted and dropped as the pilot inside was put through his paces and sweat from the stress poured off forehead and palms. In retrospect, the fellows said, time in the Link Trainer was absolutely the best possible preparation for bomber operations to come.

Before Pip's final test, not in the simulator but in open sky, a young army officer asked the instructor if he might fly as a passenger just for the experience of it. When Pip was put through some limited acrobatics, the officer belted into the rear seat sat quietly enough, but during the rising gusts and downdrafts through the Rockies' foothills, up came the passenger's most recent meal.

The instructor ordered Pip to land immediately, clean up the mess and let him know when the odour was gone. The army officer disappeared at a trot behind the hangars and stayed there for quite some time. Pip dealt with the janitorial work, then went up again with the instructor and passed the test handily. Boarding a civilian flight years later, Pip and the army officer unexpectedly met, and Pip blurted out: *"Son-of-a-bitch!"* They shook hands and had a good laugh.

With roughly 120 additional hours in his logbook after four months at Calgary, Pip went home on leave with a pal before the Wings Parade. No more gratifying event than the RCAF Wings Parade could be imagined for a young military pilot just about to become a newly commissioned Pilot Officer.

Pip learned after Wings Parade he was assigned to No. 3 General Reconnaissance Unit in Charlottetown for additional navigation training before going overseas. Because he was being sent to fine-tune his navigation skills over open water, he was guessing his operational assignment might be with Coastal Command, perhaps on the huge Sunderland flying boats, but what they got instead was Royal Air Force twin-engine Avro Ansons. A few of the old bombers had been modified for nav-training use: a navigator's position had been set up in the main cabin, and above the map table and dangling sextant, a clear "bubble" for taking sun shots had been installed.

Ground school this time involved plotting positions with the sextant or with RDF frequencies. The ocean surface lacks cross-country pinpoints, but the pilots became increasingly comfortable taking bearings on sun, moon and certain stars, at least in clear weather, as well as working with the mathematical magic of sight reduction tables. Though all the men in the group had their wings by then, the weeding-out process never stopped, and "cease training" notification was still a possibility.

Pip earnestly wanted to fly and immersed himself in learning how. Those in the course worked in pairs during the flights, taking turns navigating. His flying companion had the bad fortune of becoming airsick too often to keep up his end of things, so Pip was left to do more of the other part of the navigation assignment than the fellow could do himself. Pip improved his skill and eventually succeeded, and to his dismay, the other man failed out.

After two months on Prince Edward Island immersed in navigation training, he was notified he'd being going to England, to No. 11 Advanced Flying Unit at Nawton Shawbury. This was exciting news for a nineteen-year-old.

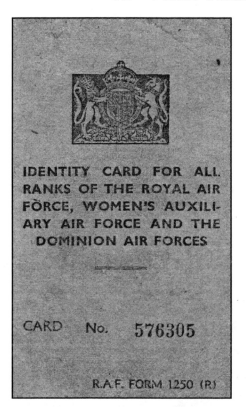

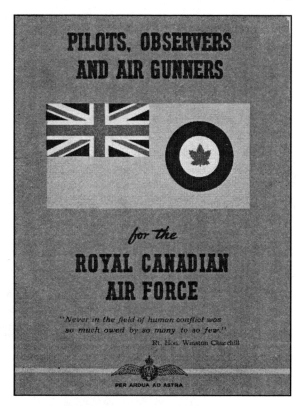

Scales of Pay for R.C.A.F. Aircrew

The following are the scales of pay for R.C.A.F. aircrew at various stages in their training:

AC2. (upon enlistment)...............................$1.30 per day.
LAC. Airman Pilot, Air Observer or Wireless Operator (Air Gunner) (Received soon after training is commenced).......................................$1.50 per day.

If you are selected for training as pilot or air observer, after completing training at an Initial Training School, you will be entitled to a special allowance of 75 cents per day, in addition to pay and allowances to which you are entitled at the time selected. This special allowance is paid continuously for the whole period during which you are undergoing flying training.

Over and above the daily rates of pay you receive, in addition, your meals and living quarters. You are also clothed, completely at the government's expense.

When you are mustered as sergeants at the conclusion of your training under the British Commonwealth Air Training Plan, your daily rates of pay, including flying pay, are as follows:

Airman Pilots	$3.70
Air Observers	$3.70
Wireless Operators (Air Gunners)	$3.20
Air Gunners	$2.95

In addition to the above rates you are also still provided with meals, quarters and complete clothing.

Upon embarking for overseas with, or in conjunction with the Royal Air Force, your pay will be in accordance with the scale of pay and allowances of the Royal Air Force. The deficiency, if any, in this rate from that of the Royal Canadian Air Force will be issued to you by the government of Canada as deferred pay, either on termination of service or otherwise in special circumstances.

For those selected as officers, the daily rates of pay, including flying pay are as follows:

Pilot Officer	$6.25
Flying Officer	$7.00
Flight Lieutenant	$8.50
Squadron Leader	$9.75

Officers are allowed $150.00 towards the purchase of their uniforms and receive, in addition free quarters and meals.

The RCAF used the same ID card (top left) as other components of the Dominion Air Forces.

*The booklet issued to RCAF recruits was **Pilots, Observers and Air Gunners for the Royal Canadian Air Force** (above). An excerpt: "To those of us charged with the responsibility of directing the great British Commonwealth Air Training Plan, the young men of Canada have provided an ever-present inspiration—the enthusiasm with which they have come forward in their thousands, the keenness with which they have carried out their training..."*

They joined up for honour, adventure and many other reasons, pay not being a main one (left).

LAC Holmes and colleague (below), at home on leave in Victoria. The white flash on the cap marks aircrew in training.

At Wings Parade, beaming Pip earns his pilots wings (right).

Halifaxes of 433 Squadron (bottom) in gaggle formation. One of the crew had a hidden camera with him on one of the ops, against regs, and later shared prints with his crewmates.

CHAPTER SIX
CANADIANS OVERSEAS

PIP'S INSTRUCTIONS WERE to proceed to the Port of New York. Another hundred or so RCAF aircrew from various Canadian locations—pilots, navigators, gunners, bomb aimers—were ordered to New York at the same time, and they converged on the embarkation wharf to board the troopship. Their convoy across the Atlantic would be led by the battleship U.S.S. *Nevada*.

Two days out, their ship started to lose speed and gradually slowed so much that a destroyer circled back and drew alongside to communicate. They were travelling under radio silence, so the agreed mode of communication was light-flicks of Morse code from Aldis lamps. The captain of the troopship had left his Aldis lamp ashore, however, so what everyone on both ships heard was a full bellow through a megaphone, ship to ship: "IF YOU CAN'T KEEP UP, GO BACK TO NEW YORK." Which they did.

With their ship in port for repairs and train tickets in their pockets for Halifax the next day, the fellows found themselves with a brief unexpected leave in New York. "Hilarious," Pip said, and left it at that. Once in Halifax, they boarded the RMS *Queen Elizabeth* and were immediately off for England. She was extremely fast and didn't travel in convoy. At thirty-four knots, no naval escort vessel could keep up for long, so her best protection was speed and an erratic zig-zag course to evade enemy submarines. "You had to be careful when you were up and about," said Pip, "because if you didn't have a good grip on something solid when she zagged, over you'd go."

Her crew complement was five thousand seamen, and she was carrying twenty thousand troops. Any air gunners aboard were put to work on the anti-aircraft guns, but the rest had no duties. Food was fair enough—two meals a day served-by-the-numbers—but walking around the crowded decks to get some exercise was nearly impossible. Pip considered himself lucky to be sharing a stateroom with only five others.

The crossing from Halifax to Greenock, Scotland, took only four days, and just before reaching harbour, Pip visited the ship's Medical Officer to report a sore throat and considerable malaise. "Have you by any chance been in close contact with many people in the last few days?" the doctor asked rather fatuously as he began examining Pip, then blanched. Pip had the mumps and was immediately quarantined to minimize further chances of an epidemic on board. As the anchor chains rattled down off Greenock, a tender came alongside, and while everyone from top brass to bottom scrubbers was kept back, Pilot Officer Holmes in solitary splendour was ferried off to a waiting ambulance bound for hospital.

The Contagious Diseases Hospital in Glasgow, not imaginatively named, was certainly an appropriate place in which to wait out a case of mumps, and the morning rounds soon developed an element of extra frisson. Rounds were led by the head doctor, a large and energetic Scot who would be trailed closely by Matron, then by Head Nurse, and finally, a retinue of nurses. At the foot of Pip's bed, the doctor would begin by carefully studying the chart, then clearing his throat in a grand way. In his broad Scottish burr and loudly enough that his voice travelled well down the hallway, he'd demand of his patient: "HOW'RE YER BALLS TODAY, LADDIE?" Morning after morning, it was cause for much tittering.

Pip recalls that he and Head Nurse, a tall and extremely thin woman, became good pals. On his second night in the hospital, she confided that her doctor had put her on a bottle of Guinness a day to fatten her up. She absolutely detested stout and got rid of it as best she could. Pip commented that if she ever needed assistance dealing with her Guinness dilemma, he'd be happy to help. She was pleased to avoid pouring it down the sink, which bothered her conscience, and he was equally pleased with the whole amiable arrangement.

When he was recuperating satisfactorily from the mumps episode, he was given a day pass—some very welcome freedom from the hospital, but only from nine in the morning until nine at night. On this first visit to the U.K., he wanted to have a good look around Glasgow and set off to reconnoitre.

In the early evening, he went into a pub for a meal and noticed a short red-haired Scot walk in right behind him and head for the bar without saying a word. The woman tending bar put out three double shots of Scotch, pulled three glasses of beer and tidily lined them up. The little Scot slapped down precisely the right amount of money and, still silent, threw back the first shot. And one of the beers. Then the second shot and a beer. And the third shot and a beer. Within five minutes, he went on his way, and what was apparently a daily procedure was complete. To Pip, it was an eye-opener.

Wanting to go farther afield on his final day of leave from the hospital, Pip decided to take a train to Loch Lomond. Over a pub lunch, he met another Canadian, an army man, and the two decided to visit the nearby castle and explore the battlements. They ended up hiking up through the hills among the sheep and forgot about the time. Pip realized he'd already missed his train and wouldn't make it back for nine o'clock, which was a chargeable offence under the King's Regulations and Orders. Matron would have no option but to charge him.

He spent a nervous night at a room in the Loch Lomond pub and caught the first train back to Glasgow in the morning. When he got to the hospital just after dawn, he was feeling miserable, but waiting for him at the hospital gates in the heavy drizzle were two of his nurses ready to brief him: what to say to Matron to avoid being put on charge and, importantly, what not to say. It worked. "I am forever grateful to those two nurses for their extreme act of kindness on a cold wet morning," Pip said.

After being discharged from hospital with a clean bill of health and no chargeable offences, he was sent to the Assignment Centre in Bournemouth on the south coast of England to wait for his posting. Men were billeted all over the place in hotels, hostels, private homes and old army barracks. Pip was lucky enough to get a hotel room for the two-week wait.

The Bournemouth stay was fairly boring, though it had its moments. Issued short passes and forbidden to leave the area, they were restless. Every so often, the Luftwaffe sent low-flying Ju88s to strafe the area. "What they hoped to achieve by strafing us, we weren't quite sure," Pip said. "All it did was remind us how ready we were to get up there and fight."

No. 11 AFU at Shawbury, Shropshire, was what he called "a real flying station"—drifts of the smell of fuel and oil on the wind, roaring of engines during takeoff and taxiing, men and women in uniform in a proper military infrastructure. To retune his flying skills after navigation ground school in Charlottetown, Pip put in seventy hours or so on the Oxford, a plane he said felt to him much like the Cessna Crane. The Oxford was a heavier and more quirky aircraft than the Crane, though, which made it a useful transition craft. Often called the Oxbox, it wasn't an operational fighting machine but a plane the recruits could use for basic flight and nav skills and that Royal Air Force pilots flew to update their skills. It was also put to work for transport duties.

One fault of the Oxford, they were warned, was that it would never recover from a tight spin, but Pip told of one student who survived that generally fatal circumstance. "Toughie" Ager had the presence of mind to fight his way to the main door against the slipstream and enough strength to counter the centrifugal forces on him and heave himself out. The parachute on his back had hit the throttles as he clambered to the door, so his empty plane at full speed did dramatic aerobatics on its own until it hit the ground in a fireball. It was an event that people at the airbase talked about for quite some time.

"Looking at my log book," Pip said, "I see most of the flights in the Oxford were short, lasting maybe an hour and a half or less. They were familiarizing us with the English weather and terrain we'd need to know for our own reconnaisance later. I soloed the Oxbox at five hours or so, with lots of circuits and bumps, then we did a whole lot of night flying." Knowing the terrain by day or night was important, because fog and rain obscured the landing aids. Some days, finding the aerodrome you wanted and landing safely were two separate tasks, both of them hard, and the frequent threat of enemy fighters near the airfields made even the practice routines exciting.

After the Oxford came the Vickers Wellington. Other than their machine guns, these light bombers could carry rockets, bombs, mines or torpedoes and were crewed by a full team of men: pilot, navigator, tail gunner, wireless operator, bombardier and flight engineer. The RAF often provided flight engineers for RCAF crews, and it was their job to make sure the plane was in all respects ready to go. During flight, they monitored the engines and could be put in charge of operating them, easing the load on the pilot. Not many flight engineers could be spared from actual operations, though, so training flights were often flown without one on board.

After five hours, Pip soloed on the Wellington and his training became more operational. With a navigator on board, he did longer cross-country flights in daylight or nighttime. For air-to-air target practice, he flew with gunners and machine guns on board. With bombardiers on board, he went through training on how to drop the practice bombs.

They weren't crewed-up permanently but were in task groups, individually honing their skills under various conditions. Each flight likely had a different crew, and Pip realized the great benefits of thorough pre-flight briefings and crisp in-flight crew discipline. It meant he knew who and what he was dealing with. He understood all the expectations for the operations and all the personalities and levels of skill at hand.

While at the OTU and flying the Wellington, Pip and his crews were told to fly over occupied areas of France to Rennes and drop leaflets over the city. "Ops" were missions that took an aircraft and crew over enemy-held territory, and such sorties, along with other support roles, were part of their training. Though he said he never fully understood how these leaflet raids urging citizens in occupied territory "to do something" would change the situation on the ground, the assignments were a real contribution to the war effort at last.

The leaflet ops also gave the crews some experience of being shot at and shooting back. The ack-ack — ground-based anti-aircraft fire — was sent up mainly by German 88 cannon, large-calibre guns that sent up multiple rounds per minute of high-explosive shells. When they exploded around the level of the planes, the shells lit up the night sky like fireworks.

During this period, they also flew diversionary missions designed to fill the airspace over occupied territory with planes that would peel off in a variety of directions, disguising the direction of the real bombing stream. The decoy planes were flying without ordnance, but the enemy didn't know which ones were or weren't carrying bombs and generally went after all of the planes with a vengeance.

––––––––––

At night and in certain conditions, the Wellington could look much like the multi-role Luftwaffe Ju88, and when a Wellington flown by Pip's very great friend Don McKay was returning from an ops over occupied France, it was shot down by a Fighter Command

Beaufighter that mistook it for a Ju88. The plane was lost, and pilot and crew were killed. The crews knew one another very well, and Don and Pip had bicycled all over northern England and become fast friends, so the funeral was heart-rending. "The lesson I learned that day," Pip said, "was that I mustn't ever again let myself enter into too close a friendship with any fellow airman during the war. Enduring such a loss was much too painful ever to repeat."

Notations in Pip's flight log are entered tidily one after the other down the pages about those sixty hours on the Wellingtons. "Those hours were intense ones," he said. Near the end of them, he was judged fit for a posting to 1666 Heavy Conversion Unit, at RAF station Wombleton in the Yorkshire dales near Nawton. "At the HCU, I was getting close to the heavy and concentrated action," he said, "and it felt really good. I was ready for the big time."

After a day or two of paperwork and orientation at Wombleton, the newly arrived pilots, navigators, gunners, flight engineers, bombardiers and wireless operators were ordered to gather in one large briefing room. The purpose of milling around chatting was to form themselves into crews that would stick together until the end of the tour, however that tour might end. Though this somewhat arbitrary method of crewing-up "seemed quite loosey-goosey," as Pip put it, the process worked extremely well. The crews formed up and fit themselves together voluntarily and compatibly.

In about thirty flying hours, he made the transition to the four-engine Halifax, older models that were "a real cow to fly." Ground crew "worked mightily" to keep them in good mechanical flying condition, and once mastered, those made every other Halifax easy to handle. "In retrospect," said Pip, "We as aircrew didn't accord the ground crews the accolades they richly deserved. The work of those hard-working and highly skilled men and women was vital to our survival, and they showed an unstinting dedication to duty in any conditions—snow, drizzle, heat and dark."

Aircraft handling procedures were considered paramount at that stage of training, and Pip was soloing after four hours of dual. After about seventy flying hours, Pip and his crew were judged ready.

———————————

Their posting was to the Canadian group: RCAF No. 6 Group, Bomber Command, and 433 Squadron at Skipton-on-Swale, Yorkshire.[43] No. 6 Group was the only bomber force Canada ever had. "Most Canadians have never realized," wrote author J. Douglas Harvey, "that in World War Two, the Royal Canadian Air Force was the world's fourth largest air force and No. 6 Group its largest fighting component."[44] Accommodation for the crews—those of 424 Squadron as well as 433 Squadron—was in functional bunkers quickly installed at the airbase. Constructed on farmland in the Vale of York, northern England, the airbase and landing strip were bounded by high hilly downs to the east and west.

The "Porcupine" designation originated with the citizens of Timmins. RCAF squadrons were twinned with Canadian cities to link those serving overseas with people in home communities, and the northern Ontario mining and forest products city of Timmins had requested a connection with a bomber squadron. When they were linked with 433 Squadron, they chose the image and nickname "Porcupine," and the fellows thus became the proud "Porcupines."

Successful performance called for teamwork at a high level of trust, and they worked together within a strict structure of system and order. "Deep bonds of respect permeated our relationship as a crew," Pip said. "There were certain barriers on base during off-duty time, mainly because some of the crew were commissioned and some were not, but when we went into town, we went as a crew." They laughed and talked together, drank together, got into and out of trouble together.

"To my mind," he said, "this sort of bond added immeasurably to the competence of our crew in the air." Each one depended on each of the others doing his job right, no matter what the circumstances. Habitual behaviours based on standard operating procedures and checklists controlled each segment: briefing, flight planning, aircraft walk-around, startup, takeoff, climb-out, altitude level reached, mission and tactics achieved, return-to-base navigation, descent, landing, shut-down, debriefing. The fundamental job wasn't to obey procedures. It was to get to the target, drop the bombs as planned and get back to base alive with the plane intact, and that involved a rather sophisticated and flexible combination of individuality and teamwork.

The RAF bombing doctrine, which was adopted by the RCAF, was quite different from the bombing doctrine of the United States Army Air Force. The USAAF flew out in daylight hours in close formation. Their main equipment was the B-17, heavily gunned and flown by two pilots. The formation of Flying Fortresses as a whole followed one leader's path and dropped the bombs on the formation leader's command, a technique named "carpet bombing." The technique as designed was based on the judgement of the lead navigator and/or lead bomb-aimer and was prone to error.

The RAF and RCAF didn't carpet bomb.[45] Improved radio and radar equipment became available early enough in the war that individual aircraft could accurately hit single targets. The expectation was that their crews had the combined skill and knowledge to conduct the entire ops profile: to navigate independently day or night to the target assigned and drop the ordnance at a specific time along a specific heading for a specific track along land or water.

While in 433 Squadron, Pip and his crew flew a variety of operations, almost all of them designed to arrive over the targets during darkness. "Gardening" was a term for laying mines in waters used by the German navy. Other assignments were to supply direct support for army or navy efforts or make planned runs to specific targets. On the night of December 4/5, 1944, for instance, Pip and crew were directed to the Durlacher machine tool factory in Karlsruhe on the Rhine.

Excerpts from Pip's flight log that night:

144 Halifaxes from 408, 415, 420, 424, 425, 426, 427, 429, 432 and 433 squadrons were joined by 46 Lancasters from 419, 428 and 431 squadrons on an attack at Karlsruhe. The crews were over the target at between 17,000 and 19,000 feet, releasing 854,000

lbs of high explosives and 678,000 lbs of incendiaries. According to reports, bombing was accurate with severe damage being caused. Among the factories destroyed was the important Durlacher Machine Tool complex.

F/O W. Mitchell from 415 Squadron was hit by flak; there were holes in the rudders, elevators and fuselage.

F/Lt. J. McAllister and crew, flying Halifax III MZ-483 coded 6U-J, was attacked by a Ju88; there was no claim or damage.

F/Lt. P. Robb was hit by incendiaries. The port wing caught fire. They dove into a cloud and the fire went out.

F/O J. Hall and crew, flying Halifax III NR-121 coded WL-G, were attacked by an Me109; there was no claim or damage.

P/O G. Sherlock landed at Elvington on return.

F/Lt. P. Holmes landed at Tempsford on return.

The men kept radio silence during operations, even during take-off. They didn't have radio communication with the airbase tower, so when they were ready to taxi out and take off, they did. The hardstand where the aircraft were parked was at one side of the airport, and because they knew which runway was in use, they simply moved into the lineup and taxied out into take-off position.

Once up and on course, strict intercom discipline was maintained. No one spoke unless there was a very real reason to do so—no comments, no joking around, just silence. "It's uncommonly strange to recall," said Pip, "that even with the engines roaring, it seemed silent during flights." But when a crew member sighted an aircraft, whether enemy or friendly, silence was broken to report its location to the pilot.

"If this occurred," Pip said, "with perhaps the tail gunner reporting where the enemy aircraft was in relation to us, I'd take immediate and aggressive action to get us out of there. This often meant a violent corkscrew toward and past the other aircraft to minimize the opportunity for them to get accurate shots at us. Doing this in the dead of night, enduring extreme G-forces often coupled with spatial disorientation, was tough enough on me, but for my crew, these violent evasive manoeuvres must have been alarming in the extreme."

On the occasional daylight operations, for not all ops were at night, evasive manoeuvres were even more violent because the pilot had visual references on which to gauge the moves. They didn't fly daylight ops in close formation, American-style, but used a looser grouping termed a gaggle.

Arrival over targets was always tense. At night, searchlights were scanning the sky to find the planes, and ack-ack fire could be heavy, so the explosions of sound and light near the plane's skin were sometimes spectacular. Avoiding enemy nightfighters was compounded by the danger of possible collision with one of your own planes.

Even the return flight was dangerous, with enemy fighters as well as one's own returning bombers to avoid. Finding the right airfield in the dark, in all weathers and winds, then fitting smoothly into the landing circuit among everyone else who could still fly were tasks done at the point the crews were most tired. Deep weariness followed their high-adrenalin-performance state, and crews deplaning after return were wrung out.

Once, a returning Halifax from their squadron had two engines on one wing inoperable and couldn't make it to the landing strip. "The pilot must have found that it called for more rudder than he could supply," said Pip, "and it gradually rolled to one side and struck the ground near a small village." Some of the crew survived, but the pilot and flight engineer, and a very young child in the village, were killed.

Handling the four-engine heavy bombers around airfields that until recently had been farm fields posed other problems. Most common was running one or more undercarriage wheels off the tarmac into the thick Yorkshire mud. As soon as the wheel or wheels left the runway or taxi-way, they'd sink deeply into the soft ground, particularly when the plane was fully loaded with fuel and bombs. Without the assistance of heavy machinery, that plane was going nowhere, and meantime, it was likely blocking the way for other planes. Although it was easy enough to do, it was a highly unpopular event.

Another nasty risk was blowing a tire. Because the brakes were holding back engine power while all the planes were waiting to reach their take-off runway, the brakes heated up. If after the pilot got airborne, he allowed the aircraft to land hard for any of several unavoidable reasons, the wheels alongside the overheated brakes would suddenly be compressed under great downward pressure as they rolled.

A blown tire might cause a spinout into the mud or through nearby structures. A rough bounce might crumple the undercarriage and produce a sliding, sparking belly landing. The rear gunner in his turret, with heaven on his side, might be sheared off and away, ending up far from the plane on the airfield, in shock but alive. At worst, such a belly landing from a ruptured tire or bad bounce could cause the four-thousand-pound "cookie" to detonate.

One witness of that kind of event said she'll never forget the sound at close quarters. It was, she remembered, an explosive roar and an enormous fireball. Others noted that the sound bounced in a very strange way, and Pip agreed. "Interestingly, the station control tower often never heard or felt an explosion of that magnitude," he said, "but windows as far as a mile away could be blown out simultaneously. Very strange." Though they realized these dark possibilities, the young crews simply continued to fly out to do their duty, mission after mission. This is what they'd come for.

When the whole squadron was confined to base, they knew an ops was due. Pre-flight briefings for night ops were done during the day. The navigators would be briefed together, usually slightly earlier than the other crew members. There were separate briefings for gunners, wireless operators, bomb aimers and pilots. When that was over, they'd congregate in the largest of the briefing rooms, where one wall was covered with cloth.

With all present, the Commanding Officer would draw back the cloth to show the target and the various tracks they would be using to get to it. The Commanding Officer gave the overview briefing, followed by the Intelligence Officer. Target coordinates and target arrival times were restated. Radio frequencies and bombing altitudes were reconfirmed. Comments were added on evasion and escape routines. And before the time came for the men to head for the planes, each crew went over the mission profile together to be sure they had it clear.

Then they'd go fetch Pinky, because ritual is ritual and mustn't be sneezed at. Pip's crew decided early on they wouldn't take off unless Pip had his toy pink elephant, which had been given to him as a good-luck gift, astride one shoulder. A tether allowed Pinky to be hung up above the pilot only slightly out of the way of the instrument panels. Though his colour faded and one of his ears started coming unstitched, the mascot elephant, among other factors, got the crew and the plane there and back during thirty-three missions.

"The year that began in March 1943 and ended in March 1944 brought the bloodiest and most devastating aerial battles," says one book about Bomber Command. "Over 2,700 bombers were shot down."[46] It was a deadly time. "Aircrew casualties during the war were appalling," states one collection of aircrew memoirs. "Sixty percent of the aircrew who served in Bomber Command during the war lost their lives."[47]

Once the engines started, they were in high-alert performance mode, but while they were waiting, they were usually restless and impatient to get going. To settle down, they had another ritual that never failed to help. After the aircraft walk-around was complete, they'd gather at the tail wheel and pee on it well and truly before climbing on board. It was a ritual with possible anthropological origins for claiming and protecting one's territory or perhaps a symbolic gesture of comradeship and solidarity with overtones of male irreverence or irony. Then again, it was practical comfort, because it was going to be a long flight there and back.

———————————

Pip woke on his twenty-first birthday in February 1945 to learn he'd been promoted to Squadron Leader. He kept heading out over Europe and kept turning up at his own airfield again, he said, but in the final months of the war as warfare technology improved, the dangers were increasing. "They were killing them off so fast the chance of promotion was pretty fair," he said, and it was true, but it was an honour hard-earned.

After a thirty-three-ops stretch of bombing, Pip, his crew and planes were substantially intact. Call it skill, name it luck, but it was an all-too-rare outcome. Updated news about someone he knew had been wounded came from the Canadian High Commissioner to London. The note reached Pip at Skipton-on-Swale airfield early in March '45 and was directed to "My dear Philip":

You sent me a very kind letter when you heard that Hart was wounded, which touched my wife and me deeply. I ought to have written long before this to tell you how much we appreciated it, but I waited until Hart was well on the way to recovery… As you say, he has been helped greatly by his own patience and courage.
Your devoted godfather,
Vincent Massey

Pip recalled for journalist Jim Hume his experience on 31 March 1945 during a daylight raid on Hamburg. In one of 361 Lancasters, along with a hundred Halifaxes and eight Mosquitos, they met the Luftwaffe dayfighter force. "Everything was going fine, when two German fighters broke cloud at five thousand feet. I said, 'What the hell is that?' They were Me262s, and we were getting our first look at Germany's new twin-jet."[48]

He added that it's difficult in retrospect to determine which challenged them most: an attack by the nightfighters—the powerful Ju88 and Me110—or by the dayfighters—the Me109 and FW 190. The most dangerous of them late in the war was the extremely fast Me262. One of Pip's gunners shot one down and got a half-credit for another. Both his gunners "were decorated after a close call with a new German weapon—the twin-jet Messerschmitt 262."[49]

During his long tour of duty, he hadn't been granted leave. He was at his station in Yorkshire on 7 May and 8 May as documents were signed to end the war in Europe, and everyone understood that the nature of the war was about to become very different. A group was being organized to take part in the ongoing war against Japan, and Pip volunteered. Many of the air crew still in England were being shipped home, their duty ended, but the men who'd volunteered for further service were given leave to return home briefly before beginning the next stage of their training.[50]

Planning just a short visit in Victoria, Pip packed a few things and handed over the rest of his kit, including his motorbike, to the care of an English church minister he knew well. During his voyage across the Atlantic in early August 1945, two atomic bombs were dropped on Hiroshima and Nagasaki. Those put paid to Tiger Force, and much else. Four days after landing in Quebec City, he was sent home to the west coast.

A reunion of Holmes brothers, each in uniform, brought together Des, Pip and Vincent. Still too young for the Royal Canadian Navy, Vincent had joined the cadets. Pip had just been demobbed from the RCAF. Des, on leave, was still serving with his regiment, the Royal Engineers, and returned overseas after the reunion.

Pip's departure from England was noticed. Another note reached him from Canada House in Trafalgar Square:[51]

Dear Philip,

I imagine you must have gone home while we were in Canada, but was sad to have you disappear out of our existence so quietly and so silently—but I hope before too long we shall meet in Canada... We always want to keep in touch with you. Give our love to all the family, and take much for yourself from ourselves.

Yours as ever,

Vincent Massey

A telegram arrived at 336 Newport in November '45 addressed to S/L P.D. Holmes. Someone at the telegraph office had added in pencil: "Mail Confirmation—Empire 7390."

UNCLASSIFIED. DFC AWARDED YOU EFF 12 NOV ANNOUNCED 16 NOV
CONGRATULATIONS FROM THE MINISTER FOR AIR AND THE CHIEF
OF THE AIR STAFF ON BEHALF OF HIMSELF AND ALL RANKS OF THE
ROYAL CANADIAN AIR FORCE.

Pip had been awarded the Distinguished Flying Cross. The initiating citation
forwarded by Wing Commander G.A. Tambling is glowing: "Throughout his many
sorties, he has displayed outstanding courage, keenness and initiative in leading his flight,
and his fearless example and undoubted ability have contributed much to the successes
obtained. Whilst on the ground, his wide knowledge of aircraft plus his untiring efforts
with new crews particularly has added greatly to the general efficiency of the squadron
and set an example of the highest order. I consider his exceptional qualities of leadership
and organization plus his fine offensive spirit in action fully merits the award of the
Distinguished Flying Cross."[52]

It was a proud achievement, and the qualities that earned it were the same ones that
shaped what he would achieve later.

Wee Donald McKay (right) was Pip's very great friend at OTU and frequent bicycling companion. Donald's plane, mistaken for Luftwaffe incoming, was shot down by so-called friendly fire over southeast England when returning from France. No one aboard survived.

"Uniform one day old!" (centre left). By Spring 1944 (below centre), the uniform and the pilot have experienced a lot but are still in good form.

From Skipton-on-Swale, the Yorkshire roads were quickly explored by bicycle (centre right).

Bottom, Squadron Leader Holmes and bomber crew pose on the tarmac.

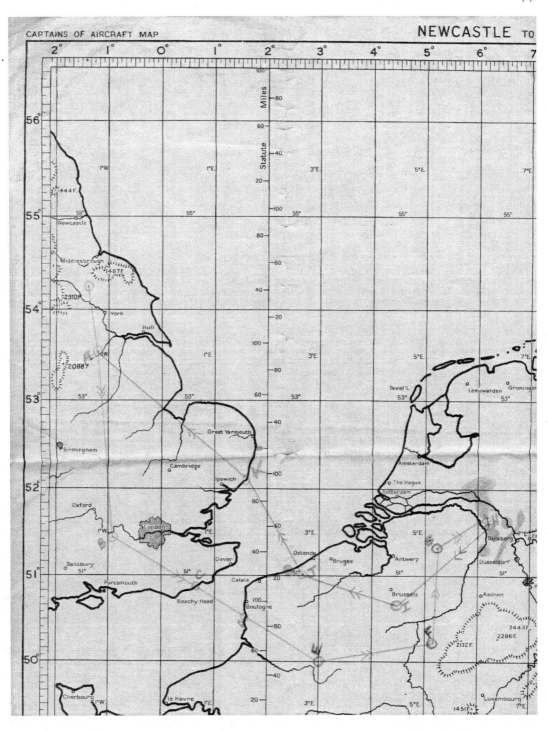

Part of a mission map, "Captains of Aircraft Map, Newcastle to Prague,"
in Pip's files with his logbook, showing target, outbound and return routes and waypoints.

Brothers in uniform at Skipton-
on-Swale, Autumn '44
(top, l-r): Jim, Vic, Jack, Dick,
Squadron Leader Pip, and Jan.
Crewmate Bob
was taking the photo.

The Distinguished Flying
Cross (right), one of which was
awarded to S/L Pip.

Brothers in uniform
in Victoria (right) at
a reunion after the
war (l-r): Vincent,
Desmond, Pip.

CHAPTER SEVEN
DESIGNING A LIFE

PIP ADVISED THE kindly English minister by mail he likely wouldn't be back for the motorcycle—"I think I told him to sell it to raise funds, if he liked, or to use it himself to get around the parish…"[53]—and arranged for the rest of his belongings to be shipped.

Though he would liked to have returned to university after the war and though he reviewed the many career routes open to him, including staying with the RCAF, Pip was well aware his father had been hoping he'd join the family company. He realized he could wholeheartedly involve himself in what his father had been guiding him toward since boyhood—judging land, working with people, invigorating his community—and make a successful career in real estate, property management, mortgages, insurance and appraisals. He made his decision and started his new civilian job in November 1945.

He set himself the task of learning as much as possible about the business in the shortest period of time. Brentwood College School had giving him solid grounding and all-round development, and the intense and efficient training procedures in the RCAF showed him that education and training produce top performance. In 1945, however, he couldn't find any set of comprehensive industry standards or formal programs of education in real estate.

Pemberton Holmes as a company, originally based on civil engineering and surveying, had repositioned itself as a one-stop real estate generalist[54] handling property management, real estate sales, insurance, mortgage brokerage and appraisals. He and his father both believed good corporate behaviour must include participation in community life and that the effect of volunteer efforts by individuals and businesses in local events was singularly beneficial for all concerned. It was good business, and it was a satisfying way to live a life. The sixtieth anniversary of the company was coming up in 1947, and the two began discussing ways to develop the capacities of the firm and its agents.

———————————

Pip's post-war emergence into Victoria business circles was marked publicly at the Gyro Club.[55] In 1945, his father Cuthbert had become president of the Victoria Chamber of Commerce when Chamber president G. Hamilton Harmon died, filling in the remainder of Harmon's term until his own term began. Major Holmes introduced Philip as a member of the club at a luncheon meeting and presented him with the membership pin given to his own father nearly twenty-five years earlier.

While Pip was turning to his business career, he didn't lose interest in the services and was one of the instigators and organizers of the Air Force Officers' Association of Vancouver Island. A few RCAF and RAF veterans got together in mid-February '46 to discuss forming an Air Force club with others recently home from the war and those who'd served during World War I in the Royal Navy Air Services and Royal Flying Corps.

Among the forty former officers present, the resolution in favour of forming the club was unanimous, and Pip was named its first president. The primary aim was to maintain and foster the friendships made in the service. A secondary objectives was "to support every endeavour that safeguards the air defence of Canada." No planes whatsoever had been visible over Victoria until a few decades before,[56] and this was true in many communities, so they decided another of their aims would be "to make Canadians more air-conscious." Membership would be open to male officers and former officers of the British Air Forces, including members of the navy and army whose duties were primarily connected with aerial warfare. The association was started and achieved its primary aim almost immediately.

Pip had declared as a boy that he loved to be mobile, and in late February '47, he set out on an extended business trip with a friend of his father's. S.J. Willis was happy enough to make the travel arrangements and take the trip but didn't like public speaking, and one result of the long tour was that Pip emerged as a speech-maker. His father had given him many a tip about drafting and delivering a rousing good talk, and at each opportunity, he practiced.

Between February 20 and April 11 of 1946, Messrs. Holmes and Willis followed their tightly packed itinerary, meeting real estate people at each stop: from Victoria over to Port Angeles, then from Seattle through Portland, Eugene, Rossburg, Medford, Redding, Nevada City, Grass Valley, Sacramento, Merced, Hanford, Porterville, Mojave, Riverside, El Centro, San Diego, Los Angeles, Oxnard, Santa Barbara, King City, Santa Cruz, San Jose, Oakland, Richmond, San Francisco, Santa Rosa, Eureka, Grants Pass, Eugene, Olympia—and back into Portland, then Seattle, then home to Victoria. After that, Pip said, public speaking didn't faze him one whit.

A death, a displacement, an anniversary and a fire characterized the year 1947. Pip's Grandfather Pem, who had been such a great friend to his grandson and source of much wonderment with his botanical triumphs, died in 1947 when Pip was twenty-three. After F.B.'s death, his executors were quick to sell the Pemberton Building[57] to Norman Yarrow, an unanticipated transaction that meant the company had to move to a new address.

The company's sixtieth anniversary of its founding was also celebrated in 1947, and its president's statement of business philosophy was distributed in a commemorative pamphlet.[58] Cuthbert Holmes emphasized that the one asset vital to acquire is judgement born of experience:

> To flourish for sixty years, to keep attracting youthful abilities in order to stay vigorous, any firm must have certain capacities and characteristics. It must have the facilities to serve its customers well. It must have the means and stability to give this good service through good and blighted years. It must put the welfare of those who depend on it above the temptation of temporary advantage.
>
> These things are not necessarily developed only through long years of service, but one asset hard to acquire otherwise is a vital one—judgement born of experience. Where important financial considerations hang on opinion—be it on investments, the purchase or management of real estate or the extent of insurance protection—the customer is entitled to expect that the counsel on which he relies is dependable. There are sixty years of knowledge, judgement and experience behind the advice of Pemberton's.

His father continued to guide Pip's training, pointedly reinforcing how their firm must relate to its customers, while immersing his son in on-the-job experience—initially with two years in property management, then several years in the liability and casualty insurance segment. Pip understood and could convey to the clients the benefits of insurance and the interrelationship of real estate and insurance, but at a certain point he wanted more formal instruction. He discovered, for instance, that opportunities were limited to learn how to handle customers' insurance contracts, and the lack of such courses added determination to his drive to develop a program of professional training in that area.

Cuthbert started his full term as president of the Victoria Chamber of Commerce with a number of ideas tailored to Vancouver Island, all of which he and Pip had discussed at length. One of his plans was for comprehensive development of roads that looped through a series of communities and back to their starting points. He suggested such systems "would achieve several purposes: economic development of the areas they served, encouragement for tourists to spend more time on the Island and magnificent recreation opportunities for residents."[59] These were areas that he and Pip often explored, together or separately. The two men knew Vancouver Island thoroughly.

The plan suggested five loops for priority consideration, and the Associated Chambers of Commerce of Vancouver Island recommended to the provincial government that funds to survey a number of routes be included in the 1948 provincial spending estimates. A decision was made to determine costs and feasibility of four loops:

1 From Port Renfrew to Shawnigan; and/or Port Renfrew to Cowichan Lake via Gordon River; and/or Port Renfrew to Cowichan Lake via Robertson River.

2 Port Alberni to Cumberland via Beaver Creek and Comox Lake.

3 Cowichan Lake to Port Alberni.

4 Port Alberni to Tofino.

It took years for the concept to come to fruition, but with a combination of public highway development and privately constructed logging roads, the loops evolved roughly the way father and son had foreseen. The route for commercial and private traffic promoted sixty years later as the Southern Island loop, for example, followed their plan for a circular connection from Victoria westward via Sooke and Jordan River to Port Renfrew, northeast to the Cowichan Valley and south via Duncan and the Malahat to Victoria.[60]

Father and son had a shock in 1947 when a fire at Brentwood College School burned down all but one of its campus buildings, and the destruction was equally miserable news for alumni, friends and the surrounding community. The Brentwood Memorial Chapel, constructed with the boys' help between 1924 and 1931 a slight distance apart from the other buildings, survived the fire.[61] The college had been nurtured by a group of Victoria business and professional men, Cuthbert among them. "It was a distinctly Western Canadian school," Pip said in an interview years later. "Strongly Western Canadian, and just a going concern... Dad and two or three others started it, you know, in 1921. At that time, the University School was a military school. My father thought there was room for another one, so he and Mr. Hope bought the bankrupt old Brentwood Hotel, and away it went."[62]

It opened in September 1923 with an "initial enrolment of fifty boys and a faculty of four," but it might well have died in the ashes. The loss of its buildings forced school operations to stop within the year, and after 1947, only a sustained effort by a group of Old Brentonians, including alumnus Pip, kept it going at temporary locations until permanent premises were found.

The economic boom in land sales and housing following the war caused the company to reevaluate its situation. One pivotal decision was whether to continue the company's practice of being agents for clients or to move into property development. Given the healthy history of the business, the decision whether to be acting on one's own interests versus acting on behalf of others wasn't a difficult choice.

The company opted for an update of its founding premise: "The decision was to retain the original course: acting as agents and in the interest of other people, exclusively. That decision being made, they looked at their various departmental operations, making sure they were up to par: negotiation of property, management of property, insurance of property, financial management. All were finely honed."[63]

Pemberton's needed a new business address and bought an 1899 office building at the northwest corner of Government and Broughton, roughly the site of the HBC fort at which J.D. arrived in 1851.[64] When Pemberton's opened for business after the move in 1948, their new space was considered state-of-the-art. One concept they adopted was to arrange the space so that clients entering their office were met by staff trained to guide them to the appropriate person for their purposes.

When the company relocated, Pip was involved in the insurance side of the business.

The numbering of the street address, which was 1002 Government when the company moved in and for decades after, became 1000 Government by the mid-'70s in a requested change at Victoria City Hall. "Same doorway, rounder number," Pip said then, but from the start, that office was for him a happy and productive base for his professional life.

While still with the Victoria Chamber of Commerce in 1949, Cuthbert Holmes began his two-year term as president of the Associated Chambers of Commerce of Vancouver Island.[65] Pip paid attention to his father's activities in those roles, and when he in time held each of the positions himself, he had the background knowledge he needed. And though he'd already been a member of the Society of Residential Appraisers for a while, Pip became a director and stayed on its board for the next six years.

By 1950, he had also considerably broadened his knowledge of mortgages. As a boy, while he and his father were touring around on excursions to look at properties, one of the many things he learned through his own experience was that reconnaissance is never wasted. He knew how to evaluate a property and was a pretty good judge of human nature, and in the next component of his working life, he started to master the financial processes.

The company normally didn't lend its own funds but acted as a trust for funds belonging to clients. It acted for and on behalf of its clients. Having lent out that money, it collected the repayments made by the borrower and remitted it as requested by the client. "When I was moved into the area of mortgages and mortgaging," Pip said, "my father's early advice again stood me in good stead. He supplied me with a fundamental understanding of the mortgaging process, pointing out that the process itself is the critical element in determining whether or not a mortgage will be recommended."[66]

During two more years' experience in the mortgage department, Pip established his credentials in Pemberton Holmes and was discovering his own financial prowess and the satisfaction of becoming known as a serious player in the business world. It was generally not understood, then or later, that while Pip studied and eventually mastered multiple aspects of the real estate world, he himself never worked as a real estate agent on the buying and selling of properties. He respected those doing it, but that wasn't the work he did.

He was scrutinizing the industry itself and where it could and should be evolving. He could see its problems and failings around the province and elsewhere and was energized by the idea of increasing the public's confidence in the ethics and professionalism of the people working in the real estate industry. "I was seized with the idea that real estate should be recognized as a vocation rather than as an occupation," he said. "The challenge was how to put that vision into effect."[67] He joined a small group of colleagues who designed a campaign to fit the challenge.

Pip explained that they needed to shift public perception: real estate must not be viewed as an activity of extreme self-interest, which it too often was, but as a community-minded activity benefiting the clients as much as the firms. The real estate firms themselves needed to be made more aware that public confidence based on real estate practitioners' ethical professionalism meant increased business for everyone in the industry. They didn't necessarily see that it was indeed to their own advantage to behave well. Pip decided he wanted Pemberton Holmes to be the exemplar of behaving well.

The strategy Pip drafted for himself in his career was quite specific: to show by personal and corporate example that representing clients' interests was good business; to provide exceptional education and training opportunities for Pemberton Holmes employees; to deliver speeches at the right times and in the right circumstances emphasizing to every real estate company the benefits of solid corporate support for education and training; to support the monarchy through his province's Lieutenant-Governors[68] as well as the RCAF and other branches of military service; and to work to help a variety of business and community organizations. Ever a doer, he promptly put his chosen strategy into effect.

While busy with the company and new ideas for the real estate industry, he was also kept active in the Air Force Officers' Association of Vancouver Island with his duties as its president. A few members, himself included, were also handling organizational details for the formation of 89 (Victoria) Squadron, RAD.

A separate but related role for him appeared on the horizon. Squadron Leader P.D.P. Holmes, who was by then twenty-six, was asked to form an air force unit, and retaining his rank in his role as its first Commanding Officer, formed #2455 Aircraft Control and Warning Squadron (Aux.), RCAF. With a strength of about a hundred men, his unit's first task was to restore to top running order their convoy of fourteen radar-equipped vehicles that had been in storage for five years. This they did.

Very soon afterward came the challenge of joining with three other squadrons in a major air exercise, which meant transporting a convoy from Victoria to Long Beach on the west coast of Vancouver Island where no road access existed. Difficulties and adventures abounded, but the effort was a resounding success. Based on what he learned during his bike trip to the outer coast and its beaches, he suggested they ship the whole convoy from Port Alberni to Ucluelet by tug and barge and ship themselves back to Victoria base the same way two weeks later. It was a thorough testing for all involved, including Pip as the young commanding officer.

By 1950, the Air Force Officers' Association of Vancouver Island was growing steadily, and Pip, first president, became its membership director. At a meeting of the association five years later, agenda notes say 1954 membership stood at seventy-six, double the 1953 figure and the best since 1946. Membership by 1964 would stand at about three hundred, with a quarter of those having served in the First World War.

When the first parade of the #2455 Aircraft Control and Warning Squadron was held at the RCAF recruiting centre under Pip's command, he announced that the formation of a second island squadron, likely based in Nanaimo, was probable. He invited women who wanted to join the local unit to report to the recruiting centre or to call them for more information.

While taking on new commitments without relinquishing existing ones, he was also determined to keep current the various skills he'd already acquired. His aeronautical map of the Nootka-Nanaimo area and of the offshore airspace is meticulously plotted in fountain-pen ink various times and distances off Pachena Point and Barkley Sound, noting: "Summer Camp, Tofino, July 1951. Time is PDST."[69]

And by way of following through on his stated intention of serving the Crown, Pip became honorary aide-de-camp to His Honour Clarence Wallace, Lieutenant-Governor of British Columbia. Pip remarked candidly years later that Wallace taught him "how to drink scotch and how not to drink scotch." Invaluable advice, he added.[70]

Memories of his childhood stay in the Queen Alexandra Solarium might have lent a poignant edge to his ongoing connection with the institution, of which he became a director, but he didn't trot it out for public view. "A cheque for $4,000, Easter Seals proceeds, was presented to Philip Holmes for the Solarium at a Friday luncheon at the Empress Hotel," one newspaper clipping says. The article adds only a short comment from Pip. "'The Solarium needs public support more than ever,' said Mr. Holmes."[71] Appropriate, and carefully neutral.

During this period of learning what he needed to know in real estate—as well as the logistics of tug-and-barge transport, the rules of order for chairing association meetings, the ways of Government House and the knowledge of scotch—Pip might also have been reviewing certain points of formal etiquette. A garden party, such as the one held at Government House in mid-August 1951—"The Lieutenant-Governor of British Columbia and Mrs. Wallace request the pleasure of your company … "—would have been readily manageable for a well-bred young man, but a visit by royalty, particularly in Victoria and most particularly involving naval participation, heightened the community imagination and the study of protocol in a singular way.

The Provincial Committee of Arrangements issued a pamphlet that outlined behavioural expectations for Premier Byron Johnson and others during the 1951 three-day visit to Vancouver and Victoria of Princess Elizabeth and Philip, Duke of Edinburgh.[72] In a town that tended to take the monarchy very seriously indeed, some of the assignments were more glamorous than others. Pip's was to be "on duty, Empress Hotel Lounge, Royal Visit, Victoria, British Columbia." Accordingly, Pass No. Thirty-Three was issued to S/Ldr. P.D.P. Holmes by the Assistant Commissioner of the RCMP for Monday 22 October 1951. With it came a Royal Canadian Navy invitation for the same day from Flag Officer Pacific Coast and Mrs. W.B. Creery, for the invitee to be presented to Their Royal Highnesses Princess Elizabeth and the Duke of Edinburgh. A lovely day was had by all.

A note from Premier W.A.C. Bennett to "my dear Squadron Leader Holmes" thanked Pip "for assistance on the public reception for His Excellency the Right Honourable Vincent Massey, Governor General of Canada … "[73] Pip's godfather had become the first Canadian-born Governor General. During this and other dignitaries' visits, his experience and connections were emerging as social and professional assets.

———————————

A new aspect of Pip's life was underway, but at a distance: the founding of an organization in Europe that would intersect with Pip's working life years later and form a major part of his career.

The French National Confederation of Property Managers created in 1945 had become, under the guidance of its first president Pierre Colleville, an association of property managers at the international level. Representatives from Belgium, Canada, Great Britain, Holland and Switzerland joined French and Danish members for the first time in 1948 to examine national and international situations in housing and rents as well as the profession as a whole. During the chaos of the war, they decided to take the organization forward.[74]

"Immediately after World War Two," Pip explained, "this international real estate organization began to take shape, and on June 2, 1951, representatives from several European countries met in Brussels to create it formally. They could see the world becoming what would later be called 'the global village' and knew their emerging real estate profession needed an international system of communication and coordination. They based it in Paris and named it the Fédération Internationale des Administrateurs de Biens-Conseils Immobiliers — the International Federation of Managers and Councillors in Real Estate."[75]

The acronym of the full French name was FIABCI, pronounced in all languages *fiab-see*. Although its name was revised slightly in subsequent decades and although Canadians and Americans generally knew it as the International Real Estate Federation, it was and is known worldwide as FIABCI. The role for which it was launched is largely unchanged from its first years, though its activities have expanded exponentially.

"FIABCI was founded in Paris in 1951 with the object of providing a forum and exchange of information on all matters connected with the ownership, development and management of real estate worldwide," explained its long-time Secretary-General Alexis Noldé. "The federation is ... represented at the United Nations and at a number of the regular meetings of several professional institutions of international importance ... I should perhaps emphasize that FIABCI is not in any way political, although it rightly and inevitably has an influence on matters of public importance by improving the knowledge of its members on matters that are fundamental to a civilized society."[76]

Cuthbert was in hospital in July '53 and, as he often did, wrote a note to his son Pip:[77]

I woke 1/2 hr ago with some pain, a slightly stuffy head and feeling chilly. Head Nurse says too late to have another sleeper. However, I've had five hours of sleep nearly. The real point of this is to tell you how GREATLY I appreciate the work you have done ALL YOUR LIFE and now for me. I always feel you left the Air Force, where you had done so brilliantly and to the head of which I think you wd likely have risen, because you felt I needed help in the office. I am most grateful for that and for all yr long, unselfish, continuous devotion ... Bless you and all yours, always. When I come back the one thing I wd ask you to do is to keep me posted regularly on office results. God Bless ... C.H.

This intermesh of business and personal matters was natural for them. The same comfortable blend pervades a 1955 exchange of notes with family friend Alice Llewellyn-Jones, who lived in Parksville. She was concerned about a large property on the Chemainus River that Pip knew from his duck-hunting days and whether it was being supervised or had been resold.

Addressing "My dear Pippy," she wrote, still calling him by his baby name, "Are the fields full to the fences with thistles? Do they need a farm manager? Wouldn't bother you but this could be business." To which Pip replied: " … I am only sorry I cannot help you very much in regard to Swallowfield. M'Lud B. bought it and, as far as I know, still owns the lovely place, which I gather, but only from hearsay, is in pretty rundown condition. Nevertheless, if your friends are really interested, we would certainly be delighted to look into either Swallowfield or anything else for them … "

Pip was immersed in a series of beginnings. He'd married for the first time in Victoria after his return from Europe and, during these years, happily became the father of four children.[78] These were the times of car trips and camping treks, large gatherings for extended family of several generations, his first sailboat, always more social occasions and new aspects of the PH company business and auxiliary reserves. He was receiving invitations to join boards of trustees but was particularly focusing on development of new ideas for standards and education in real estate.

As aide-de-camp, 1950-53 (right), to Lt.-Gov. Clarence Wallace.

Wearing his DFC (below), a chat with godfather, now Governor General, Vincent Massey.

A civilian at the office (bottom).

In a fine old Cowichan sweater, dock-sitting contentedly (top) with daughter Susan.

A brace of ducks and a dirty dinghy to show for a day's hunting (far left).

*Another kind of **Duckling** (left), first of his four boats.*

Cuthbert Holmes at Maltby Lake with two of his granddaughters (below).

October 1957 at Lambourne, Pip's parents' house at Cowichan Bay (top). Standing (l-r): Pip, his son Craig, Yoda Moyle ("a cousin of Philippa's"), Amy and Jake Pemberton ("Jake was Philippa's youngest brother"), Jack Moyle (Yoda's husband), B-M ("Baby Mab, Gran's sister, mother of Penny Hett"), Cuthbert standing behind Jennifer, and Vincent at right. In front (l-r): Diana ("with her hand in front of her face"), Susan on Philippa's lap, "Gran" (Philippa), Laura McGrath (behind Philippa, "Laura being Amy Pemberton's sister").

Guests leaving Lambourne after Thanksgiving visit in 1957 (bottom), in a rush of goodbyes, hugs, waves, promises, children, dogs and cars. Cuthbert and Philippa are in the doorway.

In an onshore wind (top left, l-r): Susan, Diana, Jennifer and Craig.

Pip's children at Maltby Lake (top right, l-r): Jennifer, Craig, Diana and Susan.

Craig and Jennifer (left), called "the Bobbsey Twins," at Gran's on Maltby Lake.

Craig and his sled (above) at Knockan Hill, north of Portage Inlet, Victoria. "Knockan Hill," anglicized from the traditional Songish name Nga'k'un, was labelled on J.D. Pemberton's 1855 map for the Hudson's Bay Company.

CHAPTER EIGHT
INDUSTRY RESTRUCTURED

NO MANDATORY QUALIFYING exams for licensing existed in British Columbia's real estate industry in the late 1940s, and it would be nearly another decade before they did. The province's first real estate act had been in force since 1922 and individual real estate boards had been established for decades in Vancouver, Victoria, New Westminster and elsewhere, but it wasn't until 1949 that the B.C. Association of Real Estate Boards was founded.

"Back from World War II," Pip said later, "came a group of thoroughly feisty, capable fellows bringing with them ideas, determination and some mental side arms carried in well-greased holsters. About that time, the Real Estate Institute of Canada grandfathered in its initial members—distinguished fellows, to be sure, but certainly not a lot of them in British Columbia. That started up a bush fire."[79]

The practice of real estate was under scrutiny in the mid-fifties, and it did need scrutinizing. For many years, all that was needed to get a licence to sell real estate was payment of a ten dollar fee to the government, with no qualifications necessary and no governmental power to refuse the licence.

A pamphlet about an upcoming conference of the B.C. Association of Real Estate Boards reached Pip at his office in October 1957. Vancouver's Herbert R. Fullerton was listed as one of the members on the afternoon panel discussion covering licence law.[80] Pip and colleagues listened with interest as Fullerton told B.C. sales agents that before the profession could govern itself, according to licence law, it needed a uniform code of ethics and a uniform educational level.

Pip already supported suggestions to train sales people properly and already believed real estate could become a genuine vocation. He was thirty-three and eager to participate, so he introduced himself to Fullerton, who was also chairman of the conference banquet that evening. "I was not going to light the fire of change with my single match," he wrote, "so the general idea appeared to be to work with the right people who might become a team." In talking about this with his associates, he found that many felt the same way. "We were well aware of the number of mistakes already made—and still being made—in the real estate field. We knew it had to be improved."

The fundamental spark, Pip said, came from Herb Fullerton, and it was he who designed the procedure they needed to follow. It was complex and had a number of essential interlocking components.

In a later speech, Pip explained the sequence of steps. "The B.C. Association [of Real Estate Boards]," he said, "appointed Col. Tom Norris, Q.C., later Mr. Justice Norris, to enquire into the past and future of our vocation in B.C., and his report was submitted to the government in January 1956. By then, the redoubtable—and now greatly missed—Col. Herb Fullerton was front and centre, in high gear, armed with the Norris report and the most complex blueprint for future organization ever conceived. For the few who could grasp it, it was brilliant."[81]

Colonel Fullerton, in addition to being president of the B.C. Association of Real Estate Boards, was regional vice-president of the Canadian Association of Real Estate Boards, or CAREB, and he won the support of Dr. Earle McPhee, dean of commerce at the University of British Columbia, and Dr. Larry McKenzie, UBC's president. Dr. McPhee was thoroughly familiar with the university's policies and processes and, with Dr. McKenzie's agreement, mentioned to Fullerton the idea of endowing a chair.

Fullerton recognized that this specific structure within this particular institution would be right for the purpose at hand. "He saw it right away," Pip said. He and those around him knew that establishing what they called "the real estate chair" could provide the status, structures and focus needed to reach their long-term goals. They pursued the matter and reached agreement to create a chair in estate management in the UBC Faculty of Commerce.

Meantime, another nexus of expertise was forming to draft a new real estate act. A group that included E.T. (Tom) Cantell and Earle McPhee had been discussing the state of the industry and the need for the bill. Tom Cantell, a lawyer who'd moved into the provincial civil service and reached senior levels, was involved in the group's efforts, and his experience was applied in development of the legislation. "Tommy Cantell was provincial Superintendent of Insurance at the time," Pip said, "and he was a very great help."

Herb Fullerton was emphatic in various strategic conversations that the real estate act passed in the early 1920s was no longer adequate in the late 1950s. Fullerton, said Pip, "was big in voice, big in frame and big in ideas, and people paid attention to him. He had a big business in Vancouver, and he was a political animal, a driving force who got things done."

They sold government on the idea, advising Attorney General Bob Bonner and other ministers it was a timely bill to introduce in the Legislative Assembly. In 1958, the bill was debated and passed. "That gave us," said Pip, "the Real Estate Council of B.C. as we know it, with Irwin Davis as its secretary and Dermot Murphy alongside." Dermot Murphy from Dublin, educated there as a corporate secretary able to work with top-level CEOs, had been brought in to bolster the Real Estate Institute of B.C. Pip described him as "an extremely energetic person who combined sagacity and great wit, a man very highly trained to be front and centre in the organization."

But how to get its members elected? Their solution was straightforward. The B.C. Institute of Real Estate Agents was formed, to which all agents were automatically eligible for membership, so there couldn't be accusations of a closed shop. It elected fifteen directors who were recommended to government to represent their jurisdictions.

"The government gave the nod," said Pip, "and zap, we had a council, self-government, were responsible for administering the act and were an advisory body to the Superintendent of Insurance. It has chalked up a totally enviable record of stern but understanding fairness. This was a massive step not emulated elsewhere in Canada for years to come."[82]

Creating and delivering real estate education was the next major goal. Pip noted a comment made by H.P. Bell-Irving while he was chairman of the Real Estate Agents Licensing Board of B.C., before the days of the Real Estate Council:[83] "The *only* people who will elevate salesmen's calibre are the agents themselves."

Pip continued his explanation of the sequence of events. "Dean McPhee, who was heading the Faculty of Commerce and Business Administration," he said, "was convinced that real estate education was worthy of higher studies at UBC ... The department was to be named 'estate management' after the well-established and honourable practice in Great Britain."[84] The program was to have three parts to it—the licensing courses, four-year diploma courses and undergraduate studies—and the faculty was determined to attract an excellent person to run the program.

The "usual magic elixir of money" had to be found, as Pip put it, to fund this first such chair in Canada. The University of British Columbia said the cost to create a chair in estate management would be $50,000, a sum equal to the purchase price of five houses in Point Grey. "It was," Pip said, "a positively boisterous sum in those days." The Real Estate Council provided the $50,000 and a foundation was later established to provide further funds.

When Pip was provincial president, he and Dermot Murphy set out to meet with all the real estate boards in British Columbia. "Our mission," said Pip, "was to explain to the boards the advantages of training and education in real estate and to gain their backing for the chair in estate management. We emphasized the importance of them joining the Real Estate Institute of B.C. to make it an effective force in the industry, and that did indeed come about." The B.C. real estate community, convinced by the possibilities presented to them in Pip's speeches on the road trip with Dermot, joined in the effort.

Dermot said that whenever Pip spoke, people responded. He commented thirty years later about Pip that "he never ceased to surprise me by his innovation, his hard work and his respect for people. We travelled the province together, all of it, and while

I may have been Sancho to his Don Quixote, Pip really knew that those windmills could be tilted—and, by Jove, he tilted them! His courtesy in dealing with people was unfailing, and for all those reasons, he was a great travelling companion, leader, boss and, ultimately, friend."[85]

Prof. Philip White had been recruited from the University of London by the UBC selection board as the choice candidate to design and set up the new courses in urban land economics. "After a derring-do career in the wartime Royal Navy," Pip said in a speech, "Philip White became an academic at the University of London, where we in B.C. found him. So began in Canada, for the very first time, undergraduate and advanced studies in real estate ... "[86] Professor and Mrs. White arrived in Vancouver with their family during the summer of 1958, and the first of the courses began that September.

Educational prerequisites were a requirement of the new real estate act, which stayed in force from 1958 until it was updated in 2004.[87] The act decreed the necessity of licensing courses for salespersons and agents and presented the stages of educational courses required for an individual real estate agent to be licensed or for an individual company to practice. The UBC diploma program in real estate and appraisal was immediately adopted as a major educational qualification for membership in the Real Estate Institute of B.C.[88]

"The institute," Pip said, "promptly provided for a professional division to be a guiding light and leader and to house those who qualified. This new institute emerged with three divisions: (1) the provincial division of all licensees, which elected council members; (2) the realtor division ... ; and (3) the professional division as a home for graduates of UBC estate management and the diploma courses. In a span of five or so years, the role of real estate became a new force and dimension that reverberated across Canada."[89]

Having training regimes, industry organizations and binding legislation in place was a huge step ahead. The initiatives worked, and the methodology and structures were adapted for other Canadian provinces and, over time, a number of other countries. Pip later said he enjoyed remembering the fun it was "to put your shoulder to the wheel and feel the wagon start to move in the direction you wanted it to go. Great fun."

Pip by age thirty-four had participated in a broad reconceptualization of the real estate vocation. Elected president of the Victoria Insurance Agents Association that year, he continued to work with employees and colleagues as they adjusted to the new professional expectations on them.

Training was on his mind in other contexts. He asked the commandant of Canadian Services College Royal Roads, for instance, to address the Capital City Commercial Club about the Regular Officer Training Plan (ROTC). "The club has a ghastly sounding name, but we are precisely and exactly commercial," Pip wrote to him. "Our membership consists of a group of sixty-five younger business executives, and I am certain that whatever you choose to say in such an address would be not only warmly received but of personal interest in many cases."[90] Training processes, in whichever contexts, interested him.

He was attending to the needs and activities of #2455 AC&W Squadron, including being the conduit toward the squadron's library for two donated books, *Cinthe* and *Canada's War in the Air*. In a letter to the commanding officer of the squadron, he wrote:

"Al Davis has been kind enough to donate these books to the Mess Library … It has long been in my mind to attempt to get the Air Force Officers' Association interested in the sponsorship of a Squadron Library, because types of books such as these will inevitably never be in reprint. It seems to me the psychologically reasonable time to ask for the books, the war being far enough away now to have lost its immediate sentimentality and yet not so long away that treasures such as these are lost."[91]

Pip's professional courtesies apparently extended into clients' personal lives. At the end of summer in 1958, he received a thank you note: "My dear P.D.P., a brief note to thank you and your colleagues at 1002 for allowing me the use of the car during my holiday. The clan was indeed grateful, and, although we did not travel far afield, we were able to enjoy to the utmost the freedom associated with an auto. I wish to thank you also for all your help and guidance in the mortgage and appraisal field during my brief period in Victoria … I trust that your holiday went well … "[92]

Meantime, two organizations connected to Pip's life were moving to new locations. He maintained neutrality in discussions and absented himself from votes but was pleased with the outcome. The Queen Alexandra Solarium, proposed as a concept in 1925 and built in 1926, moved in 1958 from Mill Bay to Arbutus Road in the Victoria area, changing its name at the same time to the Queen Alexandra Hospital for Crippled Children. Brentwood College School, which had been operating hither and yon in temporary quarters since the fire, purchased the Solarium's former site beside the water at Mill Bay and began planning to reopen there permanently within the next few years.

By 1959, Pip was a director of the Council of Insurance Agents of B.C. and was pleased that his ambition for his chosen vocation was justifying the faith put in him by those before him.[93] He was expressing his views in more and more speeches and applying, in the context of land use and community planning, some techniques he'd seen used effectively in previous years. From the press report in April 1959:[94]

The Real Estate Board of Victoria has asked the provincial government to institute a firm and far-sighted planning, zoning and utilization authority to control ribbon development on B.C. highways. Victoria realtor Philip Holmes said yesterday that although the new Trans-Canada Highway from Victoria to Goldstream is only a few years old, it is a good example of spreading bad ribbon development.

He said the Victoria resolution will be presented to the B.C. Association of Real Estate Boards at a convention at Harrison Hot Springs Sunday, Monday and Tuesday for endorsation.

The resolution asks the government to control development within a sufficiently effective distance on either side of main highways. It also asks for more restriction on access roads and that consideration be given to increasing the width of major highway right-of-way to take full advantage and retain the natural splendor of lands as viewed from the highways.

This was no theoretical stance. From reconnaissance trips with his father and his own forays by bike and car, he knew the geography well.

During the 1950s, he also joined car rallies in which the young bucks would zoom around the Island in pursuit of perfect time-clock results. The races were organized once a month and were run along cleared backroads and "into the backwoods through pissing rain, mud and mountains."[95] The waypoints were set up in towns, farmlands and logging lands, with the midnight-to-midnight start and finish line in Port Alberni.

Pip remembered fondly how he and friend Mike Penn conquered one route from Port Alberni, up through Courtenay, down through Victoria, westward to Sooke and up again for the grand finale in Port Alberni. Participants teamed up as drivers and navigators in whichever cars the fellows could muster—no five-point safety harnesses, generally without rollbars, sometimes without commonsense items like food, he admitted.

Pip was often the driver and engineering designer Jean-Paul Destrubé the navigator of the team, and off into the woods they would roar in Pip's Jaguar. Peter Duke proudly drove his Triumph-with-racing-stripe, and an impromptu Renault team was formed. Through all the rally-road years, Pip claims that all the gravel-gliding sideways around roadbends never produced more than a dent or two. "It was like flying," he said, "with somewhat less of the up-and-down dimension."

Then there were the motorcycles for roads and hill-climbs. He'd been all over Yorkshire on his motorbike during the war, but even the northern England landscape is relatively gentle compared to southern Vancouver Island. Several glacier-scoured monadnocks on the Saanich Peninsula near Victoria rise abruptly from agricultural or forested land. "The best climb we did was straight up the south side of Mount Douglas," said Pip cheerfully, referring to a nearly vertical rock-and-scrub slope. "Whole lot of sand spitting around the place!"

Pip mentioned the D-type Jaguar with some longing. "Driven one," he said, "but never owned one. Sexy little car." He was philosophical but sad when his sixth Jaguar slowly disappeared backward off a cliff after its parking brake failed. "It had wire wheels too," he said. "Lovely thing." But another Jag or two waited in the future, including one he said with a happy sigh was "pale, pale mauve." The Plimley Automobile Showroom sold Pip a series of cars—Mark IVs, Mark Vs, seven in all—until such time as "a more capacious beast" was needed to haul family's and guests' boating supplies between house and dock. A station wagon was bought.

Near the end of the year, his dear aunt died: "On October 31, 1959, in Victoria, B.C., Mrs. Sophia Theresa Deane-Drummond, born in 1869 in Victoria, B.C., the second daughter of Mrs. J.D. Pemberton and Mr. J.D. Pemberton…"[96] Susie, one of her two sisters, was the carver, and she was the painter. Known in the art world as Sophie Pemberton, she had studied in Paris at the Académie Julian, was the first woman to win the Prix Julian and was recognized as an outstanding artist in 1906 when she was made an associate of the Royal Canadian Academy.[97]

The obituary in the papers mentioned she exhibited her first paintings to the Victoria public before the age of twelve and that by the time she was eighteen, she had exhibited in England's Royal Academy. No one in British Columbia before her had received the international acclaim she did at that exhibit. She'd loved Pip dearly and given him a little collection of what he called his cherished "Sophies." When she died, she left him a small monetary legacy and a heritage of genuine mutual affection and admiration.

In the early sixties, Cuthbert as company president added an appraisal department at Pemberton Holmes after he and Pip planned it out and chose the staff for it. Pip's own familiarity with appraisal processes had been developed through his father's early and ongoing tutelage, through his own studies and experience and as a member and director of the Society of Residential Appraisers.

By 1960, he had also been president of the Victoria Insurance Agents Association, director of the Council of Insurance Agents of B.C., president of the Victoria Real Estate Board. In 1961, he became a member of the Real Estate Council of B.C., governor of the professional division of the Real Estate Institute of B.C. and president of the B.C. Association of Real Estate Boards. Pip loved living this high-energy life, and it came easily to him, he said, since he was born with energy to spare. "The 5BX plan had come out from the Air Force by then," he said. "Did that, and stayed busy." The RCAF system of basic exercises, initially developed to keep airmen fit, was promoted in the 1950s for civilians.[98]

One of the people who'd set up the B.C. real estate training structure remarked that after the war, the industry had in it mainly people who were older and more mature and few younger people. The first graduates of the UBC courses in real estate were emerging from their studies into the work world and finding top-level employment as urban land economists in the industrial, commercial, investment aspects of real estate.[99] The research projects of the Urban Land Economics Division were progressing well and receiving initial wide acceptance.

The number of people in the courses at that point was not huge, but there was never really an argument that training was necessary. After the two or so years of basic training, further real estate education became voluntary at undergraduate or graduate levels, and grants were sometimes made available to assist with tuition.

"Of course, the residential real estate people were often not that interested at first," said Dermot Murphy. "They were happy just dealing with people, and the most successful of them believed they didn't need formal courses to be good salespeople. But in the commercial field and the industrial field, there you had to have the basic academic training and as much more as you could handle. You might have people in commerce degree programs, for instance, specializing in land. That training and education was essential."[100]

As the reopening of Brentwood College School approached, the Old Brentonians who kept the school intact during its wandering years were highly active, a state encouraged and inspired by David D. MacKenzie. MacKenzie had been a naval officer and flyer, a highly qualified teacher and scholar and an international athlete, all of which made him a natural as head of the school. "He was a powerhouse of spirit determined to restart the school," Pip said, "and he always kept in touch with Old Brentonians and former faculty. All of us who were contacted rallied around strongly." Brentwood reopened in September 1961 on shoreline acreage next to the community of Mill Bay, across Saanich Inlet from its original location in Brentwood Bay.

This was a most satisfactory situation for Pip. He was bound and determined to follow the pattern of service he'd learned from family — a pattern of steady participation in public service and in business at the same time — and as a side effect of his efforts, he himself was becoming increasingly newsworthy. Favourable press clippings proliferated.

The presentation of a carved presentation item, for example, merited a front page photo and caption in the *Penticton Herald*.[101] The clipping showed Pip, as president of the Victoria Real Estate Board, presenting to the president of the B.C. Association of Real Estate Boards, Mladin Zorkin, a gavel carved from the wood of a hundred-year-old holly tree. Seed for the tree had been brought from England and planted on B.C.'s west coast, and the gavel, resting on a structure in the shape of the HBC's Fort Victoria, had been carved from same wood. The photo made a splashy front page.

When UBC held an open house to show off its real estate display, P.D.P. Holmes, Philip White and Stuart Wilson were photographed examining a wall display of agencies active in research. News coverage was warranted because of the venue and participants. It was an event of interest for newspaper readers. After World War II, real estate was news.

The industry was changing. Members of the Canadian Association of Real Estate Boards, as it was still named, attended its twenty-third conference in Montreal's Queen Elizabeth Hotel. To inform themselves about an intriguing new form of apartment ownership, roughly fifteen hundred delegates attended a special session on the topic of "condominiums."[102]

Pemberton Holmes Ltd. was doing well under Cuthbert Holmes in the postwar boom. Pip, in his late thirties, was energetically involved in the company and in the Real Estate Council of B.C. He also had duties as governor of the professional division of the Real Estate Institute of B.C. and, in 1964, was appointed both to the grants committee of the B.C. Real Estate Education and Research Foundation and to the advisory board of directors of Columbia Beneficial Holdings Ltd.

In 1964, Pip wed again. His bride was Catherine Mead, an accomplished sailor who grew up in Hampshire, England, served in the Wrens during the war and, after her first husband died, worked in Moscow for Canada's Department of External Affairs. They married at the Church of Our Lord in Victoria. Established in October 1874 by the Rev. Edward Cridge, the church stands on Humboldt Street on land donated by Sir James Douglas and was supported strongly in the 1870s by Theresa Jane Pemberton, Mrs. J.D.[103]

Ninety years later, friends and family gathered on an August day in the wooden church for Pip and Catherine's wedding and, at a reception afterward, to toast their future. Dermot Murphy later remarked that "Pip married Catherine and co-opted her to assist him in pursuing his objectives ... [for] thereafter Catherine accompanied Pip on all his travels and played a very important role as a joint ambassador for British Columbia and Canada."[104] Vincent Massey's Christmas 1964 card arrived from Batterwood "with affectionate good wishes to you both."

Said Catherine: "I knew Pip had so much to offer the world." How right she was. His career was about to broaden to the national and then the international scene.

Herb Fullerton in the 1950s (top, on left), with Pip listening.
Fullerton designed the complex interlocking proposal for professionalization of the real estate vocation in B.C.

Part of the 1964 real estate display during an Open House at the University of British Columbia (bottom).
Left to right: Prof. Philip White, Stuart Wilson, P.D.P. Holmes.

On Dallas Road in 1959 (left), Pip's trusty Jag, "the grey, bulbous Mark VII," is one of dozens of tuned-up entries for the Rally Van Isle. Craig inspects one of the Renaults before the start (below). A waypoint of the rally route (centre left) was at flooded Somenos Marsh, with the distinctive shape of Mount Brenton visible. Routes followed farm lanes, logging roads, two-lane highways on Vancouver Island.

Family camping, 1950s-style (bottom), on stony river flats beside an Island bridge.

Church of Our Lord, Victoria, August 1964
(top). Back row (l-r): John Trelawny, who
gave Catherine away; the groom Pip and bride
Catherine; Cuthbert Holmes; Catherine's
cousin Betty Webb (partly hidden); Terry
Holmes, Pip's uncle. Front row, (l-r): young
David Holmes, Vincent's son; Pip's daughter
Jennifer; his daughter Susan; Philippa Holmes,
with white handbag.

Wedding reception (above left), at Cuthbert's and Philippa's
Victoria house. Pip behind the cake; Catherine in pale sage green;
her cousin Betty; and Jock Elliott, who made the speech to the bride.
Their first Beach Drive house (above), up the cliff from the road.

From Vincent Massey to Pip and Catherine, Christmas '64 (left): "With affectionate good wishes to you both." The dogs on the card from Batterwood arè Beau and Nash.

*Family friends Miles and Beryl Smeeton, of **Tzu Hang** sailing lore, with boat cat (left).*

The seaward view (below) in a photo Pip took at sunrise from their home for nearly thirty years. On the shore and around Trial Island light, rocks emerge and are covered again as strong tides sluice through the straits. "The very best sculptures," Pip said.

Daughter Susan and Pip (top).

Happy role as "Sailor Pip" (above centre).

*Miss Lee (above) was the second boat
after **Duckling**, before **Keyask**.*

*Desolation Sound (above), of all B.C.'s
cruising grounds, was a frequent choice.*

CHAPTER NINE
PROGRESS ON ALL FRONTS

CUTHBERT HOLMES RETIRED in 1965, and Pip became president of Pemberton Holmes. Between 1965 and 1989 while Pip was president, the company would experience vigorous growth,[105] with staff increasing and gross sales rising from $6.5 million to more than $45 million.[106] Pip was elected a director of Fort Mortgage Corporation[107] and became twenty-first president of the Canadian Association of Real Estate Boards (CAREB) at its 1965 convention in Edmonton.

His father wrote him a characteristically supportive note, in his emphatic style, about Pip's expanding professional role:[108]

Darling Philip,

All success to you at the CAREB CONVENTION. Mama & I are intensely proud of your fine career. We wish you also a REWARDING YEAR of LEADERSHIP. Perhaps you will think it wise & well to make all of us accept the principle that all realtors are TRUSTEES for their buying clients. In my view, THAT wd raise us ALL in public opinion & RIGHTLY SO.

Love to you both.

H.C.H.

The CAREB position added a great deal more travelling to his schedule, and multiple visits to real estate boards all over Canada gave him opportunities to encourage advancement in education and training for their members. News coverage of his speeches as he travelled around disseminated his education-and-training message beyond the real estate crowd.

The theme he would promulgate for the rest of his long career was professional education of a specific kind. As he put it, it was the need "to advance the importance that the vocation could and would play in the planning and provision of the needs of the world [and] in the variety of accommodations and total phasing and development of the urban landscape, including recreation, leisure and natural beauties—in a word, to enhance the qualities of our civilization and have Canada play a major role in that advancement."[109]

His speech as new association president to CAREB members gave a snapshot of the industry in February 1965 ranging from individual performance measurement to analysis of the demographics pushing the international economy. He noted with interest an upcoming September '65 panel concerning licensing in all provinces. The definition of "realtor" was a topic much discussed at the time, and he mentioned many other changes afoot: population growth and urbanization patterns; debates on sales commissions; real estate sales outlooks in Canada and MLS forecasts for 1966; the impetus of working women in the economy; families increasingly having two incomes; first-time home owners moving out of apartments into existing housing stock and eventually building custom homes; luxury apartments becoming more common; landowners and interested members of the public quickly adopting new forms of ownership in cluster housing and condominiums while the legislation on those forms of ownership in various provinces was still in the drafting stage.

Inflation was a major concern of the year, that and government expenses. He forecast times of high interest rates and tight money and warned about housing shortages. Public discussion on pollution legislation was heating up, and registered realtors were raising their local profiles by taking on long-term community roles. York University was instituting courses similar to those already at UBC in licence law and licensing qualifications, he said, which would increase the access to good real estate training.

Electronic communication should have been but wasn't yet a hot topic in the industry circa 1965. Pip did some research and realized what this would soon mean for private commerce and national economies. In relation to this, he became very interested in the international organization known as FIABCI.[110] It had sufficient scope as a forum for the exchange of information, which was one of the premises on which it was founded, and it was well-positioned to deal with matters connected with the ownership, development and management of real estate worldwide.[111]

The organization had been gathering new member-nations since 1951, and Japan had just joined in 1961. Representing the Canadian Association of Real Estate Boards as national president, Pip attended the 1965 annual World Congress in Brussels and was fascinated by the range of people he met. They were, by FIABCI's own membership analysis, "a wide international and professional mix, all of them in real estate—the consultants who assess the best use of property; the valuers who estimate its market value; the financiers who provide the funding; the developers who make projects materialize; the agents who find the occupants; the managers who optimize the investment; and the bankers and insurance advisors."[112]

The organization's objectives were an excellent fit with Pip's own aims, or vice versa.

As he later explained to a journalist in Victoria: "One of FIABCI's principal objectives is to attempt to solve national real estate problems through the exchange of international experience and information. This includes not only housing, but town planning, disposition and utilization of agricultural lands, progress in urban environments and overall ecological pitfalls and solutions… We are in the global village and have to share our experiences to profit from the mistakes of others."[113]

Whenever possible, he headed for the boat with family and friends and went exploring coastal waters and islands or piled in as many people as would fit into the car and went exploring by land.

Pip and Catherine often entertained family, friends and new business colleagues from various countries, and their daysails and dinner parties were lively affairs. Guests of the gregarious couple were made most welcome, one of them being Pip's father: "Dear C & Pip, For Friday's charming party, all my thanks. Good of you to ask such cheery & clever people… Love, CH."[114] Around the same time, Cuthbert wrote a separate note to his daughter-in-law: "CAH, Well well done. Party (& dinner) simply SPLENDID. CH."[115]

One man accosted Pip during a gathering at the Holmes house and, well into the cocktail hour, asked his host how he could bear to entertain and do business with people who'd been his enemies during World War II. Despite the accusatory tone of the question, the reply was businesslike. "They did what they thought was right," said Pip, "and I did what I thought was right. Now we are continuing to do the best of what we each believe." Business would be done and friendships formed, he said, on the basis of an individual's character, professional compatibility and record of accomplishment.

In a speech at the 1966 CAREB conference in Saskatchewan, Pip issued a rallying cry for the association, thirteen thousand members strong: "We are, most of all, a unified force that can achieve vast, almost inconceivable benefits for our country. [We] can change the face of Canada, if we are determined to do so… "

He added his often-repeated education-and-training theme: "Led by the national organization and now having achieved real estate licence law in all but two provinces, the eight regional associations are moving into mandatory qualifications of competency before licensing. They have established a forceful code of ethics. They have encouraged and intrigued our universities into providing advanced study and licensing courses and are witnessing the first truly professionally trained students graduating from one university and, possibly one day soon, a second."[116]

He expressed his conviction about their function, which he called the challenge of the land: that real estate industry members were not just selling property but being guardians of the land itself. He linked this with higher education and national responsibilities by quoting the well-known opening to an industry code of ethics: "Under all is the land. On the wise utilization and widely allocated ownership of land depend the survival and growth of free institutions and our civilization."[117]

He was speaking to those at the conference in a professional capacity, but what he was saying to them was what he personally believed: "The land, every acre, be it fertile valley, snow-clad mountain, green forest or the intensified measure of downtown, is the greatest single heritage of our people. From land, basically, all our wealth is derived. Who is, or who should be, guardian of this vast asset? Who has been? No one. Absolutely no one."

He analyzed for those listening to him at the '66 conference a situation that was increasingly troublesome to realtors: "Oh, ever so many people have had and do have their fingers in the pie—the politician, the developer, the speculator, the industrialist, the surveyor and engineer, the lawyer, the merchant, the planner—and even we have, sometimes… Everywhere we look, we are being infiltrated or bypassed. An enormous variety of others have expertly taught themselves skills that should be ours… None of these people is at fault, but we are—and if we do not redouble our efforts to produce the skills worthy of becoming doctors of the land, then others will."[118]

———————

As Pip's career advanced, his father encouraged his son's progress and himself continued going to the office daily. Around the time Pip became exchange director of the National Association of Realtors (U.S.A.), Cuthbert sent him this note:[119]

> Dear Philip,
> I have today given instructions that 800 of my shares in the Company be assigned to you. It hardly seems necessary, but I would like to have your approval that during my lifetime I can make use of an office at 1002 Government St., preferably the one where I am now. And with the office, the usual things that go with it. If there are any points above which you think you cannot accept, please tell me promptly.
> Yours ever, CH

Pip, Catherine and many sociable invitees around town took great care in choosing what to wear for a Centennial Ball in 1966. Held the year before Canada's national centennial celebrations, it was intended to commemorate the hundredth anniversary of the union of the two Crown colonies on the northern Pacific coast, the upstart one on the mainland and the senior one on Vancouver Island. In a community patently fond of dress-up, it naturally enough was a full-fledged costume ball. Pip devised a persona that had resonance for him from the name of his grandfather's house as well as from local geography and history. He became "Captain Gonzales" and Catherine his Spanish Lady.[120]

Though sailing in the west coast summers aboard *Miss Lee* was a fine way to spend time with family and guests or to find quiet time together, Pip and Catherine had more business sociability and less unstructured leisure by the year. While still a member of the Real Estate Council of B.C. during Canada's centennial celebrations, the year of Expo '67, he also became a member (and later British Columbia vice-president) of the Housing Design Council of Canada.

One comment repeated about Pip was that he was very, very good at getting a team lined up and rolling. The head of one of the national business organizations in the mid-1960s needed to get a group fired up about a certain project. "I must get Pip on this," he said to colleagues. "He knows how to make a team."

Pip turned forty-three in February 1967 and, with his regional and national career base established, considered the process of going international. His move into the FIABCI hierarchy began in 1967, when he became a director of its Canadian chapter, FIABCI Canada. Wanting to learn about its effective committee system, he arranged to be at its next international congress, then turned his attention to a few special events around home.

His parents' golden wedding anniversary brought the family together at the house for lunch and at the Union Club for a cocktail party in honour of Cuthbert and Philippa. Many of the party guests had been at their wedding fifty years before.

The year after the fiftieth anniversary, Major Holmes passed away. "India-born Major Cuthbert Holmes, whose father was a judge with the Indian Civil Service," wrote *Oak Bay Star* reporter Tony Dickason, "was brought to Victoria … headed the firm bearing his name and died in 1968 after many years devoted to betterment of this area's environs."[121]

To recognize his contributions to the community, the B.C. government set aside a swath of mature Douglas firs surrounding the Colquitz River and its estuary, the idea being to name it Cuthbert Holmes Park to acknowledge his strong advocacy in preserving greenbelt lands. He'd already earned acclaim for initiation of greenbelt areas and "outstanding contributions to the planning within the capital and region" when he'd been named a Freeman of the City of Victoria.[122]

Though the park proposal took a number of years to wend its way through provincial administrations and jurisdictions, under Pip's chairmanship of the Capital Regional District the Saanich park system preserved the area of forests and bird-habitat wetlands. Suburban infrastructure built up inexorably around the park's edges.[123]

Pip addressed the Windsor Real Estate Board on some prescient matters he and his father had been discussing: "The challenge that surrounds us all, today, and probably from this day hence, unless it beats us as it has various peoples before us, is environment—not just community or national environment but a world environment … What has gone before, sufficed and proven adequate is no longer viable, valid or tenable."

The ingredients of the problem were national and international, he told them, and though of varying types, had common ground. "They are social, and they are economic—but they intimately involve individuals (and even more, our children) functioning as groups … The same story is repeated over and over again: that groups with divergent interests … find that little short of miracles can be born when they sit down together to solve problems. Despite all the technological advances, we have yet to learn to communicate and communicate convincingly, to understand and to tolerate meaningfully … "[124]

Lest the earnest theme distract from his reputation for mischievous *bon mots*, he illustrated the same speech with a timely story, his context being that coming up with the right answers takes presence of mind and, usually, judgement born of experience. He told them this: a man was awakened by his phone ringing at three in the morning and was warned by a neighbour to keep his pesky dog quiet so the neighbour could sleep.

Instead of slinging back a fast retort, he waited. The next night, at 0300 hours precisely, he phoned the neighbour back: "But I don't *have* a dog."

As a director of FIABCI Canada, he and Catherine attended the 1968 FIABCI World Congress in Mexico and found the international milieu comfortable and welcoming. After the conference, they wanted to go to Acapulco by car with another Canadian couple, but the driver they'd hired insisted on dropping them off at a tiny silver shop he knew. The driver promptly went around back to catch up on his daily intake of tequila.

Realizing he had to be sobered up or they'd get nowhere, the Canadians took him for a lengthy no-drinks lunch, but that only made him sleepy. To keep him awake while he drove, they took turns asking him questions, which soon began taxing their imaginations and especially their supply of patience. Pip's friend Denny announced that if he heard another question about the name of such-and-so tree, he'd let out an uncontrolled shriek. The travellers eventually arrived in Acapulco intact and still friends.

At the 1969 FIABCI World Congress in Lucerne, after listening to the addresses and attending the working meetings, Pip knew for certain this was where he belonged. The FIABCI group, he told Catherine, was where he could achieve progress in his career and an almost unlimited opportunity to spread the message about education in the real estate vocation. Agreed that they were in it together, come what may, they arranged a cocktail party in their Lucerne hotel suite, which by happenstance or design was particularly chic, to entertain a carefully chosen group. The process was underway.

During the 1970 World Congress in Dublin, FIABCI world president John Tysen, English by birth but an American citizen since emigrating to the U.S. many years before, had been taking note of how Pip conducted himself during conference sessions and while socializing. Near the end of the week-long event in Dublin, Tysen asked Pip if he'd stand for election to the international executive committee.[125] Pip saw this as a very welcome idea and agreed that he would. He was elected to the board and served on the executive of FIABCI International for fourteen more years.

FIABCI involvement, by any measure, was an intense experience. Senior people, of course, never met unprepared. Vincent Massey advised Pip about this. "If you've got a point you want to win, never go into a meeting unprepared. Always do your homework beforehand. Ahead of time, talk to everyone who will be there. That way, you know how the vote will go." Even the ostensibly social side of the annual meetings was work for the participants and for the host, and the sociable events at the conferences, generally reflecting the character of the host cities, gave each country the chance to show itself in its best light to a high-potential group.

The 1971 World Congress was in Montreal, based at the Queen Elizabeth Hotel across from Place Ville-Marie. Built over an enormous trench that had been dug years before into the lower slopes of Mount Royal for railway tracks, the new retail and office structure wowed Pip and other delegates not for its famous cruciform skyscape as for its underground cityscape, an effective and readily applicable idea for development design.

Willy Egeli, Sr., was the incoming FIABCI president at the Montreal Congress, and he wanted to include British Columbia on his cross-Canada tour. Pip promptly organized an action-packed itinerary for his Swiss guest to meet real estate people in Victoria and Nanaimo. Pip and Catherine then took him on a driving trip across Vancouver Island to have a look at the communities on the outer coast—the westernmost West Coast.

Pip was balancing his activities at the national and international levels with commitments around his home community. In quick succession, he was named an Honorary Fellow of the Realtors Institute of Canada, later known as the Real Estate Institute of Canada, and was elected vice-president of NW Financial Corporation Ltd.[126] He was still serving on the Advisory Planning Commission of the Municipality of Saanich.

Pip's father after World War II had been president of the Victoria Chamber of Commerce,[127] and Pip now followed suit. Three fathers had their three sons later follow them as Chamber of Commerce presidents, the pairs to that point being J.H. Todd and C.F. Todd, David Ker and R.H.B. Ker, and Maj. Cuthbert Holmes and Philip Holmes.[128] The mandate of the Chamber since its first meetings in 1863 had been to support business and lobby government to improve business conditions. Victoria merchants in the 1860s had been nearly overwhelmed with selling supplies to gold-rush miners heading for the B.C. interior, and their newly established board of trade presided over the melée and helped them weather it.

The economic situation a hundred years later was worrisome in another way. A general economic downslide began in the early 1970s, and the region was losing industry. The Victoria Chamber of Commerce ten years earlier had won the government ferry service it wanted between the north end of the Saanich Peninsula and the mainland, but fare hikes during a business downturn were devastating to local businesses. Tourism advocates, active well before the advent of Tourism Victoria, were doing their best to supplement regional revenues.

Not all was bleak. Members of the Junior Chamber of Commerce, once praised happily as "Best Junior Chamber in the World,"[129] were an energetic bunch, and Clare Copeland, president immediately before Pip, had steadily been rejuvenating his Chamber configuration with new members and setting up committees led by experienced business people for younger people to learn from.[130] Pip as his successor picked up on that immediately.

"The Chamber," he said, "must be a team of sensitive, swift, imaginative and determined committees if it is to meet its role and responsibilities in a world of galloping change."[131] To do the job with any degree of inspiration took full-out energy and commitment of time, he added. Heading a local Chamber of Commerce is not a position for the tepid, since much of it involves infusing others in the community with derring-do or generosity, and often both simultaneously. Though critics are forever near, he said, the rewards of such a thorough degree of involvement in the local scene can be most satisfying.

He took his own advice. The city's first bikeathon was organized in April '71 to raise funds for the Victorian Days festival the following month, and the lanky Chamber of Commerce president surprised a few people by volunteering himself as a participant. Not a lot of people, apparently, knew his history with bicycles. Like the other five hundred cyclists entered in the event, he and his route partner Bruce Partridge, president of the University of Victoria, began raising pledges of X dollars per mile. On the day of the ride, Pip clocked off seventy-five miles' worth of road and raised a bundle of money for the cause before heading back to the office.[132]

Orientation to the highest standards of business, in Pip's value system, had to include a whole lot of fun for members of the firm in the community. The launch of the community festival they named Victorian Days took place as part of British Columbia's centennial as a province. The idea was instigated while the Victoria Chamber of Commerce was under Pip's lead, when guiding lights Helen Beirnes, Peter Tredgett, Colin Rutherford and others stepped up to do the committee organizing it takes to produce a citywide event.

Bracketing the Victoria Day weekend from May 21 to the end of the month, the Loyal Order of Victoria Enthusiasts, Pip in their midst, traipsed through events under the scrutiny of local columnist Maury Gwynne. "The idea," he wrote, "was to give Victoria its own distinctive week in which its citizens could have a fun time. If any visitors wanted to join in, they were welcome, but the week's activities, the dressing up, the feeling of 'holiday,' was for us, not them … "[133]

Credit for the success of Victorian Days, he said, "must go to those people who convinced the city's major retail firms to go flat out Victorian — to sell toppers and ruffled shirts and swallowtail coats and all the other trappings of the Victorian era." The committee members convinced local shops to stock sewing patterns for turn-of-the-century outfits — men's, women's and children's — and to feature mid-Victorian styles for sale. Organizers gradually drummed up participation on all fronts. "Enthusiasm for dressing up gained great momentum in the last couple of weeks leading up to May 24," Maury Gwynne concluded. "It was a good week in which a lot of people had an awful lot of fun … "[134]

Pip and Catherine attended the FIABCI 1972 World Congress in London the following spring, where the final night's grand dinner in the Dorchester Hotel, with the Grenadier Guards band to play for them, was done in dramatic and elegant black-and-white. "A spectacular evening," they said together. "Absolutely memorable."

In July '72, Pip was appointed to the British Columbia Chamber of Commerce. D.A.L. Tait, president of the B.C. Chamber, outlined his new task in a note: "This will serve to confirm officially that you have been appointed a director-at-large … as chairman of the committee on education."[135]

Believing that the economics of daily living should be taught in grade school and high school, with specific concentration on the relationship of business and education, Pip canvassed business leaders at all levels. In a later letter, he wrote:[136] "I don't think for a minute that one can possibly overemphasize the importance of this aspect. If we neglect it or turn our back on it, we are begging continuance of and deepening the schism between youth and our competitive enterprise system."

His committee met with the B.C. Minister of Education and recommended several things: that instruction in basic economics should be added to the elementary and secondary curriculum; that substantially more emphasis needed to be put on teaching language skills in primary, secondary and post-secondary schooling; and that an education committee should provide advice to the minister about business, labour and education.

Pip also monitored with interest the process of Brentwood College School going co-ed.[137] Over a transitional period from 1972 to 1980, young women were gradually integrated into the school environment, starting at the grade twelve level. The school matter-of-factly became the first boys' boarding school in Canada to become co-educational.

The November '72 executive meetings of FIABCI International dealt with real estate issues relating to industrial plants and large office complexes, with a new residential category called "garden apartments" and with appraisal reports that were nearly ready to be published concerning sales worldwide of shopping centres, whether urban and subterranean like Place Ville-Marie's or suburban at street-level. An invitation had been extended to the executive board to hold the annual World Congress in Toronto in the early 1980s, and the board viewed the idea in a positive light.

There was a new element. The Asia Pacific Real Estate Federation had just been formed in Tokyo. The FIABCI executive committee discussed the role that Canada might play in the new organization, and the file was designated for Mr. Holmes to handle. He'd already had the Pacific Rim on his business radar for a number of years, and he knew that brokering a connection between APREF and FIABCI would be a successful marker of diplomatic capitalism.

In January 1973, still in his forties, he was named an Honorary Citizen of the City of Victoria.[138] Like father, like son: Cuthbert had in his time been made a Freeman of the City of Victoria. Mayor Peter Pollen's post-Christmas letter to Pip, which over the decades has faded almost entirely to white, advises of the award "to recognize your considerable contribution to our community" and invites him to attend a civic ceremony on January 8 to be given his certificate.[139]

A month after the honorary citizenship event and apparently after some enticement to relocate his working life elsewhere, Pip wrote in reply to a letter from a company in a large Canadian city:[140] "Victoria is a small pond … but, for me, my roots are here. I love our 'little old Victoria' and want to see it prosper and at the same time maintain its uniqueness and beauty. It is a path laid out by my father, grandfather and great-grandfather, all of whom had vision and wisdom in progressive planning, which I wish to continue and improve upon where I can." It wasn't the first time or last that companies offered to recruit him.

He was past president of the Victoria Chamber and finishing his term with the B.C. Chamber, and the flow of ideas about his splendid Island rarely stopped.[141] Instead of taking headhunter bait when it was dangled, he reaffirmed his sense of place and took on the presidency of the Associated Chambers of Commerce of Vancouver Island, which he referred to fondly as the "Council of the Western Isles."

As Pip becomes president of CAREB in 1965, Bert Willoughby hands over the gavel (top left). Pip is wearing a voyageur sash to herald the CAREB Montreal conference the following year. At the same event in reply to a toast, Catherine makes her first speech (above).

Picking up the conference theme (top right), they dress for a Klondike Days dinner.

Rappelling in Banff 1966 (right), after a series of real estate meetings.

PHOTO CREDIT: *BRUNO ENGLER, ALPINE FILMS, BANFF*

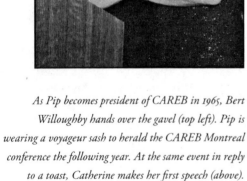

Pip addressing the 1966 CAREB conference (top) after his term as president. Montreal Real Estate Board president Jean DesRosiers, left of photo, was conference chairman. Next to him is Paul-Emile Cardinal Léger, archbishop of Montreal.

Cocktails for interprovincial sociability (above) at the Montreal conference.

Pip invented himself as Captain Gonzales and Catherine was his Spanish Lady (above) for Maj. Gen. George Pearkes's centennial costume party on 22 April 1966. It was held to mark the union of the Crown colonies of Vancouver Island and British Columbia.

The family gathered for the fiftieth wedding anniversary (below) of Cuthbert and Philippa Holmes in October 1967. Back row, l-r: Desmond, Philippa, Philippa's sister Baby Mab, Catherine, Vincent's wife Maureen, Vincent, Cuthbert.
Front row, l-r: Desmond's wife Pat, Elizabeth's husband Allan, Cicely (Mrs. W.S. Thomson), Elizabeth (Mrs. Allan Cureton).
Following this family lunch, they left for the Union Club and a large cocktail party.

Pip's dear godmother May Seale (in hat, below), holding a gift for Philippa.

Montreal cousins Jean and Charles Dupont visited (bottom right) and went sailing with Pip.

Christmas dinner 1967 (below, l-r): John Thomson, foreground left; Prue; David Holmes; Philippa; Vincent standing in archway; the Seales, Craig and others chatting in the far room; Desmond seated opposite his mother; Jennifer; Susan; and Pip's niece Vicky Plomb in foreground at right.

Christmas Eve 1967 (below), everyone opening an early present (l-r): Susan, Jennifer, Diana, Catherine.

And at Christmas 1971 (bottom), as ever, visiting with Harry and May Seale.

An April 1971 bikeathon raised money for the Victorian Days community festival in May. Pip is signing up another pledge donation (top left) while cycling partner Bruce Partridge of the University of Victoria does the same. The event was a great fundraiser and much enjoyed.

Costumes at the Victorian Days Ball (above).

The Chamber of Commerce president sets off to honour pledges and enjoy himself (top right). Few people knew his bike-trekking history.

At the end of the successful citywide festival (above), Pip is hoisted up on the shoulders of the Tourist Liberation Front.

Pip as president of the Victoria Chamber of Commerce reminds them in 1971 that in its role, the Chamber must be "a team of swift, imaginative and determined committees" (top).

At Tokyo meetings in 1972, the career gears up toward more international commitments (left).

CHAPTER TEN
BLUEPRINTS AND GREENPRINTS

THE WELL-BEING OF the west coast was always on Pip's mind in some form, specifically so in mid-March 1973 as he was sworn in as new president of the Associated Chambers of Commerce of Vancouver Island. The ACCVI delegates at the Empress Hotel convention were concerned about the energy supply to the Island and urged the provincial government to study the feasibility of a nuclear power station at a suitable location. A resolution put forth by the Nanaimo Chamber of Commerce, which wanted the plant built there, stated that power transmission from the mainland by cable had not been reliable and that alternate energy sources — thermal power was mentioned — were not yet practical for the Island. They worried about energy supply sources, distribution, costs and ever-higher demand.

Resolutions were tabled on the need to establish a tourist authority for Pacific Rim National Park and tourism to the outer coast. Pip's meeting notes show he wanted information updates on Wickaninnish Inn, Ucluelet Lodge, Tofino and Long Beach, Radar Hill, park management and Alberni connections. Years after his bicycle trip there, though not long after his look-around visit with Willy Egeli, he wanted to be current about the area's issues and growth patterns.

Interviewed in the *Victoria Times*, Pip commented that orderly economic development was vital for the future of Vancouver Island and that the search for "an economic blueprint" for the Island would be a major goal of the association in the coming year.[142] "A coherent approach is needed. Planning is no mystery, but planning Vancouver Island is complex if they're to have affairs run more efficiently, not vice versa. Planning is now needed, when it hasn't been so needed before, because of cumulative technological changes, population changes, recreational growth, urbanization."[143]

He had local knowledge from his own experience and research plus familiarity with similar situations around the world, and he wanted to apply to Vancouver Island whatever in those studies might suit. Much of what he had in mind was protection, because he could foresee its growth of population and inevitable accompanying infrastructure. He liked plotting timelines and the processes of community planning. Cross-fertilization of ideas from his various involvements gave him a useful perspective, broadly or in the details:

The basic resources of Vancouver Island are numerous, but two big ones are environmental: the forests, and the marine resources… Now, this business of being maritime. We don't look upon ourselves as a maritime province. We have no local government seriously involved, and we must get involved.

The vital area is the intertidal zone. The estuaries are the most productive and most vital part of the ecosystem, and people naturally want to use them as well. They alone are a challenging question for decision. And remember that oil spills aren't just from tankers.

Power we must have. Of course, nuclear is coming—it's just when and where—but a decision is demanded now. We must look also to geothermal energy.

What is the carrying capacity of the island? What is the saturation point? Be cautious of 'blueprint' when we might need a 'greenprint.' Oregon is approaching its development as Switzerland does, asking: what is the tolerable level of population? Can we build estuaries better than God? No, we don't know enough.[144]

Vast new resort areas on the east coast of Mexico were being built, and the word was being spread. An American real estate developer was praising one of them, for instance, as a highly promising choice for resort investment, "a haven of soft sandy beaches, undisturbed tropical vegetation and excellent climate."[145] Was this model a fit for Vancouver Island in the temperate rainforest? Maybe yes, maybe no. If not that, then what? Not sure which way things would go, Pip kept watch.

Cross-fertilization of ideas multiplied at the FIABCI Sydney Congress in May 1973. The focus there was on planned communities, and reports on the trend of "new towns" came from the U.S., Great Britain, Sweden, France, Italy and Australia. Pip was intrigued by the philosophy and the practicality of what he was hearing and jotted a great number of comments for himself: that new towns should be designed with greenbelt corridors, should be self-sufficient communities rather than functioning as commuters' dormitories outside downtown cores, and so on. Alongside, with underlines, he printed: "People *want* to live in little towns!"[146] On the next page, in his handwriting: "Town planning, cont'd. Should planning be centralized to get expertise necessary? Planning of continuous 'activity spine' set back from autoroute?"[147]

In his letter dated 20 December 1973, he thanked Roderick Fraser for efforts on an idea he felt fit Vancouver Island very well, Mr. Fraser being happily posted at the time on Regent Street in London as B.C.'s Director of the Department of Travel Industry. "I am certainly keen to keep right on going with this recreation destination concept for Vancouver Island," Pip wrote, "and for that matter, for the rest of the province as well, because I am convinced of its value. Yet it probably will not happen unless someone is prepared to push. You have helped very considerably…"[148] Recreation-destination tourism planning was still in its early stages and not widely understood on the Island.

In B.C. real estate education, by contrast, early-stage efforts to launch programs were producing results. One-day seminars on changes in legislation were being conducted, because amendments to the Real Estate Act were being drafted for debate in the provincial legislature. The Land Commission Act was also being discussed. Management seminars and an advanced salesmanship course had been held, and training courses were being run in Vancouver, Victoria, Nanaimo, Castlegar, Kelowna, Kamloops and Prince George. More than two thousand people had attended seminars.[149]

Knowing he would be away from Victoria more and more in the next decade, it was obvious to Pip that Pemberton Holmes Ltd. needed someone, other than any of its department heads, to manage the place as a whole. He needed to leave someone in command and had a talk with someone whose way with people he admired.

"I was fortunate to know a former RCN naval commander who was wonderfully qualified in every sense except real estate itself, but the departments could look after that until Commander Michael H.E. Page got up to speed, which he quickly did." Pip wrote a short note to the people at Pemberton Holmes when Page started work:[150] "I am very pleased indeed to welcome to our staff Michael Page, who joins us as my administrative assistant and will be trying to keep at a somewhat reduced level the now customary piles of paper on my desk. If you have not met him, please introduce yourself."

FIABCI Canada met in Toronto in February '73. As chair of the Canadian chapter's public relations committee, Pip clarified to the board that he didn't see his committee becoming directly involved, for example, in contributions to the association's newsletter. His thinking was more along the lines of expanding its horizons of international affairs, concerning itself with establishing the image of the organization more widely and coordinating international understanding and good will. He suggested to them that the Canadian chapter had a role to play in legislative issues such as the taxation treatment of non-residents and the proposed Foreign Review Act. This was PR of a different mien.

He brought his ongoing interest in the Asia Pacific Real Estate Federation into the agendas. The board discussed the newly created international real estate group, and he was appointed to maintain a watching brief, to monitor the development of APREF and keep the FIABCI Canada board informed.

Canada had not yet been invited to join the new group, and to the best of anyone's knowledge, neither had the U.S. "Mr. Holmes suggested that in view of the huge trade potential of the Pacific Rim countries, Canada should seriously consider accepting an invitation if it were offered. Mr. Holmes agreed to attempt to keep the Chapter informed in this area."[151]

Signals continued that he was right to set his cap for the top job, and a certain confluence of events on 14 April 1973 reinforced that. At a meeting of the FIABCI Canada executive committee in Ottawa,[152] it was noted that the Canadian Real Estate Association, formerly CAREB but renamed CREA, had contacted them about legislation pending in Canada and their desire to collect related information on other countries' experiences.

It was decided the proper approach would be to have FIABCI Canada director Mr. Holmes, who was by then on their fiscal legislation committee, take the idea forward at the World Congress in May: "The following suggestions were made to Mr. Holmes as areas where FIABCI might agree to undertake some research that would be of particular interest to Canada. The three areas were: (1) erosion of property rights around the world, and the rights surrounding expropriation; (2) zoning and planners; and (3) land banking."[153] They agreed that land banking would take priority over the rest of the topics.

His research presentation was scheduled for the World Congress in Sydney during May, and by several accounts, he did a superb job of it. He had also been selected to receive a singular honour for his overall contribution to the profession. At the International 1973 Congress in Sydney, Australia, he was awarded the FIABCI Medal of Honour.[154]

Delegates at the Sydney congress absorbed information in English, French, German and Japanese, in simultaneous translation as needed: on meeting the requirements for corporate relocation in the Asia Pacific area; the best appraisal procedures for high-rise apartments on four continents; putting the financing in place for comprehensive tourist and leisure "towns"; on the results of global market surveys for commercial and industrial properties and industrial real estate; the integration of professional training and education into real estate offices; and specialized training programs for junior personnel and, separately, basic essential training for new board members.

As Canadian representative on their fiscal legislation committee, Pip monitored discussions on the civil and criminal responsibility of members of the real estate professions. He was on familiar ground in that he was also Canadian representative on the standing committee on statutes and resolutions.

Intense work didn't mean merriment was lacking, and occasional antics became part of friends' shared lore. Besides, catching up with colleagues and friends at the annual events was considered a pleasant part of their work.

During one event Pip and Catherine attended at the 1974 FIABCI World Congress in Madrid, they related that when they'd been in Hong Kong, a friend named Geoffrey Yeh had a horse entered into races at the Jockey Club. The horse was named Naughty Naughty, and when he didn't win, those at the club instantly renamed him naughty Naughty Naughty.[155] Laughter all around, which then cued someone to suggest that now they were all gathered in Spain, the eight of them should go to dinner at the Jockey Club in Madrid.

Off they went, but no one had reserved ahead and the dining room was full. They suggested that certainly some space *somewhere* in the building might be found for them, and indeed, the club did have a small private dining room. Menus arrived, and one of the men in the group blithely proposed that the chef should put together something delicious for them and send it up. This was done. The meal was superb, and when the time came for payment, the bill was presented to Pip.

Pip took one look at the bill and thought it looked akin to the national debt, put it face down and pushed it across to Bert Willoughby. "I wouldn't pay it if I were you," he commented to Bert, who looked at it, said "Darn right," and pushed it along to the next man. In the days before "drastic plastic," they realized a moment of reckoning had come.

They dug deep into pockets and wallets, and their wives emptied their evening bags. Pip and Bert disappeared with the collection into the back of the restaurant while the others collected their coats and wraps. After a seemingly endless wait, someone asked: "What do you suppose they're *doing*?" To which Catherine answered instantly: "Washing dishes, I expect." And at that precise moment, Pip and Bert descended the staircase making mock gestures of drying their hands, to laughter all around. "Let's get a cab," said someone else. "With *what*?" came back the general response. There was nothing left but shank's pony, and in high heels and thin soles, they trudged back gamely to the conference hotel. They've laughed about the incident many times, but they learned a lesson.

In early December 1973, Pip was photographed comparing notes at the end of a working session of the executive meetings in FIABCI's headquarters in Paris, and FIABCI members reading their newsletters the world over could see the power structure made apparent. He is shown in close conversation with René-François Richardière, secretary-general, Paris FIABCI Congress; Jean Bailly, former FIABCI president and one of the originals of the organization; and Geoffrey Gay, then the FIABCI world president.

A number of FIABCI past presidents and board members had been working closely with Pip all along and helping him move to achieve what he intended to accomplish.[156] One guide and mentor was Jean Bailly of France (FIABCI president in 1967-69), who was instrumental in getting FIABCI going after the war. Will V. Egeli (president, 1971-1973), who was the first of the two Egeli presidents from Switzerland, father and son, was a strong supporter of Pip's. John Tysen of the U.S. chapter (president, 1969-1971) had recruited Pip to the executive, and when Pip was elected to the board at the Dublin Congress in 1970, John told him he'd be FIABCI world president one day.

And Pip himself knew he was at that point clear to aim at the presidency. He had firm support within the organization. Pemberton Holmes Ltd. was in good hands, and Catherine was working alongside. There was so much he knew he could accomplish in international recruiting and on education and licensing programs, and he decided to have a go at it. What he called "the great and successful adventure" was underway.

His constant drive for more education and training in real estate won attention at the September '74 CREA conference in Halifax. By the time Chairman Bert Willoughby delivered his report at the conclusion of the business sessions, all thirty member-nations of FIABCI at the time unanimously adopted a number of resolutions. Two related to Pip's work: one was adoption of an arbitration and conciliation code to settle disputes between colleagues of different nations; and another was on the need to develop new training programs with a legal aspect, recommending that the granting of licences in real estate be restricted by law only to properly qualified persons.[157]

The year he turned fifty, Pip became chairman of FIABCI Canada,[158] was reappointed for a third term to the international executive of FIABCI and became deputy chairman of the board of governors of Brentwood College School. Though it was his last year as a member of the Saanich Advisory Planning Commission, which he'd been on since 1969, he continued as president of the Associated Chambers of Commerce of Vancouver Island. He was also on the executive council of the Canadian Council of Christians and Jews, and on the board of NWL Financial Inc.[159]

"There's a bit too much to do," Pip admitted during an interview for the *Oak Bay Star*. "I seem to go from one involvement to another with tremendous rapidity." The reporter writes that despite the pace, Pip appeared "the epitome of relaxation, deceptively casual, with frequent laughter momentarily jarring a sizeable RAF-type mustache."[160] In answer to a question about advice he might offer to anyone in business, he had a concise reply. "Slog," said Pip emphatically. "Slog!"[161]

———————————

Even before 1975, which was when his itineraries really began to zoom, Pip had travelled more than a hundred thousand miles observing and evaluating real estate practices in fifteen countries.[162] He would advise people that in Canada, those who weren't educationally qualified weren't permitted to practise real estate. He would tell them how this had come about and why it needed to be done in many more places. "In the majority of countries," he said to them, "one merely has to hang out a shingle. The public doesn't have the protection of knowing the person is licensed, bonded and subject to a strict code of ethics and standards of business practice, as in Canada."[163]

He was also plumping for wider membership and participation in professional associations, including the national organizations that comprised FIABCI member-nations. "Chapter members," he pointed out, "have a unique opportunity to study legislation, construction techniques and housing around the world" and, as part of their ongoing work, were in perfect position to make the information available to their governments.

He outlined unfortunate macroeconomic aspects of some national policies: the rent control policy in Britain that was creating a manmade housing crisis; the ugly effects of ill-conceived real estate policies in various countries; and the use of the Canadian construction industry "as a marionette to deheat the economy."

He cited a theme he would carry into battle for many years—his contention that whether it's taking place within a developed or developing country, the level of real estate activity is closely tied to that country's level of prosperity. Vigour within the real estate industry, he said, creates vigour in the whole economy and increases the standard of living.

Norway was already in line with Pip's thinking about professional education and standards. Echoing the efforts in British Columbia during the late 1950s, the Association of Norwegian Real Estate Brokers was preparing a plan for a Norwegian real estate school, and Sven Menne prepared a summary document of their stance: "Whatever the political system might be for a given country, real estate brokerage is concerned with great national possessions, perhaps the most valuable ones of all. Real estate brokerage therefore not only should be, but must be, practised by professionally educated personnel as an essential component of the legal system of every society... In those cases where these two main requirements—professional education and the right to practise—have not been regularized, FIABCI should provide assistance."[164]

Pip, within FIABCI, was in a position to help steer matters the way he felt was beneficial for all: "It was a wonderful opportunity, a wonderful challenge, to spread education in real estate to all member countries."

The theme for FIABCI International's May 1975 World Congress in Paris had been set as "Real Estate Professions Facing World Development." Membership at the time was thirty-five member countries from five continents, plus seventeen observer nations, with Brazil, Columbia, Venezuela and Malaysia admitted as member-countries during the previous year.[165] Individuals from many segments of the profession assembled in France to discuss the interrelated group of real estate professions throughout the world: brokerage, property management, appraisal, counselling, mortgage and financing and development promotion.

These meetings had an extra edge, because the industry was taking stock of standing policies and adjusting for many new circumstances. The hot topic of rent controls was addressed from various perspectives, covering sixty years of frozen rents in France, rent controls in the U.S. and their effects on occupation and maintenance costs of buildings, rent freezes and consequences in Canada and, from the U.K., a report synthesizing the questionnaire replies on the actual effects of rent controls on rents, rental charges and property administration.[166] Rent controls and freezes were not looked on kindly.

Other reports at that congress included, from Nigeria, "Development in developing countries"; from Spain, "Prefabrication as a factor in the transformation of the real estate system"; from Belgium, "Discussion on the abundance of capital/scarcity of capital"; from the Netherlands, "Some main aspects of the world food problem"; from the U.S., "Marketing of agricultural real estate"; and from the U.K., reports presenting early information on redevelopment of London's docklands as well as problems of renovation and conservation in city centres by private enterprise and municipal authorities.

Presentations on professional and educational exchanges included fresh attention to the young professionals, all under thirty-five, who shared their experiences after taking part in work-exchanges set up under the FIABCI Exchange Program.

Glyn Ing reported on housing trends in the Asia Pacific area, and Cippy Ciputra reported on industrial and commercial real estate trends in the developing areas of the Pacific. Working sessions explored issues arising from the European Common Market, real estate financing, development promotion projects, residential real estate growth worldwide, real estate counselling, fiscal legislation, property management, urban planning and city-core redevelopment, industrial real estate trends, emerging issues in the Pacific sphere, reports from national delegations, successful training processes and standards, administration of shops and offices, and particularly the hot topic of international relocation services—how to make use of the services of the real estate professions for international transfers of personnel within industrial and commercial companies.

Though a certain glamour was a regular part of the schedule in each locale, and though each locale was intensely interested in presenting itself in the best possible light to the delegates, the congresses were not—as those not present occasionally assumed—some kind of week-long whoop-ups where holiday property listings in exotic locations were exchanged. The sessions were part of the global financial power network, part of the processes of shaping long-term economic and social planning and policy worldwide.

The congresses were also where those in positions of power were able to take the measure of someone's worth. By the end of the tightly scheduled week, each participant's knowledge, viewpoints, competency, skills and character had become pretty apparent to all who cared to observe.

Staff members at Pemberton's downtown office (top) have fun in the spirit of Victorian Days, May 1971.

Mike Page joins PH (left) in March '73.

The company's office building (above) has a large map of Vancouver Island painted on its exterior wall.

Will V. Egeli, Sr., presents Pip with the FIABCI Medal of Honour (right) at the May 1973 FIABCI Congress in Sydney, Australia.

Participants at the September '74 CREA conference meet on the **Bluenose II** *in Halifax harbour (below). Pip is at left, Jack Webber in the middle and Bert Willoughby at right. When he was fifty, Pip became chairman of FIABCI Canada and knew he was clear to aim at the FIABCI world presidency, which he proceeded to do.*

CHAPTER ELEVEN
TOP OF THE WORLD

JOHN TYSEN'S PREDICTION materialized when Pip was elected twelfth world president of FIABCI, the youngest yet and the first Canadian to hold the position.

A press release went out to the wire services: "Meeting in Paris at its Twenty-Sixth World Congress, the Board of the International Real Estate Federation FIABCI elected as its World President Mr. Philip Holmes FRI, RI(BC), from Canada. Mr. Holmes' period of office, which will be of two years, will cover the Twenty-Seventh International Congress to be held in San Francisco (USA) from 23 to 28 May 1976 and the Twenty-Eighth Congress in Amsterdam (Netherlands) from 5 to 10 June 1977."[167]

For celebrating his new position, he said there couldn't possibly be a more dramatic venue. The *soirée de gala* on the final night of the Paris meetings was at the Theatre national de l'opéra, where Republican Guards in full-dress uniform very imperiously greeted delegates. Guests were led to their seats for a performance by the Opéra ballet corps—all of a *Pas de Quatre* and the second act of *Les Sylphides*. Afterward, gathered into a grand hall readied for them with orchestras and buffets, they were given charming instructions to dance until dawn: "*On dansera jusqu'à l'aube dans le Grand Foyer de l'Opéra et la Rotonde du Glacier.*"

Responses to his election promptly arrived from various quarters.

From Ottawa, dated June 3, from Prime Minister Trudeau: "May I add my voice of congratulations to you as you assume the challenging role of President of the International Real Estate Federation, FIABCI. I understand that you are the first Canadian to be so honoured. My best wishes to you. P.E. Trudeau." One of Trudeau's closest political colleagues, Marc Lalonde, also sent a congratulatory note.

From Ottawa, from Leader of the Opposition Robert Stanfield: " ... You are bringing to this office the knowledge and good judgement of many years of experience in the real estate profession. There is no doubt in my mind that the presidency of this worldwide organization is in capable hands. Please accept my congratulations and best wishes."

From former Prime Minister John Diefenbaker: "The meeting of the ... Federation in Paris brings together outstanding representatives of the real estate profession from many countries ... I was impressed by the outstanding work done by the World Organization at the 1971 Congress held in Montreal ... "

From Quebec, Premier Robert Bourassa sent a telex via the Canadian Real Estate Association office: "I am extremely pleased to offer you my congratulations for your election as World President of the International Real Estate Federation."

From New Brunswick, Premier Richard Hatfield's telex was forwarded to Paris via the CREA offices as well: "I understand that this is the first time in the twenty-eight-year history ... that a Canadian has served as president of the world organization. You bring honour to Canada ... "

Notes arrived from British Columbia, both from Premier David Barrett ("Best wishes for a successful real estate congress to yourself and our Canadian delegation ... ") and former Premier, W.A.C. Bennett ("Best wishes for a successful and rewarding congress ... ").

Slightly more expansive comments arrived from provincial Minister of Housing Lorne Nicholson[168] and Vancouver's Mayor Art Phillips. Nicholson sent a telegram directly to Pip in Paris: "Best wishes to all delegates for a successful congress. Especially pleased that a British Columbian is heading the Canadian delegation." Art Phillips' telegram said: "My sincere congratulations on your appointment as President of FIABCI. This is a most distinctive honour and a great tribute to Canada. I know you will do an outstanding job."

Congratulatory letters flowed in. Jules Léger, the former diplomat who had been appointed Governor General the year before, wrote a warm note from Ottawa. B.C. Lieutenant-Governor Walter Owen, whose son Philip later became mayor of Vancouver, and Ontario Lieutenant-Governor Pauline McGibbon, first woman in the Commonwealth to represent the Queen in that role, sent their congratulations.

From Canadian Real Estate Association president E.L. Hoppe: "We know the wheel is in good hands with you at the helm. Very best wishes for continued success ... and if you feel CREA can be of assistance ... do not hesitate to call."

From E.J.W. Griffith, Jr., executive director of the Windsor-Essex County Real Estate Board: "Pip, on behalf of President Marwood Andrews and all 680 members of our board, I extend to you hearty congratulations. You have brought a tremendous honour not only to those associated with CREA but to all in this great country ... "

Notes came from Alberta Premier Peter Lougheed, Saskatchewan Premier Allan Blakeney, Manitoba Premier Ed Schreyer and Newfoundland Premier Frank Moores.

Ontario Premier Bill Davis and his staff were up-to-date on the news. He sent a trio of communications to Pip, the first of which arrived several weeks before the May congress: "It is indicative of the interest of the members of FIABCI Canada and of the respect in which you are held in the International Federation that such a strong Canadian delegation will be attending the…Congress in Paris later this month. In today's increasingly complex society, your profession is facing unprecedented demands and challenges…"

The second contact was a telex from Davis to Pip via the Congress central desk in Paris. It arrived immediately after the presidency announcement: "This honour is an expression of the respect in which you are held by the delegates…and is a tribute to your personal qualities and your considerable talents. It is also an acknowledgement of the role you and your associates have played in the development of our country…The delegates have chosen wisely. William G. Davis." A third communication from him arrived shortly afterward: "May your discussion and resolutions be highly successful and your visit to one of the world's most beautiful cities be a delight." Communications well handled on that front.

The Ontario politicos generally were well-organized about acknowledging Pip's powerful appointment. They knew what it was and knew what it meant. Notes arrived promptly from the Ontario Leader of the Opposition, Ontario's Minister of Mines, the Minister of Energy and the Minister of Revenue, the Ontario Provincial Secretary for Social Development, several Toronto-area federal Members of Parliament and Toronto's Mayor David Crombie.

Communications staff working for Metropolitan Toronto Chairman Paul Godfrey initially made an awkward assumption about Pip's home town and rushed to correct themselves. "It has recently been brought to my attention," the note from Godfrey said, "that you have been chosen as world president of FIABCI… We are proud that such recognition has been given to one of our countrymen and doubly so since you are a citizen of Metropolitan Toronto and bring worldwide attention to our community." Almost immediately, but just after the conference closed, a follow-up telegram reached Pip via the Hotel Méridien front desk: "Best wishes for a successful and stimulating 1975 Congress. Metropolitan Toronto looks forward to hosting you in 1982."

Pip delighted in the moment when his new business card was produced—"Philip Holmes, World President, International Real Estate Federation"—and looked forward to his two-year term with great anticipation. His campaign to rise to the top of the industry had succeeded, and he could proceed with communicating his training-and-education drive.

Canadian real estate industry press carried news of Pip's appointment with satisfaction—"Holmes becomes head of FIABCI"—and showed him in Paris flanked by CREA president Georges H. Couillard and retiring FIABCI president Geoffrey Gay.[169]

FIABCI's quarterly magazine of course carried its new president's statement, which was a long piece re-emphasizing the importance of property ownership to strong, stable economies. "FIABCI with its member countries," Pip said, "has to positively identify itself with and represent the interests of this immensely powerful but quite leaderless sector of society—those who believe in property ownership." He added that while "increasing our own standards of competence and practice," it would be "necessary to know and publicize what is happening and recommend better solutions."[170]

He wasn't speaking theoretically. Zambia that week had unexpectedly decreed a state takeover of land ownership. The wire-service story put Pip and others involved with the industry on high alert: "President Kenneth Kaunda of Zambia announced Monday the nationalization of all privately held land, movie theatres, nursing homes and the country's main newspapers. He said it was necessary because of economic difficulties and to stop land speculation…More than 90 percent of Zambia's foreign exchange earnings are derived from copper, which has been hit hard by falling prices…The president also earmarked a number of other areas for state control. These include privately owned rental housing [and] tobacco factories…"[171]

The news story continued. Effective Monday, Kaunda said, freehold titles to land in Zambia would be abolished. All land held by freehold farmers would now be held by the present titleholders only as leasehold for a hundred years, and unused farmland would be taken over immediately. In urban centres, freehold titles would also be converted to hundred-year leases.

Real estate agents were ordered to close their offices immediately, and all the land they administered would be taken over by local authorities or directly by central government. Compensation wasn't top-of-mind in Lusaka: "Kaunda made no mention of compensation for any of the areas of outright nationalization, but in the case of partial takeovers, he said he has ordered negotiations with existing owners."[172]

The Zambia situation was troublesome because it wasn't the only country inclined to abolish freehold title. Other countries had already publicly or privately expressed interest in much the same thing, and no one knew whether this Lusaka announcement from Kaunda would precipitate others to act. In Pip's first post-appointment interviews, after restating his belief in real estate training and standards of practice, he detoured to refer deliberately to FIABCI's heightened watchfulness on property ownership rights and then proceeded on with his original text.

Pip said in those first 1975 interviews as he began his term that he was looking forward to meeting as many FIABCI members as possible over the next two years. And meet them he certainly did.

The travel agent's finalized bookings for one trip show departure from Victoria on September 18, 1975, for Seattle, Taipei, Manila, Bangkok, Singapore, Djakarta, Sydney, Canberra, Sydney again, Auckland, Los Angeles, Vancouver, Winnipeg, Vancouver, and into Victoria again on October 14.

One of Catherine's letters among the business papers filed for early September 1975, several months after Pip began his presidency, gave a personal view of this:[173] "I think in many ways we shall not inwardly digest these trips until the two years are over and we can relax and think over the details. They are, of necessity, very *organized*. There is no time to mosey round even when in meetings. Still, that's all par for the course, and travelling in the capacity in which we are has its pros and its cons. One interesting facet is that one immediately meets the core of the progressive and forward-thinking people, and one learns a lot about the economic and political problems of the country... Our next trip is in September to the Far East... Very rushed, unfortunately, but that cannot be helped... "

Work would be continued for two or three weeks in Victoria before the travels resumed. "In November it's down to the States, and in December back in Europe again—Paris first for executive meetings and then the Scandinavian countries. We shall have a couple of days in London as Pip is addressing the British Chapter, so we will give you a call and at least have a chat... "[174]

The workload and the travel to accomplish it were intensely scheduled. In 1975 and 1976, for instance, one sequence of Pip's meetings covered France, Germany, Holland, England, Monaco, Italy, Switzerland, Austria, Spain, Canada; then a round of September and October meetings in Japan, Taiwan, Philippines, Thailand, Singapore, Indonesia, Australia, New Zealand and central Canada; followed by another cycle, to France (in Paris), Denmark, Sweden, Norway, England, Israel, Greece, Crete, France (in Verval), England again, Ireland, home to Canada; then for good measure, out around once again to Latin America, South America, through the Caribbean, the U.S. and across Canada east to west, then home.[175]

Pip had decided to go listen to what was on the minds of real estate people in all the FIABCI member-countries, and in each country, they were more than glad to oblige. Denmark, one of the two founding countries of the prewar form of the organization, was put on the schedule for mid-December 1975, [176] and the agenda there was the sort of thing arranged for him in most of the countries.

After an informal meeting with the president of FIABCI-Denmark, Pip addressed members of the chapter and continued afterward on topics of shared interest in small-group and one-on-one discussions. A banquet in his honour had been arranged with the Minister of Commerce and Copenhagen's Lord Mayor, as well as leaders of the national political parties, directors of the finance houses and banks, chairmen of trade associations and the Estate Agents Commission, the majority of the Estate Agents Association executive, senior officials from several ministries and the executive of FIABCI-Denmark. Pip listened to all and, as well, updated them on FIABCI's worldwide work. Always, he dwelt on the meaning and importance of education and training in the real estate field. FIABCI's aim was a proper university education, he told them, of the sort still found only in a few countries.

After Denmark: meetings in Stockholm. On December 16, he and Catherine flew from Sweden into a thick coastal fog blanketing southern England and were diverted to Birmingham. They were given a long bus ride to London and the committee of management meeting of the British chapter of FIABCI. Immediately after arrival, Pip gave a speech at a luncheon attended by eighty members "on the need for the profession to protect the right to the ownership of property, a worldwide problem." There followed an evening reception, and only then, bedtime.

By December 18, they were at the Hilton in Jerusalem, with Monsieur Philip Holmes being praised for *"son brillant exposé sur l'importance des objectifs que les professions immobilières doivent atteindre..."*

He travelled steadily, with purpose, in a great variety of circumstances. On one trip, the Holmeses were taken around all over Israel, for instance, by David Blumberg, who they called a huge force in Israeli real estate. A South African Jew with a passion for Israel, "a person not afraid of man nor beast," he had been a major in the tank corps and turned up on occasion at the annual conferences with his head bandaged or arm in a sling.[177]

Travelling with David, said Pip, was an experience all in itself. Once, Pip and Catherine were taking a few travel photos of a pretty-looking valley—a picturesque scene that turned out to be a sensitive military position—and were suddenly challenged by militia who emerged from nowhere. Blumberg deftly defused the situation, rescuing his guests from bureaucracy or worse.

Another day, when he was touring his two guests through an old section of Tel Aviv at a snail's pace, drivers of the dozen or so vehicles blocked behind his car were honking and trying to push past in any way they could. Blumberg glanced back at the hubbub and commented: *"They* have the problem." And he drove onward at exactly the same pace as before.

The three went together, Catherine said, "to all the famous places connected to stories in the Bible and walked the paths that Jesus walked," and though they found some of it "terribly touristy," she remembers it as a marvellous experience. Security enforcement was everywhere, but their host was widely known and apparently well-respected. He was full of daring and courage and loved a good fight—such as, let's say, Entebbe. When Blumberg was later in charge of the 1993 FIABCI World Congress in Jerusalem, Pip said, "things were pretty well run."

After Christmas visits with family and friends in England, they were in Ireland in early January 1976. Staying at the official residence of the President of the Republic, he was scheduled for luncheons and discussions with the president of the Irish Auctioneers and Valuers Institute (IAVI). There followed chapter meetings, receptions and banquets. Pip was giving speeches, answering questions and asking just as many or more. Near the end of the visit, he was presented with honorary membership in the institute, which pleased him.

Then they'd be home in Victoria to unpack, catch up with messages and obligations, see their family and reconnect with Pemberton Holmes, community goings-on and local friends. Hobbies listed on Pip's biography handout at this juncture were sailing, photography and music, and perhaps amid the furore of obligations, there really was a bit of time to devote to music and other gentler arts. Pip had a notably good eye for colour and loved their home's watercolours, sculptures and other *objets d'art*, especially glass. He said he saw much during his travels that was memorable: "just wonderfully done by someone, beautiful."

Though he gave a great many interviews in those first six months and did a great amount of travel through the whole period, plentiful sociability continued unabated at home. Dinner invitations Chez Holmes during their brief periods in town were mailed well ahead of time, so that after each of their sweeps through various countries, their friends in B.C. could come visit, dine, chat and generally stay in touch. In the flurry of work, good friendships became even more precious.

If people didn't know Pip or hadn't worked with him, his easy social abilities sometimes obscured his determination. Mark Ricketts, writing an "In Person" profile for the *Financial Post*, recognized it. "If Philip Holmes had to jostle for political power," he wrote, "one wonders whether he could turn off his pleasant disposition and slay fellow aspirants. As world president of a 600,000-member association of realtors, a quick assumption is that he could. But then, why should he? Moving through a succession of leadership roles in an ever-widening vortex of local, provincial and national real estate associations, the presidency of the world organization was not only inevitable but a fitting reward."[178]

Ricketts interviewed Pip at Pemberton Holmes downtown. "Comfortably ensconced in his office overlooking B.C.'s Victoria harbour, he looks the part of a wartime ranking officer and chats with a lighthearted vigour that inspires friendly confidence. With his bushy eyebrows raised in intelligent amusement, he says, 'I like people.' And he could easily have continued by saying, 'I like living too.'"

Pip's agenda for the *Post*'s readership that week, stemming from his experience with chambers of commerce, was that governments simply didn't understand how fundamental real estate investment was to a vibrant economy. As Ricketts wrote it, "Holmes plans to oil the machinery to help realtors make themselves heard in government circles around the world." Pip clarified that he wanted to see realtors invited to participate in discussions with governments whenever those governments contemplated legislation that would have economic effects on real property markets. Another of his objectives related to that, he said, was to improve research capabilities in the organization.

He wanted to begin realigning FIABCI's direction, and when he gave the keynote address at a meeting of the Real Estate and Stock Institute of Australia in Canberra, he outlined his plan. "With noteworthy exceptions, FIABCI has to date concentrated largely on organizational and internal professional problems. This is natural. To a large extent, all our member national associations have done likewise, and it is just as well. We've built foundations."[179]

By the 1970s, however, postwar economic expansion was lagging after thirty years. The nationalization of land, taxation increases at all levels, labour strife, shortages in housing and rent controls were chewing at the market system. Pip gave them the Zambia example: that in one day in June that year, by the stroke of a governmental pen, real estate agencies were ordered to close their doors by the following morning and freehold property was abolished. He added that in the previous two and a half years, FIABCI had successfully prevailed upon two Western European governments not to outlaw real estate brokerage.

He explained what he saw happening. "Now we face the challenge of a real-life game.

Out there, in each of our jurisdictions, live people who have the deepest stake in their community and their country: the landowner, the property owner and the person who hopes to be one. Vast in numbers, of great collective wealth, [they are] earnest and greatly concerned citizens. Politically and economically, they are not represented. No one is looking after their hard-earned investments, their rights to their home, the farm, the cottage, their apartment, commercial or development property—and their hopes for independence."[180]

He suggested a community-based process of engagement. Through continuous local-level liaison in regular meetings of residential housing committees, he said, the conclusions and all consensus reached locally could be carried forward. He urged members' participation in their own communities so that an overall housing policy could be developed on a continuous and evolving basis and, when the policy was formulated, urged the Real Estate and Stock Institute in Canberra to promote it on behalf of the owning public and young would-be property owners.

"Through this process," he told his audience, "the profession not only suddenly becomes politically viable but it means that contributive leaders with a voice will be heard…" Carrying these local, regional and national policies into the international level, he said, would mean the real estate professions of the world would become the major component in leadership of real estate policy and forward planning. They were certainly most qualified for it.

A young Australian realtor, Ian Wallace from Perth, met Pip at the CREA conference in Winnipeg and began excitedly reporting on his five-month exchange visit in the U.S. and Canada, where he had been hosted by various FIABCI members in small rural firms and in large commercial offices operating nationwide. Ian was near the end of his work-study stint in FIABCI's Professional Exchange Program when he met Pip, who was four months into his term as president.

Ian said he was getting an advance view of the trends set by his host countries that would arrive in Australia, he guessed, "some time in the future." Among those trends was the fact that in North America, there were so many highly competitive women in real estate: "It took some time for me to get used to the different experience of finding so many females in the real estate field. It's a complete reversal of the situation in Perth."[181] It floored him.

Ian summarized his discoveries in the exchange program—differences such as the North American capacity for working long hours, the independence of each sales employee working within a firm's guidelines, the novelty of a public authority being able to impose environmental protection controls on development, and in particular, the requirements for education and training.

In the two years he was head of FIABCI, Pip visited each of the member-countries, some of them several times. "It was a huge load to carry," he said. Each of the six-week "sweeps," as he called the trips he and Catherine took, needed preparation in great detail. Schedules and agendas were tightly packed and had to be right. Because he custom-tailored his speeches to the audiences and their situations, research for each of the speeches to be delivered en route had to be current. Creativity was needed on how best to convey the omnipresent education theme as well as other specific information in each venue.

These commitments even when he was based at home all but precluded Pip's active participation in Pemberton Holmes Ltd. for long blocks of time, but he had to trust that all was running smoothly while he concentrated on what he himself was meant to be doing. He gave credit where credit was due: "I could never have given this time nor accomplished all I did if it hadn't been for a dedicated and loyal team in the Victoria office. And without having Mike Page at home looking after the business, it would have been utterly impossible. He led with zeal, organizational prowess and integrity, and I had complete trust in him and his abilities. He never let me down."[182]

The March 1976 travel schedule had the Holmeses flying in quick succession from Victoria to Vancouver, Los Angeles, Mexico City, Bogota, Carracas, Brasilia, Iguassu Falls, Sao Paulo, Rio de Janeiro, Curaçao, Kingston, Montego Bay, Chicago, Seattle and Victoria again by April 6. The flight bookings covered PWA, CP Air, Argentine Airlines, Lufthansa from Bogota to Caracas, Varig into Brasilia, Viacao Aerea to Sao Paulo, Cruzeiro from Iguassu Falls to Sao Paulo, VASP from Sao Paulo to Rio, VIASA Venezuelan Airlines, Dutch Antillean Airlines, Air Jamaica and United Airlines.

Their longest stay was three nights in Sao Paulo near the mid-point of the journey. In Rio, Pip had good working meetings with the chairmen of two national real estate organizations, CRECI and ABADI, and at the reception at the Jockey Club there, got a good laugh by telling the tale of the dinner-bill dilemma in Madrid.

The hospitality was generous and a large photo was run in the *Sociales y Personales* column of the newspaper *El Universal*[183]— *"Visita do Dr. Philip Holmes ao Brasil."* Amid flutters of good-bye hugs, several fond farewell notes were handed to Señora de Holmes y Philip Holmes from people they'd met, even though briefly: "Hope you enjoyed Brazil!" and "My best regards to Philip, and I hope to see you again in the next future." Their "next future," actually, was downtown Chicago, and the jollity of Brazil fell away at once.

The FIABCI medallion (right) is worn by its world
president during the term of office.

The new business card (below) delighted Pip,
who used "1000 Government" on it.

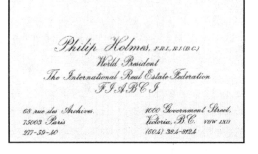

Alexis Noldé (left) and Baïa Noldé, both based at the Paris headquarters of FIABCI
International, were central to Pip's progress there and to its ongoing operations.

Pip wearing the FIABCI medallion (above) during the two-year term.

Maj. Gen. the Hon. George R. Pearkes and Mrs. Blytha Pearkes (left) greet Pip in mid-1975.

Korean café fare (bottom) with his host's family. Pip was determined to visit each FIABCI member country.

CHAPTER TWELVE
FIABCI AND THE ASIA PACIFIC

A TELEX FROM Jack Pontius was waiting for them at their Chicago hotel.[184] Pontius was CEO of the National Association of Real Estate Boards, or NAREB, the U.S. national organization. "Earlier I wired you in Bogota," he wrote to Pip, "but I doubt the telex reached you... Have arranged for a briefing with you and members of our staff on Monday [and] on Tuesday morning I look forward to the opportunity to review with you policy and any proposed statements we may want to submit... to the International Habitat Conference in Vancouver..."

The FIABCI executive had been alarmed to the highest degree by a proposed agenda item—a resolution for debate from "the Habitat people"—at the upcoming United Nations conference several weeks after the twenty-seventh FIABCI World Congress.

"That was the BIG FIGHT in 1976," Pip explained. "Some of the Habitat '76 people proposed a motion that all land should be owned by the state, with no private ownership. Imagine the impact if this had gone through! The very idea of denying individuals the right of owning property flew in the face of all I held dear, and in every fibre of my being, I thought this motion wrong." If discussed and passed, the motion would become a resolution of the United Nations for worldwide application.

It was Pip's battle to fight. As world president of FIABCI and therefore connected with the United Nations Economic and Social Council, he was Head of Delegation of FIABCI to the World Habitat Conference in Vancouver.

Though he was still in transit from the South America trip, he began the next round. The FIABCI executive and members of the delegation to the Habitat conference set up a meeting to make a plan. The first item was to organize the research and gather as much information as possible about the situation. Next item was to have Pip get in touch with the presidents of each of his organization's national committees and talk with them about the state-ownership motion being proposed. Their intention was to speak as a single collective voice.

This could be made to work, because they were all about to converge in San Francisco's St. Francis Hotel for their 1976 World Congress. The week-long congress from 23 to 28 May "was beautifully organized," Pip said, not by FIABCI in Paris this time but, as their own preference, by the Americans themselves. The theme had been set as "The Real Estate Professions Serving the Public," but the service being rendered to the public turned out to be far more broad-reaching than most would ever realize.

On the first day delegates were assembling, a Wild West Show was scheduled at the Bay Meadows Race Track. One of the San Francisco organizers took Pip aside there, spoke to him briefly and led him away. Catherine noticed but thought no more about it. When the entry parade for the show began, there was still no sign of Pip. Cowboys dressed in glittering white entered on six rearing black horses. Cowgirls dressed in glittering black entered with all possible drama on six white horses. Showmanship!

Then onto the track in front of two thousand people trotted a stocky black and white pony, and in the saddle, with Stetson waving aloft and his long legs tucked up in short stirrups, was their world president. The one silent moment in which Pip was announced was followed by an enormous roar out of two thousand throats and rolling laughter that didn't stop. They adored it and were talking about it years later.

At the official opening ceremonies in the Masonic Auditorium next morning, Carla Hills, the assistant attorney general and free trade negotiator who had been named Secretary of the U.S. Department of Housing and Urban Development, welcomed those present and gave her keynote speech. She was followed by Pip delivering the dramatic message on which much hinged: that "the basic right and freedom of property ownership faces inhibition, even abolition, by governments following a path to a new form of feudalism, where every state is supreme and man is again slave, this time to a state."[185]

He told the real estate professionals they had a choice of two reactions: to continue the industry's well-established introspective role or to mobilize themselves, "to assume leadership toward the survival of the profession and the rights of private property ownership." Few people understand, he said, how much depends on the rights of property ownership — not only home owners but property owners in business and industry as well as beneficiaries of investments of insurance companies, annuity and pension plans, the union funds and the social benefits agencies touching national and international populations.

"Real estate is a major factor in redistribution as well as creation of wealth," he said. "The tragic fact is that no group represents the interests of this real-estate–dependent sector of the public. Our profession must fill the void." He called for "a vast program of communications" within their industry through which FIABCI could define and analyze problems, determine long-term and short-term solutions, report national situations to international committees, garner support for the industry's viewpoints and serve the public in a more effective way. They already had the necessary structure within their organization, and the technology they needed for research and quick worldwide communication was increasingly available.

Their resolution's wording stated that governments alone could not satisfactorily solve the world's housing problem without a substantial contribution from the private sector. It said governments should develop sound plans for land utilization, plans that included provision for the production of adequate housing, food, raw materials, energy, transportation and communication, and that such plans should provide for projected population increases.

The resolution then restated FIABCI's belief that the tendency of all levels of government to restrain business and industry from operating in a free economy would not lead to the improvement of the human lifestyle. It urged further discussion on these matters within the year and pledged broad support toward any agreed solutions.

The backgrounder documents were studied and national chapter executive boards in home countries consulted. The Canadian Real Estate Association continued helping wherever it could. Pip dispatched a letter with the resolution text to all chapters, and the presidents of the national chapters supported him, name after name. Every one of the national chapter presidents signed the submission document for the resolution and supporting brief.

Immediately after the San Francisco World Congress closed, preparations ramped up for another major event, the UN Conference on Human Settlements in Vancouver, often referred to as the World Habitat Conference or as Habitat '76.

FIABCI issued a barrage of purpose-directed communications, including Pip's statement in a June 1 press release. His public message was this:[186] "A solution to the world's growing housing problems will be achieved only by an enlargement of private and public cooperation ... " His statement was accompanied by a fifteen-page briefing paper on the essential role of real estate professionals in the solution of human settlements problems.[187]

The briefing paper provided a succinct presentation of who and what FIABCI was and what its responsibilities were, plus its international code of ethics. It put forth an overview of human settlement situations worldwide and set out a prescriptive take on what adequate housing might entail. "There are four billion humans on Earth," it said in part, "and providing adequate housing for everyone poses enormous political and economic problems. Twenty-seven large countries in the world own 75 percent of the Earth's resources and represent only 25 percent of the world's population."[188]

FIABCI stressed that the need to preserve the right to own and enjoy private property must be a paramount consideration, always bearing in mind that greater co-operation with government agencies was an anticipated goal. Governments, furthermore, should not acquire private property without just and prompt compensation.

Because Pip and the international executive committee were able to present to the World Habitat Conference at the right moment a document signed by chapter presidents in thirty-six countries denouncing the concept, the effort to promote state ownership of property was defeated.

The American chapter understood clearly what had taken place during May and June '76 in successfully combatting the motion and, in appreciation, had a bronze plaque cast to present to Pip and Catherine: "in grateful appreciation to Philip P.D. Holmes and his wife Catherine, for their outstanding contributions in serving the real estate professions and the public among the free nations of the world."[189] Insiders in the national chapters appreciated the urgency of the situation and realized how far it could have gone against what they wanted.

Alexis Noldé, FIABCI secretary-general in Paris, sent a memo on a number of business matters to Pip later that summer and commented on other information subsequently emerging from Habitat '76. "I was amazed," Alexis wrote, "when I read in the newspapers in Caracas that the main discussions during the two last days of the [Habitat '76] conference concerned a resolution condemning Zionism, on a Cuban proposal supported by Algeria, and that this resolution was finally adopted by seventy-seven votes to zero and twenty-two abstentions! This shows, certainly, the spirit of the attending delegates and what can be expected on problems like land use or private property."

Alexis was proud of what had been accomplished, as well he might be. "Nevertheless, I see that our small FIABCI team made a great job under your leadership and succeeded by using all possible ways (or even perhaps impossible ways) to bring our resolution forward. Bravo! I can easily imagine how tired you were after all that coming in, plus of course our Congress."[190]

Pip wanted to stay involved with shelter housing in some way and, among other actions, became the FIABCI representative in Geneva of the Sixth Session of the Committee on Housing during the meetings of the Building and Planning Working Party on Housing, part of the Economic Commission for Europe. He began to assemble project files related to a shared effort that gained momentum. With many others' work over the next two decades, that shared effort emerged as FIABCI's Global Housing Foundation.[191]

Yet what many people remembered from that period—actually, all they knew of what was going on—was Pip arriving on the pony. Alexis Noldé's wife Baïa sent a note to Catherine in August saying someone they knew in common had sent to the Paris headquarters "a very big picture of Pip on the horse at the rodeo" and suggested they might have it framed.[192] Pip nixed the idea on the grounds of cost, but it remains a famous image.

While the planning and research continued for the next sweep of countries in the fall, their summer in British Columbia was, as ever, a sociable season. An August '76 note from Catherine to Baïa Noldé in the Paris offices illustrated what the Holmes household considered leisure:

Enclosed is our itinerary for the Asian trip... How we are going to survive the thirty-two-hour trip from Christchurch to Quebec City I'm not quite sure. But we have no alternative, as Pip doesn't want to leave New Zealand until after the nineteenth but has to be in Quebec City for the CREA conference on the twenty-first... As you know, Habitat followed the Congress, and then a flow of different guests, which I didn't altogether appreciate because I was trying to get all the work completed...

My cousin and her husband stayed ten days, and we had a marvellous time with parties, sightseeing and cruising in the boat at weekends... Then Pip's cousins arrived [and we] drove up the Island and took the northbound ferry that goes through the inland waterways of the B.C. coast—very spectacular scenery, extremely similar to the Norwegian fiords—to Prince Rupert on the mainland, and drove to a northern town called Smithers.

We met up with my cousin and her husband there, and the six of us [went to] a wilderness park... We saw lots of wild game—moose, caribou, beaver. So wonderful to see them so close in their natural habitat. Pip and I drove leisurely down through B.C. to show them the different types of terrain and scenery.

Now we are back to work again—Pip behind the office door three-quarters of the time and never home for dinner before 7:30 or 8 p.m. Oh, well, it's all a stimulating life, and we are lucky to have happiness and our health...[193]

At Paris headquarters, Pip's thinking on some new FIABCI methodology was being put into effect. Alexis Noldé gave a hint of the changes in a letter to Denis Hayes of the Worldwatch Institute in Washington, D.C., to provide him with backgrounder information. Mr. Hayes would be delivering a paper to the FIABCI Congress in Amsterdam the following June. "A Congress is held in a different member-country each year," Noldé told Hayes, "and although the attendance figure varies, we expect around two thousand in Amsterdam."

He elaborated. "Until now," he wrote, "the Congress has tended to be somewhat self-centred with an emphasis on professional education, but the board has decided on a change of format for 1977 onward to give the delegates a chance to vote on resolutions that may be noted by governments and others in authority—i.e., that FIABCI is to speak when it has something worthwhile to say."[194]

Of necessity, realtors watch the economy the way farmers watch the weather, and one worry during mid-'76 was the unsavoury coexistence of inflation and recession. In Singapore, the president of the two-year-old Asia Pacific Real Estate Federation was commiserating with members about their situations: "Every government has to steer between the evils of inflation on the one hand and the spectre of recession on the other."[195] The president of the Real Estate Institute of New Zealand added that the world was seeing both these economic cancers growing and that almost everyone was suffering to a greater or lesser degree. "New Zealand is no exception," he said, "and the housing industry in particular has felt the cold wind of crisis."[196]

The third APREF Congress was set for Christchurch, New Zealand, 17-20 October 1976, and Pip was scheduled to speak. The overall theme of that year's meeting was "new town" development, and its agenda covered state development as well as private enterprise development in the Asia Pacific area—sociological problems and benefits of new-town development, high-rise/low-rise design factors, marketing approaches, construction and management, analysis of state versus private development and, an ever-increasing element, environmental considerations.[197]

As the sessions rolled out, one speaker would put the case against new towns and another would just as adamantly support them. One presentation was on high-growth areas within Australia. The usual heated discussions erupted on social and financial aspects of high-rise living and on whether shelter housing was to be considered as foreign aid or a charitable obligation of conscience. Twelfth in the sequence of fifteen items they planned to discuss was proposed cooperation with FIABCI.[198]

Out of the San Francisco congress had come a decision to seek closer cooperation between FIABCI and APREF, and FIABCI, through Pip, needed to express effectively to the APREF board during the New Zealand meetings this wish for cooperation. The Asia Pacific Real Estate Federation members by 1976 were Australia, China, Indonesia, Japan, Korea, Malaysia, New Zealand, Philippines, Singapore and Thailand. Observer status was held by Guam, Hong Kong and Papua New Guinea.

An alliance with FIABCI to form a world-spanning network had potential benefits for all participants. Pip's main difficulty with his chosen objective, which was to convince the Asia Pacific seaboard to join forces with a Europe-based professional group not yet widely represented in their part of the world, was that the cooperation he was proposing was fairly low on the APREF priority list.

Well ahead of the conference, he started with casual questions to the chairman of the event about dinner jackets and requested a bit of background related to planning his presentation. The chairman wrote back to Eileen Goulet, Secretary to Mr. P.D.P. Holmes, an equally casual letter from Australia: "There will be no occasion where a dinner jacket will be necessary during the APREF Congress in Christchurch. My recollection is that dinner jackets have never been worn at APREF meetings and therefore I do not expect that anybody will create a precedent on this occasion. Perhaps you could tell Mr. Holmes this and also tell him that I have had no further reaction or information concerning the APREF views on liaison with FIABCI. It will be necessary to wait until they arrive, apparently, to find out what the APREF position will be."[199]

During the time in New Zealand, Pip talked systematically about possible terms of a cooperation agreement between FIABCI and APREF and listened during discussions for ideas on increasing coordination and avoiding duplication of time, money and efforts within both organizations. His ability to get people working together, in this instance at the international level, did produce negotiations and eventual success, and he said he suspected he was able do this in an international situation because of his Canadian viewpoint. "This is where the strength of Canada shows," he said.

It wasn't by any means a solo campaign. It was lifted and carried along by the suasion of architect-engineer Ir. Ciputra, a most dynamic entrepreneur based in Jakarta, and Glyn Ing of Taipei, a man who was Ciputra's and Holmes's equal in energy, was also immensely knowledgeable about regional realities. Each of them was essential during the complex and delicate process of finding a fit between the two organizations that both saw as mutually beneficial. With others involved also playing their respective parts, Ir. Ciputra, Mr. Holmes and Mr. Ing worked together very, very well.

At a brief meeting for questions and answers, the document to establish a joint committee was considered and discussed. In an instinctive expression of overt trust, FIABCI President Holmes formally signed the document, and waited. Later the same day, APREF President Hanson Kwauk put forward his document agreeing to cooperation, and their plans to meet again during the 1977 Amsterdam congress were arranged and confirmed. "FIABCI and APREF were on the move," said Pip.

Pip also was able to report to the FIABCI executive council at their next meeting that the Real Estate Institute of New Zealand filed a formal application to become a full member of FIABCI and that they too looked forward to being officially admitted in Amsterdam.[200]

———————————

Victoria's community life continued at its usual relatively placid pace, but between 24 September and 24 October 1976, Pip and Catherine were out of town. They left Vancouver Friday 24 September for Tokyo, lost a day at the International Dateline and so arrived in Korea on Sunday 26 September. They flew back to Tokyo on 4 October, and after a memorable stay, continued on to meetings in Hong Kong, Bangkok, Kuala Lumpur and Singapore. They flew into Sydney, then on to Christchurch for the APREF Congress from 17 to 20 October.

That satisfyingly productive segment of the trip was followed by the thirty-two-hour journey from Christchurch to Quebec City (departing out of Aukland, transPacific to Los Angeles and then Vancouver, the transcontinental flight to Montreal, then another into Quebec City) for Pip to deliver a speech upon arrival to the Canadian Real Estate Association meeting. They carried on after the speech to a short series of meetings and visits in Montreal, Toronto and Vancouver and, on 24 October, reached home in Victoria. "Been away?" a local resident asked when she spotted them in town again just before Hallowe'en. "Anything interesting?"

In short, yes. To single out four days of the trip, they were in Japan for informal discussions with the Japan Chapter from September 30 to October 4. Pip's schedule included meetings, luncheons, real estate development presentations and press interviews. He and Catherine toured the frenetic urban neighbourhood and park in the Shinjuku district of Tokyo and went to have a look at the resort area of Nikko, where schoolgirls hiding their faces behind textbooks giggled about Pip's moustache. They'd apparently never met such a moustache before—or for that matter, any moustache. When he winked, of course, the giggling doubled.

Pip and Catherine accepted several invitations to private venues while they were in

Tokyo. A teahouse party was sponsored by Mr. Nakada, and they found it to be a calm and very civilized setting for cordial conversations. One invitation was extended to visit the guest house and garden of Mr. Mitsui, and another for a walk and tea in the garden of Mr. Watanabe.

The grounds around Mr. Mitsui's guest house were landscaped with trees and mosses of varying textures and habits showing every colour of green.[201] In Japan, this was not unusual, except that Mr. Mitsui's land, appropriate to his top position, was a one-acre garden in the middle of downtown Tokyo.[202]

Mr. Watanabe, head of Mitsubishi and one of two FIABCI deputy world presidents during Pip's term,[203] also had property in Tokyo, and his had a lake within it. "A small lake," he demurred—but one with rather special koi and perfectly groomed plantings circling its rocky circumference. Pip and Catherine took photos of the koi being fed and were provided with stout walking sticks to continue their gentle stroll.

They were shown the Mitsubishi think tank, a freestanding building in the garden containing one austere room with high windows, completely without distractions, and the walking paths surrounding it were perfect for slow walks to clarify the mind between concentrated sessions of shared corporate thinking. "Then we walked onward, and he took us in for tea," said Catherine. "The whole ceremony."

They were also taken to a very good restaurant by their hosts and noticed in particular the slightly scented breeze flowing past them as they entered. Out of every window was something beautiful and natural—black-stemmed ferns in a tiny moss garden, an aged bonsai gripping a rough boulder, a miniature waterfall with silver-black koi in a pool. This was a created environment seven storeys underground.

During another phase of the month-long trip, Pip and Catherine found themselves walking beside the gates of a small Korean shrine. "We often went exploring around, communicating with dictionaries and sign language," Pip said. The monks of the shrine led them through the temple and courtyard, and Pip gave them whatever money he had in his pockets to help with the shrine's maintenance.

The small group sat in the temple's shady courtyard "conversing" with facial and hand gestures plus phonetic phrases from a guidebook until their colleagues from the real estate association found them and joined the group. Their guide, a real estate executive, had shown himself more than eager to try speaking English, so the afternoon's plans were altered. He and the monks and the travellers carried on happily communicating under the trees in the courtyard without most of them knowing much more than a half-dozen words of the others' languages. Pip, comfortable everywhere, enjoyed the afternoon thoroughly.

A touch more drama than usual attended their Thailand visit between October 6 and October 11. During the Bangkok visit, their host was their friend Sukhum Thirawat, president of the Thai Real Estate Association and advisor to the king and the prime minister. "The visit is fitting," he had written to Pip in September, "since Thailand now becomes a full member of the FIABCI."

Arrangements were made for them at the Amarin Hotel in Bangkok, where the

Thai Real Estate Association maintained its headquarters, and a formal call on the Thai Premier (who was also the Minister of Interior in charge of the national Housing Authority) was set up. "Apart from the usual formalities," Mr. Thirawat advised Pip, "some topic on the FIABCI role could be suitably injected. I will submit to you in advance a memorandum on the current situation in Thailand."

He sent his daughter Charuwan Ingwasu to pick up Pip and Catherine at the airport, and he also sent his apologies for not being there himself because there'd been a coup.[204] From the Pemberton Holmes office in Victoria, repeated telexes from Michael Page were arriving: "Are you all right? The papers are reporting a revolution." In her letter dated Wednesday 6 October, one of Pip's daughters echoed the concern: "We're all thinking of you back here at the home front … Actually, this AM's news brought word of a military coup in Thailand, and we all figure you're probably in the thick of it, so that's food for thought."[205]

Throughout the touring around with Charuwan and her husband, a professor from India, they glimpsed only quick indications of political disruption. Without incident, they moved on to Pattaya on the Gulf of Thailand to be shown land developments there, then flew out from Donmuang Airport to their next stop.[206]

So around the end of October, when the Victoria woman asked genially if they'd seen anything interesting in their four-week absence, each of them could have given her a long answer. To such questions, they agreed it was often best to give a straightforward but vague reply: "It was absolutely *fascinating*. And what's been going on here?"

———————————

Two weeks later they were in Houston, Texas, at the sixty-ninth annual convention of the National Association of Realtors, where Mr. Holmes as FIABCI world president was delivering a plenary session speech to a collection of America's real estate elite. And at the end of November, they left for Paris for the annual executive meetings there.[207]

Executive committee meetings of the FIABCI officers were held every year in late November and early December. It had been agreed the previous year, December 1975, that in the face of some nations' activities concerning land ownership, FIABCI must take up the worldwide fight for the defence of the profession and of private property. The previous March, Pip had created a working group to study practical means of achieving this, and he addressed his executive committee on the FIABCI action taken at Habitat '76 the previous June to support and sustain this right to private land ownership.

As world president of the organization, it was he who welcomed the board members to their first meetings. Eleven new vice-presidents of FIABCI recently elected by their chapters were introduced and applauded, and the revised five-year plan was outlined. Pip reported on his travels throughout the member countries, and their summary report on the Pacific sector that year noted his success in gaining approval-in-principle of the cooperation agreement between APREF and FIABCI.

Pip also pointed out to the committee that the most effective expansion of their resources lay in using the tremendous capacity of the national organizations through their chapters, a perception soon to be a policy direction that stood the organization in good stead. "FIABCI is their organization," he said. "It is not a separate international club but the extension of their national organizations into the international arena."[208]

After Paris, the Holmes pair went by train to Luxembourg and then Brussels. In Brussels, Pip and the Belgian prince discovered common cause:[209] "World President Philip Holmes was granted an audience by H.R.H. Prince Albert of Belgium on the occasion of his four-day visit to FIABCI-Belgium. H.R.H. seemed extremely interested by the impressions President Holmes got from his recent trips around the world … and was also deeply concerned with the future of housing, environmental and social problems in the world."

From Brussels, they went to Geneva, then circled back to Belgium. By mid-December, they were with colleagues, family and friends in London.

*A well-known moment in FIABCI
lore (left): the introduction of Pip on
the pony.*

PHOTO CREDIT: ARMEL NUTTER

*Pip with Carla Hills (left), head of the U.S. Department
of Housing and Urban Development, at the 1976 FIABCI
World Congress in San Francisco.*

*Apollo 7 astronaut Walter Cunningham (above) admires
the whole-world insignia on Pip's FIABCI presidential
medallion. With them (photo left) is H. Jackson Pontius,
Secretary General of FIABCI/U.S.A.*

FIABCI

68, RUE DES ARCHIVES
75003 PARIS, FRANCE

FEDERATION INTERNATIONALE DES PROFESSIONS IMMOBILIÉRES
INTERNATIONAL REAL ESTATE FEDERATION
INTERNATIONALER VERBAND DER IMMOBILIENBERUFE
FEDERACION INTERNACIONAL DE PROFESIONES INMOBILIARIAS

This Resolution and the supporting Brief
is submitted to

HABITAT
United Nations Conference on Human Settlements

By the Member National Chapters of the International
Real Estate Federation (FIABCI), Meeting in Congress at
San Fransisco, May 28, 1976, and the signatures of the
Presidents of the National Chapters appear hereunder.

Alexis Nolde
Secretary General

Philip Holmes
President

FIABCI AUSTRALIA

FIABCI BELGIQUE

FIABCI BRAZIL

FIABCI CANADA

FIABCI COLOMBIA

FIABCI DENMARK

FIABCI DEUTSCHLAND

FIABCI ESPANA

FIABCI FRANCE

FIABCI GREECE

FIABCI INDONESIA

FIABCI IRELAND

FIABCI ISRAEL

FIABCI ITALIA

FIABCI JAPAN

FIABCI KOREA

FIABCI LUXEMBOURG

FIABCI MALAYSIA

FIABCI MEXICO

FIABCI NETHERLANDS

FIABCI NORWAY

FIABCI NIGERIA

FIABCI OESTERREICH

FIABCI PHILIPPINES

FIABCI SINGAPORE

FIABCI SUISSE

FIABCI SWEDEN

FIABCI TAIWAN, R.O.C.

FIABCI UNITED KINGDOM

FIABCI U.S.A.

FIABCI VENEZUELA

Signatures from each of the FIABCI chapter heads
supporting their research brief and resolution to defer and defeat
a 1976 motion against private ownership of property.

The American chapter had a bronze plaque cast after Pip's success in defending the right to own property: "In grateful appreciation to Philip P.D. Holmes and his wife Catherine for their outstanding contributions in serving the real estate professions and the public among the free nations of the world..." Douglas Morrison (top left), president of FIABCI/U.S.A., presents the plaque to Pip in San Francisco, May '76.

Dian and Cippy Ciputra (above);
Cippy's sketch of Pip (right) on a New Zealand menu.

Mr. Watanabe's Tokyo garden astonished them (top) in October 1976. The austere building behind them is the corporate think tank for Mitsubishi.

Near the forest teahouse in downtown Tokyo (right) with Mr. Watanabe and Mr. Hashiba, Pip and Catherine admire the lake's old and rare koi. Smaller koi in another garden's pond (centre, above) rush toward a handful of food.

CHAPTER THIRTEEN
FOR THE HUMAN SETTLEMENT

DURING THE COURSE of 1976, Pip became a Knight of the Military and Hospitaller Order of St. Lazarus of Jerusalem. When asked years later about this, he explained briefly. "It's an international organization," he said, "one of the hospitallers' orders that go *way* back, one of several, and there's a huge history attached to all of them. I suppose they were set up to get the crusaders back home in one piece. Now they meet as a group at certain times and places all over the world. They're a good bunch, still meeting for good purposes—another method of tucking-under-the-wing."[210]

This "tucking under the wing" by the organizations has been extensive enough to be a significant force in humanitarian activity, and the Order of Lazarus is one of the oldest of these respected confraternities. In recent years, its members have been actively engaged in service programs, and while Pip didn't expound further about the order, its own sources clarify some of the ongoing work: "Millions of dollars worth of food, clothing, medical equipment and supplies have been distributed in Poland, Hungary, Romania and Croatia."[211]

In a chivalrous way, Pip diverted a further question about one of the Who's Who entries in which KCLJ and OMLJ appear after his name between his list of medals and his list of professional designations. He looked out the window for a moment to watch three gulls riding the onshore wind and then simply started another line of conversation.

OMLJ is Order of St. Lazarus of Jerusalem, in which he was a member, and KCLJ signals the rank of Knight Commander, reserved for heads of jurisdiction and the merited members of the order, so he could therefore prefix his name with "Chevalier" and use the postnomial letters. Other people sometimes added them when listing his honours and affiliations, but he generally didn't.

This was part of the quieter side of international service work. Brief comments on these interests and activities were given when sought but weren't discussed unless the activity had first been identified in other material. Part of the range of involvements might be suggested by handpainted plates from Turkey and eastern Europe on the wall beside the Holmes front door and the Christmas card they sent one year with his photo of a carefully restored chapel on a rocky hill, somewhere near the Adriatic. Or it might simply be a liking for ancient motifs and traditional artisanship, plus a penchant for repairing little chapels.

While they travelled, their second boat *Miss Lee* was listed for sale through a yacht broker in Maple Bay north of Victoria,[212] and near there, Brentwood College School in Mill Bay was looking for land. In 1976, the school began purchasing property north and south of its campus as it became available on the market, eventually more than doubling its grounds and facilities to accommodate double the number of students.

Around that time, the directors of Pemberton Holmes Ltd. agreed that adding a new director to the board was appropriate, and it was Pip's role to approach the person chosen. Accordingly, Pip wrote to Michael Page that the directors of the company "unanimously and enthusiastically voted" to invite him to become a director of the company effective from the date of his acceptance. "The company continues and will continue to grow in strength and size. Your efforts and loyalty have contributed greatly to that growth."[213]

Page's acceptance letter specified the date he would like the appointment to start: "It is both my pleasure and my honour to accept the very gracious invitation ... I would be pleased if you would make the effective date of this appointment the second of February 1977, as it is a date I find easy to remember."[214] It was Pip's birthday, and for years afterward, Mike and Pip celebrated together on February 2 with lunch or a drink.

Supporting the Shoal Bay Area Ratepayers Association, Pip was getting more and more involved in the vociferous local dust-up some called the Battle of the Oak Bay Pumping Station. Even after a year of controversy, sharp comments were proliferating from (and often about) individual homeowners, local community associations, various newspapers, B.C. Premier Bill Bennett and the provincial pollution control branch, the decision-makers of the Capital Regional District, the sewage treatment advisory committee of the Municipality of Oak Bay, and a small army of project engineers and consultants. The battle was about the possible location of a sewage pumping station somewhere along the Oak Bay waterfront.

The ratepayers association, 650 of whom put their names on the initial petition, emphasized in one handbill the importance of the family unit in Canadian society, citing the preamble of the Canadian Bill of Rights. One of the hundreds of letters quoted the provincial Municipal Act for city councils to stop nuisances that "tend to disturb the quiet, peace, rest, enjoyment, comfort and convenience of the neighbourhood." In league with the ratepayers association, Pip weighed in by writing a letter to the editor:

The moment is overdue for the greater community of our wondrous Victoria to have its eyes opened to the latest proposed plunder of our natural beauty. This concerns the siting of a 10,800 cubic foot (thirty-foot-high) sewage pumping station for the northeast trunk sewer. It is unbelievable in this twentieth century that the engineering consultants have recommended to the Capital Regional District that it be on a beach—Shoal Bay Beach—at, or near, the foot of Transit Road where it meets "scenic" Beach Drive.

Will it smell? Yes. Will it make a noise? Yes. Will it create dangerous explosive gases? Yes.

Are the representatives of the Capital Regional District unaware that Shoal Bay is one of the few beaches used all year round? That it is an area of dense population with the nearest home only feet away? That it is on the scenic route for tourists and citizens alike? That it is a heavily used and enjoyed waterfront for walking, jogging, bicycling, sitting, lunching, birdwatching and for children to play? That it is south-facing and that 90 percent of the wind is onshore toward homes, walkers, beach-sitters and sightseeing buses?

Of course there are alternatives, far better ones. It is high time the people of Greater Victoria spoke up, and time for the politicians of all levels of government to stand up for environmental rights instead of political expediency...[215]

The Minister of the Environment replied directly, asking Pip to appreciate that pumping stations are a normal and essential facet of sewerage schemes everywhere and, in particular, that such facilities at or near shorelines are common. "Your concern appears to be one of land use planning," the minister said, and Pip's letter was bumped over to the Capital Regional District.[216]

Pip's notes during the sewage-issues meetings weren't centred on the fighting words as much as the cost-and-performance numbers: "44.3 cu. ft./sec. in NE sewer"; "1 x 1,000' long to handle 15 cu. ft."; "$900,000 thus saving $2-$2.5 mill"; "more flow inevitable." Other notes on the triple-folded paper show that his mind was on two other tracks at the same time. On the second panel, he was writing reminders about the imminent World Congress ("Amsterdam—ticket, room, work, 1 wk hols") and on the third part of the folded paper, he was drafting a speech on women in real estate ("Women—Future in RE, Ins., Other"). He had promised to speak at the installation ceremony of new officers of the Victoria Real Estate Board and the Victoria Society of Real Estate Salesmen.[217]

D'Arcy Kavanagh interviewed Pip in his Pemberton Holmes office for the *Daily Colonist*:[218]"One question and he's off, articulating information and opinions gathered from decades in the real estate business and his almost two years as world president of the International Real Estate Federation (FIABCI). As world president, he visits, advises and delegates the eighteen-member committees to do various studies..."

Pip expressed concern to Kavanagh that the real estate profession wasn't making enough gains in education and didn't yet have enough discipline. "When Holmes speaks about the upgrading of his profession, there's a hint of urgency in his tone as if it must happen soon or else. 'Some of the countries in the federation,' he says, 'suffer from grossly inadequate management.' That inadequacy shows itself as fouling up in a variety of areas. 'It could mean ruining a mass transit system or destroying a natural environment. It covers a tremendous number of areas but, purely, it means urban and individual settlement problems.'"

En route to Amsterdam and the '77 congress there, Pip and Catherine went in mid-May to Finland, where ten representatives from that country were preparing for the Amsterdam meetings. The president of the Finnish Real Estate Brokers Association advised that accommodation had been arranged for their two guests at the Hotel Kalastajatorppa, built like a fisherman's house at the very edge of rocks over the water but in design anything but rustic. Their hosts explained the luxurious choice: "all prominent guests appreciate pauses for relaxing and breezing in private peace."

They also took Pip and Catherine for "a little motorboat trip to show them the countryside," somewhat as people might tour B.C.'s Gulf Islands by boat to see farms and private homes. *Uusi Suomi* ran a brief item about the Canadian guests: "FIABCI today has members from sixty-four different organizations in Europe, Africa, America, Australia and Asia. President Holmes has in his own enterprise about fifty employees."[219]

Pip had in hand good briefing notes about FIABCI-Finland and had prepared a list of questions, since gathering information, whether travelling or not, was something he did by habit. "You will meet the heads of our association, the officials—among them the Minister of Trade and Industry, the Ambassador of Canada plus FIABCI chapter members and the press," he was told.[220] "Unfortunately, the political situation in Finland is at the moment most complicated..." He was not one to commit political gaffes.

During a lunch for about a dozen people given by the Minister of Trade and Industry and another lunch given by the Canadian ambassador, as well as in his other conversations, he continued his fact-finding: relations between banks and brokers; the percentage of value for mortgage calculations; amortization schedules; current interest rates; the situations concerning rent control and tenant protection or restrictions on capital.

FIABCI president-elect Woodrow "Woody" Weight would soon start his two-year term, but Pip was still president of the organization until 11 June 1977. Their time in Sweden was set up to be private, since they needed to regroup before the Amsterdam events. Swedish friends Puck and Lennart Ljungquist took them by boat to their cabin on Ronnkob Island, where they rested and treated themselves to a herring lunch.

———————————

More than fifteen hundred hundred delegates from thirty-six countries, plus observers, were attending the June '77 World Congress, which to the Amsterdam organizers' great satisfaction was officially opened by Prince Bernhard of the Netherlands.

Though Pip would deliver the opening report, two leading speakers had also been invited. Denis Hayes of the Worldwatch Institute was first on the program for Monday, and Thursday's sessions would begin with Willem Schut, former Netherlands Minister of Housing and Town and Country Planning.

New Zealand's Edward Harcourt, president of the Asia Pacific Real Estate Federation, and Mr. Tadeo Mitsui of Japan, the APREF Secretary-General, were there to formalize the cooperation agreement between APREF and FIABCI and the entry of New Zealand into FIABCI.

Pip had written to Ted Harcourt earlier in the spring. "I am delighted to know you are clearing things away so you may attend in Amsterdam," he wrote. "It is vital to me to know that you are still keen to see a clear-cut and sensible, productive liaison being established between the two federations, leading down the road to a union." This was one of Pip's highest priorities in FIABCI, but only a few months before Amsterdam, a great deal of work remained.

"There is work to be done in both federations," he continued to Harcourt, "and the enthusiastic pressure must be maintained... Obviously, the completion of the agreement is the principal order of business [and] my deepest conviction is that there is no time to lose, for it is while you are President of APREF and Woody of FIABCI that this great stroke can be carried off... "[221]

Pip's quick notations during a meeting in Manila the previous fall show his tally of the positions taken by individuals and national organizations involved.[222] Various dangers, actions, adjustments, possibilities and solutions are meticulously, if cryptically, outlined. Tracking APREF viewpoints from Australia, Republic of China, Indonesia, Japan, Korea, New Zealand, Philippines, Singapore, Thailand and Malaysia, as well as FIABCI Pacific Committee input from Indonesia, Korea, Australia, Japan, Taiwan, Malaysia, Philippines, Hong Kong and Singapore, his notes show the processes of moving toward agreement.

Part of the final negotiation process is reflected in the minutes of one of the meetings. When one man suggested the merger might be possible in perhaps four or five years, Pip replied this would be too long and the dangers too profound. The point he emphasized was that the merger would see everyone winning and nobody losing: that FIABCI would gain the Pacific and APREF would gain the world, and the alternative was that both would lose.

Reports on the congress in industry publications or press reports didn't have the story of the inner workings. What goes public is only the results. Finally, ink. On 3 June 1977, the two-page agreement for co-operation and mutual assistance was signed by Holmes for FIABCI and Harcourt for APREF.

In the opening address, Pip re-emphasized his conviction that democracy is founded upon the rights of individuals to own property. Referring to the events at the conference in Vancouver the year before, he said it might be useful now and then to be reminded of the foundation of democracy—private ownership of property. Fully evident only in retrospect, he said, the logic of the FIABCI campaign before Habitat '76 was clear and the risks of losing the resolution plain to see.

The theme of the twenty-eighth congress in Amsterdam was "Man's Environment in the 1980s." Picking up the concept, Pip's address to the delegates and observers pointed to a new worldwide concern over the human environment and suggested that the real estate profession had a key role to play in helping society achieve its goals.

An *Estates Times* special issue on the Amsterdam event ran coverage of the speech,[223] and

Blair Jackson, one of the more than a hundred Canadian delegates and their wives, wrote a lengthy commentary on Pip's speech in the Canadian Real Estate Association's magazine.[224]

Jackson reported that Pip "dwelt at length on the areas he perceived were of most concern and most common among the member nations from six continents" and that a shift in social infrastructure and governmental capabilities was one such area.

"Governments have tended to believe themselves capable of assuming and efficiently operating virtually any of the productive and distributive systems," Holmes noted. "That fallacy becomes increasing apparent... The process of returning responsibilities of entrenched governmental institutions to the private sector is going to be one of the longest, most painful and expensive transformations for tomorrow's society...

"These ventures by government have become increasingly expensive for the taxpayer and have grossly depleted the capital resources available to the private sector. The counterbalance has been the creation of the giant corporations, including the multinationals and giant unions."

Small business and the public and national economies have suffered, he said, and it is small business that provides the marketplace flexibility so needed during times of rapid change. "Real estate is part of the small business component, while also representing a major economic foundation stone... No government at any level is able to solve the problems until and unless it is prepared to sit down with business." The time for ad hoc unilateral governmental solutions was over.

Commenting on the United Nations Conference on Human Settlement in Vancouver the year before, Holmes noted that the total living environment of man was the overriding concern of all countries: "For the first time, it has been made quite clear that whatever happens anywhere on the surface of the world—land, water, air or ice—relates to man and to his environment. That we are in the midst of the greatest and most urgent process of groping for truth and techniques to deal with the human settlement, there is no doubt. There is no question either that, even faced with a world population that will double by the end of this century, the answers have not been found. Peace and prosperity depends on their discovery.

"When I speak of peace, I include peace at the urban level, for in our large cities, there is now unacceptable danger and conflict. By 2000 A.D., there will be ten times the present number of urban centres of more than one million... We recognize that the availability and choice of decent housing, quality in planning, urban design and environment, with development of spaces for employment, business and industry, and markets to serve the public, is our responsibility.

"Real estate was still primarily concerned with the meshing of gears between supply and demand," he said, but was now extending beyond that "into the entire physical realm of the human environment, involving the cause, the consequence and the cost of the land component and utilization."

"The professions and government must start work together as a team with a division of responsibilities toward established national objectives. It is clear that no longer may the global land masses be managed by well-intentioned amateurs."

When Pip finished after an hour, the delegates rose in a standing ovation. Veteran members of the International Real Estate Federation, said Blair Jackson, ranked Holmes as one of the most outstanding, articulate and effective presidents since the organization was originally formed in 1943, and their applause reflected that.

Pip would return to these themes two years later in Japan in a parallel speech that was more of a retrospective evaluation than this one in 1977. These weren't trendy speech topics but his own beliefs: "If our profession does not defend and promote the rights of the property owners, who else is to do so? It is we on behalf of the public, for whom we act in real estate, who must insist on the right to ownership of property as a basic freedom of the individual and his family or corporation. It is we who must demonstrate that this right is fundamental to economic, social and political stability in a free society."[225]

As the audience in Amsterdam settled down, Pip took his seat and settled in to listen to the next speaker, Dr. J. de Vries, past president of the Bredero Group, Utrecht. He was a man whose perspectives interested Pip, and in his address he expanded on the theme of man's environment in the 1980s while Pip made tidy notes on the back of the printed program of the opening ceremony:

- Need specific insights in 1980s; mechanisms that are historic will not be able to cope with problems.
- Individuality expresses itself in housing.
- Half the world still uses firewood. Ancient wisdoms on techniques using shade, south walls.
- Lighting consumes half the electricity produced. Office buildings have to be cooled from lighting's heat.
- Solar heat does not need much transportation. Ethanol is being produced in Brazil. Solar towers could generate electricity and/or hydrogen but need to ship it.
- Object is to reduce energy dependency for a more stable economy and stable international relations.
- The Japanese are ahead of the rest of the world in air conditioning, solar-generated. The U.S. uses more electricity for air conditioning than China uses in total. Sweden uses as much oil as India.
- The USSR has enormous natural gas and coal, etc., and also is going nuclear; has 56 percent of all fossil fuels remaining.
- Nuclear advancement is dangerous in an unstable world.
- Fair liaison internationally in FIABCI.
- End of age of cheap energy. There will be obsolescence.
- Building codes will be important—and this has hardly started yet.

In his notes attached to the text delivered next, Pip categorized the issues:[226] "Wealth distribution and quantity; land distribution; social, economic and political stability, awareness and participation; society, the people who control the government and its bureaucracy and the institutions of both capital and labour—lost control?; urban design, the planning and use of landscape; energy problems and food problems; tap unlimited resources of space, particularly energy; the competition for the limited resources on Earth — the cause of so much conflict will be minimized; urban illness, free market — a right of choice, a right of title; human identity in urban life — value of rural and agricultural life-flows; choose "utopia or oblivion" — Buckminster Fuller's point; we need people on the side of hope and action; frustration, so get out of bed!"

The quality of information during these annual gatherings was always high, and organizers and delegates paid attention. To the congress in Amsterdam, the Federación Argentina de Entidades Profesionales de la Propiedad Inmueble sent an observer, Sr. Ricardo J. Pérez Centeno, and Italy and Kenya also sent observers. Before electronic global communications changed the industry utterly, the variety and scope of discussions at these congresses functioned as one of the main systems of trusted-source information interchange. Excerpts from daily congress reports illustrate something of the process:[227]

- "Representing Thailand at their first Congress as full members of FIABCI, the president of the Thai Real Estate Association, Sukhum Thirawat, will be stopping off in London on his way home in a bid to persuade British industrialists to set up in his country. In this, he has the full backing of the Thai government, which sees co-operation with the real estate profession as increasingly important."

- "Another country where cooperation between the government and the profession is increasingly strong is Malaysia. In a bid to solve the country's housing problem, the government invited local property men to join them in discussions. As a result, both the public and private sectors agreed on long-term housing targets and are cooperating to make sure these are achieved."

- "Tadao Hashiba, who is organizing the 1979 Congress in Tokyo, could be seen deep in conversation with Carl Franzen, who is in charge of next year's Congress in Hamburg..., both speaking in English. Next to them, a delegate from Nigeria was explaining to some British colleagues how his country was attracting substantial funds from Lebanon..."

- "While worldwide inflation rates may be a few points lower than they were last year, the effects of inflation are still hitting delegates hard. It's not only the British who are appalled at Amsterdam's astronomical hotel and restaurant prices. Even the once big-spending American delegates can be seen scouring the streets looking for somewhere cheap to eat."

Just before relinquishing his role to president-elect Woody Weight of Australia,[228] Pip was deeply pleased to be able to present to Cippy Ciputra, with whom he worked so well, the FIABCI Medal of Honour that year. He thanked all those who'd worked as a team toward the organization's achievements. "Included on the team and in my appreciation is our dedicated staff under the Secretary General [Alexis Noldé] and the staffs of our national and chapter organizations. Together we form a powerful force for betterment."[229]

Pip usually wrote his speeches between midnight and two in the morning, he said, "because that's when it was absolutely silent." At all hours, he made notes as exact and compact as those in his air force logbook. He'd jot while listening, while planning, while travelling, at home or on the boat. He said the notes he made for his own speeches clarified for him the thousand thoughts running through his head but that he also took notes while certain people spoke. The handwriting remained elegant and precise, staying legible despite a variety of circumstances.

The hunt for ideas never stopped, and fluent speeches emerged from cryptic notes: "Partnership with government to solve problems; political horizons versus the horizons of the *people* of the nation; social systems advanced to point of insulation of people from national economic circumstances; double standards; development of profession – education, responsibilities; meshing of the gears behind the engine of demand and the wheels of supply; cause, cost, result, real estate land management; partnership with social institutions, including government; real estate is basically a national industry— i.e., it develops raw material, then to the finished product, is labour-intensive, is a need, is a creator of capital wealth."

From those particular notes, for example, came the speech at the opening ceremony that earned the ovation. He set out six areas to cover: "the public we serve; human settlement; government and the economy; FIABCI; the future; our profession." However it was done, it worked.

As he and Catherine left Amsterdam on 11 June for London and the Queen's Trooping of the Colours, people were responding to his performance during the two-year term. Congratulatory letters, including one from Cippy Ciputra, began to fill what became a thick file.[230] Murray Bosley, chair of FIABCI Canada, was fairly effusive: "... what a superbly diplomatic and effective world leader FIABCI was fortunate to have." Tom Molesworth, president of the Real Estate Institute of New Zealand, wrote: "Philip, please accept my full congratulations for a magnificent effort during your term of stewardship ... Yours was a maximum effort, and you carried on the office with absolute aplomb."

The letter from R.W. Frewin, director of Chambers & Frewin in Hornsby, New South Wales, was similar to many letters received: "This note is to add my personal congratulations to you, Pip, and to my favourite WREN Catherine on the wonderful job you did for the world of real estate during your two years in office."[231]

Pip replied to each note. To Mr. Frewin, he wrote: "It is impossible, of course, to get a clear reflection of what one has or has not achieved in any mirror in one's own hand, so thank you for assuring me that the effort resulted in progress. Actually, I have finished my term of office with far stronger convictions about the profession and where it must go, what it must achieve, and what responsibilities it has to assume than I ever held prior to election. It was a great experience..."

In Finland (top) at the cabin of
Vilgo and Ritva Heinonen, Pip
continues to listen to ideas in
each FIABCI member country.
He and Catherine also needed
time to prepare for the June '77
meetings in Amsterdam.

Puck and Lennart Ljungquist
in Sweden keep a cabin on
Ronnkob Island (right).

Catherine with friends Puck
and Lennart (bottom) at a
herring lunch in late spring,
needing shelter from the wind
off the water.

Prince Bernhard of the
Netherlands (next page top)
guides Pip toward the main
hall for his opening speech
at the FIABCI Amsterdam
congress in 1977.

Pip presents Ir. Ciputra (next
page bottom) with the FIABCI
Medal of Honour, June 1977.

Pip addressing the International Real Estate Federation in Amsterdam, 1977, summarizing his two years' work as its world president and his discussions with people in its chapters worldwide. The flags are those of the FIABCI member countries.

Congress organizers in Amsterdam scheduled a brisk walk on the polders (left) as part of the program. Meantime, one of the FIABCI committee groups (centre) sorted out policy reports indoors. After the presidency, Pip continued with World Scene committee work, which interested him greatly.

Keyask (bottom left) was the third boat and was pointedly not a wooden hull. They took off to cruise Desolation Sound after Amsterdam.

Gorde Hunter drew **Keyask** leaving Amsterdam (below), which became their Christmas '77 note card to friends and colleagues.

PHOTO CREDIT: GORDE HUNTER

CHAPTER FOURTEEN
CYCLES OF CIVILIZATION

THE SUMMER OF '77 was restorative. Pip generally moved forward and took on new roles, including the start of a four-year stint on the Victoria Central Business District Advisory Committee. One old familiar role that summer, though, was as host welcoming overseas visitors, since connections with people met within the FIABCI network continued when Pip and Catherine were home again on Vancouver Island.

Tadeo Hashiba, auditor of the Mitsubishi Estate Co. Ltd. and Secretary-General of the FIABCI-Pacific Committee, was planning a British Columbia visit.[232] "Many thanks for your letter of July 5," he wrote to Pip. "Indeed, the establishment of the FIABCI/APREF Joint Investigation Committee was solely owing to your enthusiasm and leadership and was appreciated very much by our colleagues within the Asia Pacific region... As for our trip schedule [to Victoria and Vancouver], we will follow your suggestion. We are looking forward to seeing you very soon in Victoria."

Mr. and Mrs. Hashiba spent some time that August with Pip and Catherine and sent photos in a letter filled with praises soon afterward.[233] "These wonderful experiences shall never vanish from our memory...," they wrote. "The times we spent with you at your residence on Beach Drive, the lunch we had in your wonderful summer cottage at the Highland lake and the reception in your gorgeous yacht *Keyask* at the Royal Victoria Yacht Club, all were wonders to us... Further, the meeting with the Hon. Walter S. Owen, Q.C., Lieutenant-Governor of British Columbia, was most significant, and we sincerely wish for his good health and prosperity."

By October, Blair Jackson of the Canadian Real Estate Association and Pip were delegates and participants in an Ottawa event of considerable interest to both of them. It was about worldwide housing, or more accurately, the lack of it, and was held under the auspices of the United Nations Economic Commission for Europe. This was the Seminar on the Impact of Energy Considerations on the Planning and Development of Human Settlements, and for the real estate industry nationally and internationally, the sessions brought together expertise on what was known and set up protocols for future work.[234]

When he travelled, Pip took walks whenever he could to see how and where people lived. He had decided during Habitat '76 he wanted to keep track of information on basic shelter housing. He was strongly interested in applicable designs and practical measures for the spaces and systems that people need — housing, transportation, neighbourhoods, towns, megacities, or all of them together. When told at one point his concepts reflected the pattern language developed by Christopher Alexander, he nodded. "Absolutely," he said. "Different drummer, that one. Understands what works to make the places that people sense are *right*. Works in a lot of ways, on a lot of levels."[235]

By the end of the first week in October, Pip and Catherine were arriving at Donmuang Airport in Thailand and descending the ramp from the plane into early evening warmth and scent. Alexis Noldé from FIABCI Paris headquarters met them with briefing papers on FIABCI activities and real estate affairs in Thailand and to discuss their week's schedules.

Mr. Sukhum Thirawat called at their hotel the next morning to continue the briefings and consultations. He was for Pip definitely an advisor in the know on the Thai front, being simultaneously president of the Bangkok Land Development Co. Ltd., president of the Thai Real Estate Association, board member of the Thailand Protection Foundation, chairman of the program committee of the National Security Organization and a member of Thailand's Senate.

The Thai Real Estate Association hosted a grand Chinese dinner that evening for the Holmeses and at dawn next day, they flew to Chieng Mai to visit the Forest Department Arboretum atop Doi Suthep mountain and tour the Phuphing Summer Palace, His Majesty's experimental station for temperate plants, then to stop briefly in the hill tribes' villages. They were taken into houses on stilts where ravenous silkworms were creating threads of Thai silk. Despite the intense heat, Pip and Catherine stayed a long time watching workers throw handfuls of mulberry leaves into small tubs where the industrious silkworms were making short work of the leaves. "The leaves just *vanished*," Catherine said.

Considering his wartime mascot, it might be thought that at least some of Pip's guardian spirits took the form of elephants, and he very happily spent the next day learning more about them on a trip to Lampang and beyond. The royal forest department and the Forest Industries Organization arranged to show them natural teak forests as well as the teak plantations, very unlike Vancouver Island's cedar and Douglas fir forests and coastal logging methods. They watched the elephants deal handily with huge logs and were told about the process of training them for forestry work. There was much to discuss.

Holmes itineraries were seldom leisurely, and after a short foray into Lamphoon, they left Chieng Mai in the late afternoon for Bangkok and flew out next morning to Kuala Lumpur.

Pip kept working on updating FIABCI's communications reach, inbound and outbound. He wanted to base it more broadly across continents and to leave it in a generally accelerated state, and he very much meant what he said when he pronounced that FIABCI was on the move. After his term as its world president ended and he'd taken on the presidency of its World Scene Division, he involved himself in more committee research.

He consulted as usual with colleagues and mentors, one of whom was Jean Bailly, a wise and supportive presence in Pip's life. Bailly initiated the FIABCI idea before the Second World War and with Pierre Colleville and others sustained the concept until the right circumstances for the organization's formal founding.

"My dear Pip," Monsieur Bailly wrote in reply to Pip's letter.[236] "Further to your request regarding the World Scene, I am submitting to you herewith a few thoughts ... to be added to the overall considerations that will be expressed in Hamburg in this connection."

Bailly provided Pip with clear-minded briefings in four areas: the effects of oil reserves and distribution costs on real estate; observations on post-war housing expectations and urban constraints; concern about multinationals acting exclusively in the service of profit, particularly in the field of world food; and assessment and predictions on the phenomenal growth of computers.

Concerning computers, he foresaw what he called a geometrical advance. "About ten years ago, on the occasion of a FIABCI Congress," he told Pip, "I stressed the increasing importance that data processing would be bound to take throughout the world in the years to come. It has already progressed tremendously, but this is nothing as compared to what it will be with a geometrical advance throughout the world in the coming decade. We have to consider that the use of computers is going to transform our way of life, the employment market, human relations on the level of local, regional, national and international communities."

Bearing in mind the multinationals' tendency "to deprive economic relations of their human side," he warned Pip that if the ethic of service to the public were to be continued, those in the real estate profession had a duty to develop policy and enterprises locally, nationally and internationally "to serve men and not exclusively profit, which would lead to a world without humanity."

Pip wanted to convey that perspective to his audience at the British Columbia Real Estate Association's annual convention in May 1978.i He compressed his analysis into one hefty speech on what happened during and after Habitat '76, covering more than the property-ownership issue that had been his tour de force at the time. He spoke about the cycles of civilization and the global village and showed their specific application to B.C. He was trying to bring home to them how much was out there to be learned, and he wanted to fire up the generative power of teamwork in those directions. His speech:

Enrique Panalosa, Secretary-General of the United Nations Conference on Human Settlements, or Habitat, says this in his introduction to Barbara Ward's remarkable book *The Home of Man*: "The case for the second half of the twentieth century…is not only, or even mainly, that it is an era of unremitting and inescapable upheaval—in population, growth, technology and political transformation—but that the fact of universality has overtaken us before we are politically and socially able to deal with it."

It is in this context that a forward-looking and challenging discussion of Habitat is worthwhile. Because the dust of that enormous conference held here in Vancouver two years ago has now settled, the principal issues have emerged, and they are being dealt with, piece by piece, in continuing United Nations seminars.

At these seminars, as at Habitat itself, we play our part through the contributive participation of the Canadian Real Estate Association with FIABCI, your International Real Estate Federation, which is accredited to the UN as an international non-governmental organization. To Habitat itself, FIABCI presented not only a comprehensive resolution but a supporting fifteen-page brief, which still stands today as a clear position paper or charter for our profession. It is worthy of continual referral.

What was the essence of Habitat? As Pip told his audience, it was primarily a statement of the universality of the human settlement, and secondly, a diagnosis and suggested treatment needed for the problems posed by the contemporary human settlement. These problems and the treatment, he continued, were categorized under the heading of the developed nations and the developing countries, each with its own agonies, each with its own interrelating difficulties, neither with obvious nor easy solutions. The issues were spotlighted within sixty-four recommendations for national action, subsequently produced in a special report called the Vancouver Action Plan. He evaluated Habitat's effect:

Was Habitat a useless, futile gesture, or was it an expression of realism and acknowledgement? Do we find an answer in anything that has happened since then? Yes and no. Yes, the UN plods on as rapidly as intergovernmental machinery can move, with its seminars—on "Energy" in Ottawa, on "Water" (that cry for clean water), and now, in Stockholm in two weeks' time, the philosophical clash, "Land Use." No, in the sense that the tensions are still there, possibly worse now and more widespread, and while recognizable and defined, are incapable of instantaneous solution.

Did and does it mean anything to us—in this maple-leaf mosaic of Canada, and in British Columbia and to us in this infant profession? Again, the answer is both yes and no. Yes, it gives us an opportunity to serve a critical purpose, probably our greatest opportunity. And no, because we have not taken up the challenge… Do we then give a damn what happens?

Do we have knowledge with which we can help? Do we have convictions that stretch beyond our pocketbooks, our contented existence and beyond the popular misconception that government alone will provide the answers?

Before he dealt with these questions, Pip gave the BCREA group an overview of the world and its history as he saw it:

The first element of complexity, the most impelling and the subject that's so explosive it is not mentioned, is the "civilization cycle." We are part of what is called "western civilization." Like others before it, it is moving in a cycle from conception to oblivion. Where are we now on that perimeter? The signs do not fill us with confidence. They point to gross waste, overindulgence, permissiveness and shunning of obligations. Around us we see the adversary stance and tension, rising even to the point of seemingly uncontrollable lawlessness. The behemoth of government is having responsibilities thrust upon it for which it was never designed and is unable to cope…

Secondly, we must be more than merely aware of the gulf of disparities in our global village. The rich and the poor glare at one another. The fat and well-fed do not seem to be able to feed the starving, who themselves appear unable to produce food. Many in the world simply switch on air-conditioning while others wince at the heat from tin roofs. "Need" lives beside "plenty," and we, with all our technology, are not creating sufficient goods, any means of distributing them or a financial system able to respond.

Finally, while populations surge upward, our land supply is exhausted and environmental qualities are in jeopardy. In certain knowledge of future demands on farmland, it is still being urbanized by sprawl that defies the realistic relationship between people and their countryside.

It is said that four million acres a year are being reclassified to desert. Water supplies are still fouled. The riches of the Earth are still being wasted. The quality of air and even the vast seas are suffering neglect. Additionally, both the human and geographical environments within the increasing number of major metropolitan concentrations are in a state of friction.

And his encapsulation of the Big Picture in 1978? Bleak indeed. In fact, he said, the twenty-four "big thinkers" at Habitat came to Vancouver with the declared intent of making the largest fuss they could.

As Lady Barbara Ward, leader of the self-styled Vancouver Symposium Group, said: "We will be behaving outrageously." They took that lead not out of despair but out of a determination to rattle the world's teeth and to get its peoples and its governments to pay attention, then to listen and, subsequently, to act. They were right in doing so — even if much of what they subsequently said, and led others to believe, was eggheaded.

How did Habitat itself react? It declared as recognizable all these problems. It said governments must get to work and get together. It admitted the problems were so immense that governments alone could not solve them. Because of its political colorations, it made little reference to private enterprise, personal initiative or individualism, much less the market economy or human incentive — yet these are the ingredients that have produced for the Western democracies today's advantages.

Carl Marx himself admits that not only was capitalism the world's most impelling revolution, it proved what man was totally capable of accomplishing through the historic sense of mission. There is no recognition that the gross inequities created by that revolution are steadily being stamped out.

No magic or universal formula for the ideal human settlement environment existed, Pip said, nor could there be a single definition for the quality of life. He instead zeroed in on where he saw this worldwide urgency fitting into a British Columbia context.

We have to create our own ideals in the context of our own geography, demography, political and economic system. Certainly, we must as well make a concerted effort to forecast our future so that definition and action are not based solely on the contemporary circumstance.

Having created our model with the assistance of the wealth of human and informational resources we have, the Habitat "Recommendations for National Action" is amended so it will read "Recommendations for Action in British Columbia." By way of flying a kite or perhaps of casting bread upon the waters — I'm not sure which — we might even bring into our "orbit for action" other neighbouring or nearby Canadian jurisdictions to make it even more exciting, though not if it will slow us down. Time is not on our side.

The temptation to enumerate a score of areas crying out for attention would be presupposing and presumptuous. Let me simply state categorically that the $20 million seminar on human settlement, here in Vancouver, had much to say to us here in this province. I will also remind you that even though our professional life is the human settlement, there was not one single licensed realtor picked by the Canadian government to serve on the huge Canadian "Habitat team." That fact, particularly here in Vancouver, where sophisticated real estate education started in our university twenty years ago, should be challenge enough to us.

Why do we not meet that challenge through the initiation of a "Habitat B.C. Task Force"? A mass of identification effort has already been done for us. We need to use it to create our own goals and objectives, then work toward them. It is my belief that we need such a dedication to achieve our place in the sun and to serve our public and our country in multitudinous ways at the same time.

Such an effort will serve as a worldwide example of the capability of the profession, the power of collective thought, the validity of the market economy system and the supremacy of the free individual when it comes to guiding the well-being of human destiny.

He asked them to let him know the date and place of the first meeting, "an epic moment and giant stride in our history." BCREA president O'Leary responded that Pip's message had been received loud and clear. They'd be giving the matter grave consideration at their next meeting and determining the kind of committee to be struck. But Pip and Catherine had already flown to another round of events. A cordial reply letter was sent in Pip's absence from E.M.R. Brulé (Mrs.), Secretary to P.D.P. Holmes: "Philip is…on his way to Hamburg today to attend FIABCI's annual Congress."

The program at the Congress Centrum Hamburg ran from Saturday 3 June to the evening of the following Friday. "It was run impeccably," Pip said. Bearing in mind Jean Bailly's comments, he paid particular attention to a computer system exhibit set up in a side room. The display was related to a specialized lecture on the real estate profession and communication sales, and the equipment and a technician were standing ready for inspection and questions each afternoon.[239] The equipment was listed.

Data processing: IBM System/32
Word processing: IBM MC 82
Typesetting: IBM Composer
IBM copying machine, desk calculator 5100
IBM monitors
DeTeWe shows the DeTeWe Conline 4/10 telephone installation.
"Other firms will show modern mechanical equipment for the office in action."

Voice recognition was done by simultaneous translators, human ones, who were then still irreplaceable. Sessions of the congresses were translated into and out of English, French, German and Spanish, and participants at the congresses would generally shift in and out of languages to suit the best interests and comfort levels of the conversations at hand.

Pip said he remembers being asked if he and Catherine were familiar with boats, since one of their tour program excursions was a trip along the Alster, the river running through Hamburg, ending with a visit to Poseldorf, a high-end shopping area. Since Catherine knew the Solent like the back of her hand and Pip had been around B.C. boats since boyhood, he allowed as how they would probably be able to handle it.

They shifted from Hamburg to Stockholm, where Pip was due at meetings of the Seminar on Land Use Policies, Economic Commission for Europe. When in Victoria again, he commented to Dennis O'Leary at the BCREA:[240] "I have only just returned from Europe… In regard to the Habitat mission I recommended, I am of course pleased that you should take it seriously. I certainly meant it seriously… What one continues to hear about the inroads socialism is making, to the detriment of particularly the small people in our 'free' world (such as at the Land Use Seminar), the more one is convinced that there really is a mission and a dedication that we not only have to recognize but do something about."

With an eye to the election of the European Parliament, new intranational and international liaison relationships were being sought by organizations, and shared endeavours and cooperation initiatives were being planned within FIABCI as well. It was seeking common ground with professional associations of developers, for example, as well as with insurance providers, architects and town planners. This process was of great interest to Pip.

During the summer, FIABCI and a European group of seven national associations of developers agreed, among other measures, to establish permanent contact at the highest level, effective immediately.[241] A FIABCI representative at a congress in Spain later in the year reported them having reached a cooperation agreement at the level of principles, with "the main concern for both associations being the defence of private property."[242]

———————

At the start of Henry P. "Budge" Bell-Irving's term as Lieutenant-Governor of B.C., he asked his colleague Philip to resume the duties at Government House he'd had to relinquish in the busiest of the international years. Pip was willing and able. When in late July '78 it happened that the Canadian Real Estate Board's directors scheduled their annual meeting in Victoria, opportunities arose for Lieutenant-Governor Bell-Irving and his aide-de-camp Philip Holmes to be part of the welcome.

The four days of Victoria meetings, each with a full slate of topics and resolutions for discussion in the sessions, incorporated some distinctively regional special events. The meetings coincided with a government-sponsored Captain Cook festival that brought a number of world-touring Tall Ships to the Inner Harbour, and the Vancouver Island Real Estate Board set up "horse-drawn appraisal inspection tours" along an appealing route through heritage streetscapes, parks, harbour views and ocean lookouts.

The BCREA invited all delegates to an English music-hall type of show inside the Empress Hotel, and local CREA director Eric Charman held a reception and buffet on the lawn of his home, Donnington Farm, with Fiji's Governor General Ratu Sir George Cakobau as a special guest. Lieutenant-Governor Bell-Irving and the hospitable Holmes welcomed them all to a reception at Government House on its hill overlooking the Strait of Juan de Fuca.[243]

CREA members' reactions pleased Norman Ross, president, and Blair Jackson, executive vice-president. Some directors had originally expressed misgivings about mid-summer meetings, particularly those in venues other than Toronto, but the consensus after the annual meeting was that "the quality and quantity of the Victoria reception and activities more than compensated" for them having to rearrange their summer plans.

Pip was by then an honorary member of the Fraser Valley Real Estate Board, and a 1978 photo shows him once again in his aide-de-camp uniform standing with colleagues chatting at their AGM dinner[244]—Bob Chaplin, executive officer of BCREA, past president Eric Trygg, honorary member Terry Carlow and, not least, Henry P. Bell-Irving. That was also the year Pip joined the McPherson Playhouse Foundation. Two years later, he became its vice-president.

The touchy topic of sewerage came around again, and after objections from residents, it was decided to try putting a short outfall into Enterprise Channel. The experiment would be monitored. "If beaches were being polluted, half of the sewage would be diverted to Clover Point, and if beaches were still polluted, then all of the sewage would be diverted, with pumping stations at McNeil and Transit and at Fort and Foul Bay." Thus ended that round.[245] The beaches were not consulted.

Pip again showed himself as a numbers man by his reactions during the meetings about a new conference and trade centre at the Inner Harbour. His bookmarks in Ken Stratford's research report on the matter are wedged into the pages at revenue analysis, specific revenue projections and the event revenue summary.[246]

Numbers were a language he spoke well, and only with solid numbers would he discuss feasibility. "A great deal of public and tourist industry discussion over a period of years," Ken Stratford wrote, "has demonstrated the desirability and overall financial advantage of a conference centre to be located in the City of Victoria. The enclosed brief is in response to a study initiated by a group of Victorians, the purpose of which is to begin to determine the feasibility of a medium-capacity conference and trade facility to be located on Victoria Harbour."[247] It had numbers, and it had comparables.

Edmonton had given approval in principle to a new downtown convention centre.[248] Calgary's convention centre was reporting a 70 percent increase in revenue year over year with only an 11 percent increase in operating expenses, so they were declaring themselves most satisfied.[249] Urban decision-makers in Vancouver had been talking for ten years about how to build trade and convention centre there and were still talking.[250] Victoria's conference centre wouldn't end up at the harbour after all, so Pip ostensibly didn't get what he wanted, unless what he actually wanted was debate on local land use, a good hard look at local zoning and an airing of what people valued for their downtown.

Around his fifty-fifth birthday in February 1979, he was still living a third in the world of FIABCI, a third in the world of Victoria and a third just about everywhere his work took him. He had been adding to his commitments without relinquishing very many, and the quantity of obligations, plus the quality of what he wanted to deliver, was a heavy load. He didn't go to Nairobi when the UN Committee on Human Settlements convened, though he later said he paid close attention to its proceedings because the field interested him greatly.[251] Nor was he in Jakarta for the opening of a certain project that produced thousands of units of low-cost housing, though he was kept well aware of the situation by colleagues and monitored the project's progress from afar.

A piece in the *Indonesia Times* explained the Jakarta housing:[252] "State Minister for Administrative Reform Dr. J.B. Sumarlin called on business entrepreneurs in this country to think about solving their employees' housing problem... The call was made yesterday when the minister inaugurated 5,200 low-cost houses built by PERUMNAS (National Urban Development Corporation) at Karawaci Tanggerang, 32.9 kilometres from Jakarta."

According to the minister, the country's housing problem "could not be solved by the government alone but should be handled together with private business entrepreneurs."

A young elephant and Pip meet and greet in Bangkok (top).

Sukhum Thirawat of the Thai Real Estate Association (right) welcomed and advised Pip and Catherine during their visits to Thailand.

Elephants shift teak logs at Chieng Mai, Thailand (below).

June '78 daysail on the Alster River (top left). **Shanty**, *belonging to Mr.
and Mrs. Hans Otto Noack, was docked in Hamburg. Pip at the Hamburg
FIABCI World Congress listens intently on earphones to presentations in
translation (top right).*

*Tadeo Hashiba and his wife are taken around Victoria by the Holmeses,
with drinks on the boat at the RVYC and a woodsy walk to the A-frame
(bottom left, and bottom right).*

CHAPTER FIFTEEN
PHILOSOPHY CONSOLIDATED

STARTING IN JULY 1954, FIABCI had a role advising the United Nations on property activities and policy concerning property matters, including "the thorny problem of the homeless or that of the property business and the environment." The link was by means of a consultative status arrangement with the United Nations Economic and Social Council, as an NGO, with the Committee of Housing, Building and Planning of the Economic Commission for Europe.[253]

Agreements among governments, private real estate enterprises and the UN were done within a framework that was eventually called their "global compact," with FIABCI defining sustainable development in four areas: problems of the homeless, property rights, environment and codes of ethics.[254] It also began charity property initiatives of its own.

Years later, after strong urging from United Nations agencies and others that the real estate industry contribute further skill and resources toward solutions to homelessness and basic housing, and with FIABCI sponsorship, honorary deputy president René Frank launched the Global Housing Foundation.[255] Pip, from afar, applauded its appearance.[256]

He absorbed and took personally the meaning of the FIABCI symbol, an image of a city with six towers in its walls, plus two keys. "Saint Peter's keys," he said, when asked, and pointed to the information published about the symbol: that the real estate profession must "plan, build, manage and protect the city to keep it in good order for the best welfare of its inhabitants."[257] He wasn't sure, he added, about what was said concerning Saint Peter being the patron saint of property managers. Fishermen, shipwrights, masons and bridge-builders, maybe, but property managers? "Maybe that too."

Pip and Catherine attended the 1979 World Congress in Tokyo. "In a broad sense," he wrote later, "my speech to the international federation when it convened in Tokyo in 1979 largely sums up what the vocation and its objectives added up to in total."[258] The text of speech, by "Philip D.P. Holmes, Past President," was reprinted in the conference papers and does draw together many of his themes.[259]

Today, after some years of active participation in FIABCI, the International Real Estate Federation is an important and integral part of my business and professional life. I will tell you how and why this has happened.

Firstly, it is an integral part of "organized real estate." Within a short time after the start of one's career, it becomes absolutely clear that business does not and cannot operate in isolation and that strength and progress depend on a united organization with collective thought and action at the local level.

With increased experience, one learns that there is need for a regional and national organization. Finally, national associations must unite and work together at an international level in these days when we are in fact citizens of an interdependent global village.

The global village concept applies as imperatively to our profession as it does to the United Nations of government. At the international level of real estate organization, I have found many answers to professional problems based on the experiences of those from other countries. It is a "trade fair" of ideas and experiences that is invaluable.

A second part of the need for organization is to deal effectively with government. Governments at all levels, from local to international, intrude further into business, continue to move toward socialistic legislation, add to the cost and difficulty of business, detract from individual and corporate freedoms and impose more inventive and punitive tax levels. My business remains dependent on the rights of private ownership, of property, reasonable taxation, just compensation for only necessary cases of expropriation, and non–counterproductive land use … These matters have to be guarded and fought for at all levels, including, most importantly, the international scene.

These points focus on my third point. If our profession does not defend and promote the rights of property owners, who else is to do so? It is we, on behalf of the public for whom we act in real estate, who must insist on the right to ownership of property as a basic freedom of the individual and his family or corporation. It is we who must demonstrate that this right is fundamental to economic, social and political stability in a free society.

We must also address ourselves to the planning, use and preservation of agricultural and recreational lands. We must be concerned with the development of our urban framework, the enhancement of the environment, energy conservation, the production of living space for homes, business and industry and the vitality of the urban core areas. These endless, massive problems are beyond the powers of government to solve in isolation. Government needs the real estate profession.

One may say: "What do these things have to do with me personally?" The answer is simple. If you wish to maintain a profitable real estate business, if you wish to live in a free country as a free person, if you wish your children and their children to live in a prosperous and free country and a better world, then it is the direct and personal responsibility of each and all of us to see that it happens through being involved.

Let me now come to my fourth point: what do I get from FIABCI, and what is it to me and my business? FIABCI has provided me with a broader international group of professional acquaintances, many of whom have become personal friends. These fine people are in the same business while also representing many specialties within the practice of real estate. They are prepared to share their experiences in practice, management and techniques, which may often be adapted to apply to one's own organization.

The annual FIABCI Congress is in a different country each year, so there's the opportunity of seeing many aspects of real estate and its practice in that country. This provides exposure to the practical application as well as the theoretical side of the profession. Meeting regularly at the FIABCI Congress also provides the opportunity of keeping a finger on the pulse of changes and trends in finance, development, marketing and management. Knowledge of these trends often allows one's own business to plan and project ahead of those without FIABCI contacts.

Involving the company in international business is, in many ways, quite another matter. FIABCI has great value whether or not the company gets involved in international real estate transactions. If it is involved, personal connections through FIABCI and the reputation of involvement with FIABCI provide every possible opportunity. The personal knowledge of real estate practices, investment opportunities, tax structures and currency criteria in other countries becomes invaluable.

The fifth and final point of the importance of FIABCI is the advancement of the profession itself. We are too well aware that the advancement and high reputation of the profession depends on the long-term success of those in our business and the success of our companies as well. To this advancement, FIABCI is not only dedicated and making progress but in an international sense is uniquely able to do so. The world and its human settlement is in great need of a stronger, more capable and responsive real estate profession.

When categorized as one of his city's most influential citizens by a Victoria journalist, Pip evaluated what the term "influence" might actually mean in the context of downtown and economic development. "I look at 'influence' from the perspective of actually being able to influence what happens in the city, what sort of growth and development take place, what kind of place Victoria will be five, ten or twenty years from now..."[260]

Another journalist announced Pip's return to Victoria, if such it was, as a restart. "Philip Holmes has been to the summit and back, but at fifty-five, he feels he is far too young to think about taking it easy," said the article. "That's why he is starting all over again."[261] More accurately, Pip was not starting but continuing, and at the local level, he was also adding. He was still honorary aide-de-camp at Government House, still active with the Victoria Central Business District Advisory Committee, was newly elected as vice-president of the McPherson Playhouse Foundation and had just taken on the presidency of the Victoria Downtown Business Association.

He made a list of what he wanted to see happen in Victoria: (1) the convention centre as top priority; (2) parking, with a plan for a five-storey parkade in the theatre district; (3) moving the bus terminal to a larger site; (4) burnishing up Victoria's old town as a tourist draw; (5) developing a database for orderly growth of downtown facilities and needs.

However he was viewed around town, he was bringing his energies and ideas home to the Island and getting involved in groups going in directions he thought were good. In 1979, he joined the Regional Visitor Industry Development Committee and the Task Force for the Victoria Conference and Trade Centre. Press reports mention him attending multiple meetings of the Pan Pacific Conference and Trade Centre Society,[262] and his files for this became voluminous.

Commentaries about him in the local business press sometimes went over the top: "Holmes ... is actively involved in real estate organizations worldwide. He has been given honorary life memberships in just about every real estate board in B.C., and at one time or another during his thirty-five years in the business, he has been president of just about every real estate association in existence."[263]

Maybe there was local muttering about movers-and-shakers, as is often the way, or a few twinges of jealousy or cases of professional inertia. Maybe it was just the old familiar question of how you're going to keep 'em down on the farm once they've seen Paree.[264] He had indeed seen Paree and quite a lot else in his travels, so a decompression process might be expected in the circumstances. Pip phrased his thoughts carefully. "With the slower pace and casual graceful living in Victoria," he said, "there is great temptation to continue the conversation long after the decisions have been made. The prime example is a convention centre, which according to local legend was first proposed in 1898 and has been revived as an issue every ten years since."

But many a truth is spoken in jest, and judicious wielding of humour was a Pip trademark. When he was asked to say grace at a Chamber of Commerce luncheon, for example, he took a quick swipe at interprovincial relations. As a squib in the paper put it: "It isn't often that a prayer has an audience rolling in the aisles with laughter, but leave it to Victoria realtor Pip Holmes to take a whack at it. The occasion was Wednesday's luncheon of the Victoria Chamber of Commerce at the Empress Hotel. Guest speaker was Calgary mayor Ross Alger. Holmes was asked to say the prayer, and he started off innocently enough. 'Bless this food and our rich land,' he said, adding: 'And make Albertans cognizant of the needs of others.'"[265]

Though he'd been immersed in new ideas and fluid circumstances, his grounding in southern Vancouver Island never budged. Pemberton Holmes was still his business base, where brothers Des and Vincent were actively involved. The *Daily Colonist* was quite precise about it: "Pip's older brother William Desmond Cuthbert Holmes and his younger brother Edgar Vincent Buxton Holmes are also associated with Pemberton Holmes, as is Richard Harry Cuthbert Holmes (who is Desmond's son), now a realtor with the firm."[266] A *Business Life* piece was prescriptive: "Richard Holmes, the fifth generation in the firm, will likely ensure that Pemberton Holmes will still be family-owned and operated into the next century of operation."[267]

Continuity in the business community since J.D. Pemberton and F.B. Pemberton might well have preoccupied the two local newspapers, which were in the process of combining forces.[268] The *Daily Colonist*, started in 1858 as the *British Colonist*, merged in 1980 with the *Victoria Daily Times*, started in 1884, so the activities of Pemberton Holmes Ltd. and its constituent staff and family members would thereafter be monitored and recorded by the new entity known, at first with its hyphen and later without it, as the *Times-Colonist*.

By 1980, Pip was involved in meetings on all fronts, though his main project—a convention centre by the harbour—either wouldn't or couldn't materialize. He was also appointed to the Provincial Capital Commission, which had been set up in 1956 as the Capital Improvement District Commission, and it suited him well. "P.D.P. Holmes has been appointed to the Provincial Capital Commission by Finance Minister Hugh Curtis. The eleven-member commission is responsible for beautification of the capital, with emphasis on planning the precinct of the Legislature buildings."[269]

He liked what the Crown agency was generally designed to do: "to aid municipal and civic interests by supplying advice, capital funds and impetus to undertake projects that might not otherwise have been realized."[270] Through outreach initiatives provincewide, it was a vehicle "to foster all citizens' sense of pride and ownership" in the B.C. capital.[271]

By the time Pip joined, it had grown past its original representation of the four core municipalities—Esquimalt, Oak Bay, Saanich and the City of Victoria proper—to take in all of the Saanich Peninsula and the Western Communities as far as Sooke and Port Renfrew. It held stewardship of a number of provincially owned properties and heritage buildings in the capital region and was tasked with tending them well enough to keep them intact for the future. The PCC was also expected to undertake new projects in the region.

"He loved projects along waterways where people could walk along a creek or the Inner Harbour," Catherine said. "He just loved the Bowker Creek project, for instance, and excitedly took me walking along beside the creek as soon as it was done. And he was absolutely jubilant about St. Ann's when it was saved—just thrilled."[272]

Funding for projects during his years with the PCC went to the Arm Street Park Project in Esquimalt, Chinatown development, Brentwood Bay's Pioneer Park, Bowker Creek's walking paths, the Fleming Beach walkway, improvements for Reay Creek and Lochside Drive, and the building and grounds of St. Ann's Academy. Victoria Inner Harbour's south shore promenade got some attention, as did the former CPR ferry terminal, the Black Ball terminal and the arcaded rock wall at the foot of Wharf Street.[273]

The World Congress that year was held in Greece. Apart from the June working sessions on the theme of the importance of real estate property in the world economy, the schedule included "Sound & Light, and Folk Dancing, at the Acropolis" plus a day cruise to the islands of Aequia, Poros and Hedra aboard the *Saronic Star*. Pip and Catherine agreed: "Athens was a good one."[274] During their post-congress holiday, they had come across the British fleet anchored in the particularly capacious harbour of an island where crews and officers always anticipated a good game of cricket against the locals and assorted expats. A letter from Tokyo arrived in Victoria weeks after the congress sending best wishes and photos: "I was very glad to meet you [and] enjoyed the days in Athens and the sailing to Mykonos. I enclose a picture of you both, taken in the lobby of the Hilton ... "[275]

They were in Paris again in late November for the FIABCI executive board meetings in early December, since Pip was involved in its world scene division. Wide-ranging reports from the Americas, Latin America and the Asia-Pacific, UNO Geneva and UNO New York brought board members up to date. Also, a new documentation centre that had been discussed earlier was in the process of being set up, its mandate not to be a mailbox but to render a service as a conduit for permanent dialogue with the national organizations. Administration of the steadily growing FIABCI structure needed to be scrutinized, including matters related to its 1981 budget, dues and membership directory as well as new publications such as *Housing Terms in Four Languages*, which was much in demand.

The board discussed contemporaneous events and entities other than FIABCI: the Habitat International Council; the report of the Commission on Human Settlements to UNESCO; the fact that the IMF was closely scrutinizing its own policies on reserve funds and drawing rights; considerable discussion on new leadership in the World Bank; and an update of the most recent World Economic Survey. From Group 35, the young entrepreneurs, came an announcement that FIABCI was "a bulwark of freedom," which to their satisfaction seemed to bode well for their individual futures.

Well before the December meetings, Pip and Catherine had decided to spend Christmas in Crete, as they told friends, "for some winter sunshine." When they stepped off the plane, Catherine was presented with an oversize bouquet of flowers but apparently no car, cart or donkey for transportation, so they staunchly set out on foot with the bouquet and the bags. They were led to where they'd arranged to stay — out past the tarmac, along through town and down by the harbour, eventually arriving at an old gate in a wall and — yes! — a white house in the promised olive grove. The old couple in the other half of the house were the live-in caretakers. It was the man's fiftieth year of playing cricket against the British Navy, and over the holiday, he related to them everything he could remember about each game. As for Christmas sunshine, they met with terrible weather. "We nearly froze to death."

Pip added another commitment to his roster when he was appointed for a three-year term to the University of Victoria's board of governors by provincial order-in-council. After about a year as new boy on the board, he became vice-chairman. In another context, he was made Honorary Lieutenant Colonel of the 11th (Victoria) Service Battalion, and began work there.

He was also delighted to receive an honour from his peers in the B.C. Real Estate Association. Two such awards were given at the BCREA convention in early 1981. Lieutenant-Governor Henry Bell-Irving, long-time realtor and BCREA's first honorary life member, awarded life memberships to Pip and to Tommy Cantell, both of whom had active roles in setting up training and provincial standards for B.C.'s real estate industry.[276]

Around the time the two were being presented with honours related to the processes leading to the 1958 Real Estate Act, the subsequent Real Estate Amendment Act was being debated in the Legislature.[277] Discussion on the bill was sparked by an overheated market, alleged flipping of properties, new categories of ownership and, during sales transactions, problems over full disclosure or the lack of it.

Some realtors weren't disclosing facts about options on properties they themselves held. They were after quick money, ethics be damned. "What we have seen out there in the last year and a half," boomed Mr. Macdonald, representing the riding of Vancouver East, "is a wilderness of speculation in real estate that has driven prices up and where commissions have been made on an incredible scale ranging from 4 percent to 7 percent. I've even seen 7.5 percent."[278]

Sharp debate arose on the unfamiliar notion of time-sharing and whatever its ramifications might be. The Hon. Mr. Hyndman, who spoke last in the sequence during the debate, was in favour of the concept but demanded clearer rules: "A number of members opposite represent constituencies in which time-sharing is, or is about to be, a very important part of tourism or the economy of those areas ... We do believe that if it is to continue in this province, its rules should be clearer, more comprehensive and strengthened in terms of consumer and public protection ... "[279]

He drew a parallel between time-shares and other relatively new concepts in B.C. real estate: " ... condominiums and strata titles have developed over the last fifteen years, after a relatively rocky start, into what is now a reasonably perfected and, in many cases, quite attractive and sophisticated form of real estate offering ... "[280]

The 1981 Real Estate Amendment Act passed first reading, second reading and clause-by-clause debate. By the time it was given Royal Assent and came into force, Pip and Catherine had left for the 1981 World Congress in Stockholm, where Pip was responsible for another role. As had been suggested, decided and announced five years earlier, the FIABCI board was depending on Pip to chair its 1982 World Congress set for Toronto.[281]

Tokyo 1979. Pip's progression addressing a group, stages progressing from "what we're trying to achieve," to
"this is the essence of the problem," to
"options, out-of-the-box suggestions, even some solutions," to "so very delighted we'll work on this together."

Audrey Bennett and B.C. Premier Bill Bennett (left) greet Pip with pleasure. Bennett was elected in September '73 and became premier after the 1975 election, serving until '86.

"Paris every November…" This was a Holmes annual trip. Vendors sell small bags of hot roasted chestnuts from sidewalk carts under Christmas lights (left).

Lt.-Gov. Bell-Irving (above) holds a Government House function, with Pip present and accounted for.

CHAPTER SIXTEEN
RECESSION VERSUS DREAMLAND

FULLY ENGAGED WITH FIABCI's world scene division and determined to make the 1982 Toronto congress run seamlessly, Pip was increasingly concerned with an ugly economic wave affecting another front. Though recession was not worldwide or even fully countrywide, it was certainly swamping British Columbia. As resource revenues plummeted, the province was pushed into full recession. Municipalities were suddenly in a very tight position regarding land use and regional district planning.[282] Buyers simply stopped looking at properties, and in 1981, the real estate market fell steeply: "Revenues of Pemberton Holmes fell 77 percent between the first half of the year and the second."[283]

The provincial government and B.C.'s municipalities began restructuring some jurisdictional responsibilities and making efforts to get markets on an even keel for the long term. "In 1982, the municipalities agreed with the province to a Partnership in Restraint program, cutting costs and changing revenue-sharing distribution, including finally removing welfare as a municipal responsibility. In 1985, a provincial-municipal partnership program provided tax relief and lost-revenue reimbursement to local governments ... In 1983, planning powers were taken away from regional districts; new land use regulations were introduced in 1985 and 1987; and regional district reform was undertaken in 1989. Other key issues of the decade were assessment and property taxes and liability insurance."[284]

Pemberton Holmes, like other west coast firms, had to fight through the worst part of the recession in 1981-83 and emerge intact. They decided that instead of resorting to layoffs, they would try to keep everyone working and institute salary cuts across the board. Most salaries went down 10 percent. Executive salaries were dropped by 20 percent. The directors systematically pared down the company's processes to retain clients and maintain or increase revenues.

Pemberton Holmes touted far more actively than before its reputation for service based on long-term experience. The firm had been in the community for nearly a century and prided itself on being trustworthy whether the economy was healthy, overheated or moribund. Its president was able to apply FIABCI perspectives for its corporate strategies and its management during his absences was solid, but the firm had a tough time in that recession-era market, with little relief from higher costs of doing business.[285] The company was well-positioned, but getting its revenues back to previous levels took many years of sustained effort.

Instead of being in Victoria or in Prince George at the end of May as the Cariboo Real Estate Board hosted its Gold Rush '82 convention,[286] Pip had to be in Toronto tending to two thousand FIABCI delegates as they grappled with "Resources as They Relate to Real Estate," a congress theme tailor-made for Canada. The last time FIABCI had come to Canada was 1971 in Montreal, and the CREA contingent was hard at work for this event eleven years later.[287]

Pip and his organizers could obviously make good use of venues in Toronto for their meetings and socializing—"We thank you very much for your kind invitation for cocktails at the Royal Canadian Yacht Club, Saturday, June 5, 1982..."[288]—but what Pip relied on for events management was skill within the FIABCI administration. Since 1970, when John Tysen wisely installed them there, admin at the top was handled by Alexis Noldé as the CEO of FIABCI and Baïa Noldé as his executive assistant. They knew perfectly well how to handle multilingual, multicultural, high-demand delegates from thirty-seven countries, and they thoroughly liked working with Pip. In his remarks to delegates at the closing session, Pip noted that the 1982 congress was the only one since 1970 in which Baïa hadn't lost her voice—and those attending, in admiration for all she did with the organization, applauded energetically.

Pip said that if he thought he could do a good job of something and cared about the people and the cause involved in whatever-it-was—locally, regionally, provincially, nationally, internationally—he generally said yes to it. He also made use of the process of synergy, he added, so participation in separate efforts could often be made to dovetail and benefit the whole lot of them incrementally.

In Victoria a short time later, Pip recommitted himself to his service as honorary aide-de-camp at Government House. The new Lieutenant-Governor being sworn in was His Honour Bob Rogers. And with an apparently full plate, Pip added another commitment as well. In 1982, he agreed to chair the board of the Victoria and Vancouver Island Corps of the Canadian Corps of Commissionaires.

"They're retired service people, thousands of them," he explained. "They provide security at Government House and are on duty everywhere. They patrol airports, offices, do high-tech consulting. They do anti-counterfeit stuff—all kinds of fun things." At their annual dinner, he said, there were people from all over Canada and from all walks of life—a publisher, a surgeon, and so on—and "the one common factor they had was having been in the services." As to his role as chair of the board: "As in any organization like that, there's many a decision to be taken. All kinds of things come up, are discussed, resolved and used as guidelines."[289]

For good measure, he also moved from being a member of the Provincial Capital Commission board to being chair of it.

Yet the urge simply to mess about in boats was getting stronger, and the long travels and the daytrips he and Catherine took were increasing his love of photography. He also thought he might like to paint, and though there was never time for classes or lessons, he began to play around with watercolours. He admitted in an interview to a secret lifelong ambition "to capture nature on canvas like Churchill in his quieter moments."[290]

In the same interview, Pip floated the idea of his own retirement "someday," but everyone in the firm was still working flat out to counter the effects of the recession. "One of the things we are determined to do," he said, "is to keep the family connection going in some way. We want it to survive for another hundred years."[291]

He still found it satisfying, he told the interviewer, that his two major business concerns, real estate and insurance, both played a vital role in people's lives. "We began selling fire insurance ninety years ago this year. We were one of the first companies here to do so. Think what it was like before fire insurance was offered…"[292] His own company's building had burned down in 1909, which emphasized his point.[293]

Over the Easter weekend, Pip and Catherine anchored the boat off Pender Island—South Pender specifically—and hiked up for a picnic atop Mount Norman. En route, they arrived at a rustic church built by island pioneers in the late thirties and were delighted with it. They'd already intended to invite other sailing friends along for picnics around the Gulf Islands, and this discovery of the Church of the Good Shepherd[294] led to a number of repeat visits. In league with Reverend Littlejohn, a plan was afoot.

But duty called, so they both packed their files of papers and their suitcases for the 1983 FIABCI Congress in Jakarta. After the World Congress closed, they stayed on for a short time in Indonesia. "The population density there was unlike anything you might see here, *anywhere* here," Pip said, "and who you saw there in the 1970s were the very rich, the very poor and not a lot of people in between. And what's the essential element in building a nation? Development of a middle class."[295]

They thought they'd been getting to know Jakarta fairly well but were surprised at a change that had been happening on an immense scale. They were amazed how quickly a middle class emerged. From not being visible in the social and economic structure during their 1975 visit, a new demographic group was by 1983 becoming broadly established. Pip investigated how and why and decided that much of the impetus emanated from Cippy Ciputra. "He created such a basis for them—the really solid development, the essential development, of a middle class where none had existed," Pip said.

Cippy and Dian were well-travelled and highly educated, as were their children, and

Jakarta was their home. "He was an engineer and architect, certainly a developer on a very large scale," said Pip, "but he also instigated all sorts of fascinating, ingenious ways of sparking this development of a middle class."[296] One way he was doing this was by sponsoring scores of bright young men and women in universities, through the professions as doctors and as engineers, and through trades training and the fine arts as weavers, carvers, artists on canvas and highly skilled artisans.

Cippy's name rhymes with "Zippy," as his friends were fond of pointing out, and people said they thought it suited him perfectly. Cippy Ciputra was busy launching the big projects he preferred.[297] One of his early developments in partnership with the Indonesian government was a self-contained community named Dreamland, for which a huge boggy area was drained and replaced by an equally huge park for residential and tourism use, the biggest in Southeast Asia at the time.

High-security housing for professionals and a secure area of visitor cottages around a saltwater swimming pool were already in place when Pip and Catherine were shown around. Starting every half-hour, waves for surf-splashers were generated onto a sandy manmade beach beside the water slide, and in a landscaped swimming track around the circumference of the enormous pool, a strong one-way current created by powerful pumps allowed swimmers to exercise either with or against the current. Children of visitors and residents could buy snacks in a special area near the hotel and rental apartments. Food supplies could be bought on site or provided by hotel kitchens.

Ciputra lent the Holmeses his own cottage, and Pip often declared it one of the best cottage designs he'd seen.[298] A sleeping loft facing the ocean was invisible from the banquettes in the living room below, and between the cottages, high berms planted with security fencing and flowering shrubs allowed unobstructed views over the water with privacy in all other directions.

As much as possible, the furnishings for the whole development were crafted locally. A chandelier in the hotel foyer, for instance, was a cascade of local shells lit from within by tiny light bulbs. In the ballroom, dozens of miniature teak ships with white parchment sails lit by more tiny bulbs sailed freely around the perimeter of a ship's wheel hung from the ceiling. Around the hotel plaza, simulated boat wrecks made to look as though they'd hit a reef were air-conditioned private dining rooms, each table with a clear view of elaborate evening presentations of traditional dance.

The long-term legacy of Dreamland, however, was its social engineering. As well as the job-training done during construction of the project, the creative hub of Dreamland was a market for Indonesian weavers, carvers, painters, embroiderers and jewellery makers. They were given workrooms and display space rent-free for six weeks in prime tourist areas and were expected to prove themselves and the appeal of what they produced within that time. If so inclined, the artisans could bid for another six-week period at the market, and the process was working extremely well. The level of skill was high, and the entrepreneurial spirit was higher. That was the point.

Catherine and her friend Nancy Ing went touring in central Java to Borobudur, the long-lost temple city built of volcanic rock. The ashlar, quarried from mega-volcano Krakatoa and other nearby volcanoes, can be readily carved and was shaped centuries ago into a complex of statutes and twenty-six hundred bas reliefs showing Gautama Buddha's life. Nancy, ever the researcher and writer, wanted Catherine to see the restorations the Indonesian government and UNESCO had been doing during the previous eight years.[299]

Indonesia was a place Pip and Catherine eventually visited seven or eight times, and their home in Victoria has Asia-Pacific artwork alongside family pieces, some from Catherine's father's travels in Africa and elsewhere and some from Pip's side. Pip remarked that once upon a time he'd daydreamed about having "a smallish Van Goggghhhh" but later came to prefer having around him the artworks and objects they'd collected in their travels. Those are what's significant to you, he said, like a personalized museum collection of stories connected to objects, and he loved living among daily reminders of certain times and people. It was one of the paintings in their living room that evoked his explanation of the artists' kiosks set up by Ciputra to encourage entrepreneurship and create a middle class.

Cippy also dreamed up an occasional project just for himself. "My determination," he said to Pip at one point, "is to see, in my lifetime, a new house for my family in the centre of Indonesia's first championship golf course." He loved golf, it seems, so he built a world-class golf course around his new home and invited many, many friends to the housewarming. "What an absolutely wonderful party *that* was!" Pip said.

———————————

Functioning on the theory that his many activities dovetailed and created happy synergies, Pip moved from one country to the next, one responsibility to the next, without any apparent ill effect. "You look so well and full of energy," wrote friends Lennart and Puck Ljungquist in a mid-summer letter after one FIABCI congress. "It was so nice to see our 'family members' in Jakarta. Best wishes to all our friends in Victoria and looking forward to seeing you in Cyprus."[300]

Cyprus? It must have been so. Catherine was looking through a file for that year and found the old boarding pass. "Yes, Nicosia," she said. And in a December '83 letter, Woody Weight commented: "Sounds as though you have had a marvellous summer. Hope the trip to London and Cyprus was good ... "[301]

Recession or not, offers to buy out the family company came in periodically from national investors, but links with the past and the desire to keep control local defused the overtures. "We feel very strongly," Pip said, "that decisions affecting the lives of people should be made here and not in the east. A local company has a greater sense of responsibility toward the community—at least, it should have—and we've tried to maintain that high level of community involvement."[302]

By the time Pip turned sixty, Pemberton Holmes Ltd. had three offices—downtown Victoria, Salt Spring Island, Sidney—and the plan was to build up a network on Vancouver Island.[303] Company literature was restating how proud it was that it could offer to any member of the public the chance to walk in and sit with the top bosses to work on problems and decisions, which was something that couldn't be done if the bosses were based in Toronto.[304] The same, it said, applied to bank loans: local power works best.

As the recession waned somewhat, company staff were still battling its effects. When asked for professional advice from people he knew in Victoria, Pip put in extra time and effort. To advise on one couple's real estate situation, for instance, he set up his research files and jotted eight pages of notes as the basis for a six-page letter to help their decision-making: "I did so enjoy the opportunity of seeing you, and your kindness in taking me around your home and wondrous garden was greatly appreciated. The statements and reasonings that follow are, I hope, neither overly subjective nor coldly objective, and are put forward to you so the alternatives may be discussed. My main concern is that they should be of value to your ultimate decision."[305]

He reviewed their expressed wishes and provided a valuation of the property, copies of assessment maps, six options in detail for them to consider, plus his recommendations on the overall situation. They were encouraged to choose their course of action according to their own wishes, but they did so prepared.

The FIABCI World Congress returned to London again in 1984. Pip was leaving the presidency of the world scene division and for the first time in years would therefore be off the executive board. Ralph Pritchard, who soon afterward became FIABCI world president, praised Pip's approach to his work, including efforts for more shelter housing.

"It was a pleasure to be with you in London," Pritchard wrote. "I wanted to drop you a note to express another member's appreciation for the devoted service and high degree of intellectual integrity you have brought to FIABCI during your long tenure on the executive committee and as its world president. You are truly a remarkable individual, and the impact of your personality has been extremely important to FIABCI's growth over the last few years… We are looking forward to October and a new giant step in the direction of international cooperation in housing. Thanks for just being you and for having the ability to make such an impact on the 'world scene.'"[306]

Another thank you came from the RCAF Association No. 800 (Pacific) Wing parade coordinator: "…and thank you for your participation as Reviewing Officer for the subject parade. Your ready acceptance to take part is very much appreciated…"[307] And another thank you for his public speaking, something he'd enjoyed right from the start: "It was indeed a pleasure for all of us in attendance for [Prime Minister Harold] Wilson's address to hear a really professional introduction. Your delivery and insight into the man and his background was truly superb… Pip, I would very much like to have you address the membership of the Spokane Board of Realtors in the future…"[308]

Jakarta '83 (top left, photo left to right): Pip, Catherine, boat's skipper, Cippy Ciputra waving, and Phil Smaby of FIABCI/U.S.A.

A 1983 side trip to Borobudur, an Indonesian treasure (left, photo left to right): Suzanne Beaudoin, Nancy Ing, Catherine, Glyn Ing and their archeologist guide.

Marking the Battle of Britain (below), on a parade review stand at the Inner Harbour in September '84, Pip takes the salute.

Queen Elizabeth and Prince Philip arriving in Victoria, 1983. Top (l-r): Jane Rogers; military man; Her Majesty; Prince Philip behind her; Brian Mulroney; Bob Rogers; Mila Mulroney; Pip with his back to camera as he salutes. As aide-de-camp, he helped with private and public royal visits, of which there have been many.

Fulford Valley, Salt Spring Island (above), from Mount Maxwell.

At the Salt Spring Island office of Pemberton Holmes in the late 1970s (above), the group included Jake Javorski (photo left) and Ann Foerster (second from left), beside visitor Pip. Manager Gus Bolton (photo right) hired Ann to join Jake in sales soon after the office was opened. Ann's daugher Diana (on step) was helping out at the office.

Once the west coast Canadian Navy participants learned Pip enjoyed being zipped across in breeches-buoy practice, they zoomed him on a cable from ship to ship. HMCS **Provider** (508) seen from HMCS **Saskatchewan** (264), under way (below left).

Pip recorded the 1988 naval exercises in the Pacific (left) and entering port at Mazatlán (below right).

In Mazatlán (bottom), during Pip's usual walkabout to see where and how people live.

*At Quinta da Eisa Velha in Portugal,
workers harvest grapes (right).*

*Pip's cousin and cousin-in-law Peter and Kate
from Devon, England, went to their
Portuguese vineyard (below) every year for the harvest.*

*After marching to the drums comes dancing
to the squeeze-box and other instruments
in a **lagar** full of grapes (bottom).*

CHAPTER SEVENTEEN
HEART OF THE DRAGON

PASSIONATE ABOUT COMMUNICATING positive spirit, Pip started revving up the company, the community and himself for Expo '86 in Vancouver, two years ahead. Preparing a speech for the Chamber of Commerce about transportation, which was the theme set for the exposition, he jotted on one of his triple-folded sheets of paper: "Ferry system—nineteen million people will attend Expo '86 in Vancouver; B.C. Ferries can and will handle that. European fares go as high as nine times those of B.C. Ferries... We are a maritime province... Have highways we can be proud of. Air, too, we lead... Transportation is vital to Canadian development. Transportation in B.C. stands up to any world comparisons, equals the road to resources... B.C. Ferries should be a number one tourist attraction, as is Washington State Ferries system."[309]

Then an unexpected element. "In '84 I was told I was seriously endangering my health with that workload," Pip said rather casually during an extended conversation about the University of Victoria and related matters. "The medical directive was that it was absolutely necessary to cut everything back, so I had to resign from the university's board of governors. Felt very sad about that."

He'd already been treated in hospital a few years earlier with a severely painful pinched nerve in his shoulder he'd been told was stress-related. A heart attack in 1984 was delivering the same message: that after enforced rest in hospital and at home, he must redesign his life. A piece in *Times-Colonist* advised its readership he was making some changes.

"Philip Holmes said Tuesday he is resigning his major public appointments," it read, "including the chairmanship of the Provincial Capital Commission, 'to reduce the workload.' Holmes said Tuesday he will leave the thirteen-member commission Nov. 30 after almost five years, two and a half years as a member and two as chairman. The sixty-year-old Holmes had already attended his last University of Victoria board of governors meeting when the board was told of and accepted his resignation ... Holmes, who served several terms as vice-chairman of the university board, said he was leaving 'purely and simply to reduce the workload.'"[310]

Whether or not they knew the reason, and most didn't, best wishes flew in.

Provincial Capital Commission members and the Hon. Hugh Curtis each signed a "token pictorial record" of the work of the commission and sent it to thank him for his years of service to the capital region. Probably not aware of the true extent of his activities, they noted the increased workload specifically in the PCC. "History would indicate that the passing years have brought increased demands and challenges before the commission, and it is against this background that your valued participation is to be measured ... For our part, we offer you our deep appreciation of your leadership and sincerest best wishes for the future."[311]

President and vice-chancellor of the university, Howard Petch, wrote a warm note: " ... it saddens me to receive your resignation, but I most certainly appreciate the time you have devoted to serving the University of Victoria in this way. I look forward to a continuing relationship over the years."[312] And from a member of the university board: "We'll all miss your experience and perspective ... "[313]

Pat McGeer, who was then the province's Minister of Universities, Science and Communications, wrote that he was sorry Pip resigned from the university's board: "I can, however, quite appreciate the reasons behind your decision, and ... thank you on behalf of the university and of the provincial government for the substantial contribution you have made to the good development of the university ... "[314]

Bill Bennett sent an appreciative note. "Dear Pip ... Not only as Premier of British Columbia but also as a personal gesture, may I extend a very grateful thank you for everything you have done for your city and for British Columbia. Kindest personal regards and every good wish in the days ahead."[315]

Every year for fifteen years in late November and early December, often when Paris was cold and wet, Pip and Catherine had gone to FIABCI headquarters. When he was president, they'd be there for three weeks. When he was on the committees, they'd be there for ten days. With this new need to put health first above all, one comment reflected the feelings in the Holmes household as he gradually recuperated: "Thank God we didn't have to go to Paris this year!"[316]

Pip retained the presidency of the family firm and his role at Government House, as well as his connections with Brentwood College School and the 11th Service Battalion. He was awarded the Canadian Forces Decoration in 1984, which he described as being "federal recognition of service rendered,"[317] and in 1985, had to learn two most difficult things: to learn to take things easy and not to render quite as much service. Neither of those appealed to him very much, he said, but he did ease back.

Sailing was allowed, so off they went again next spring to the anchorage below the

South Pender church. This time they were in company with several more friends and several more boats. As before, they attended the Easter service and stayed on to do repair-and-maintenance work. Someone in the small flotilla noticed and announced that the rather muted bell in the steeple was "being rung with a skinny little string," and Pip made a note on his list.

By late spring, some long-distance travel was allowed, and off flew the Holmeses to the 1985 World Congress in Rome. Not being in charge of events, they were freer to enjoy themselves among people they knew and liked. Still attending the working sessions but at a much more relaxed pace, Pip needed to be part of the discussions, daytrips and socializing but do it without exhausting himself.

Organizers in each venue always put on a grand effort for the last night of the congresses, and Rome's was memorably dramatic. "We had an absolutely fabulous final evening in a local castle," Catherine said, "where we were led up wide stone steps lit by flickering torches and through the arches into a huge courtyard for the banquet. It was simply spectacular!" During one of their city walks a day later, they were jostled by pickpockets. As Pip put it: "Been there. Done that. Got robbed."

On 1 November 1985, Pip had been working forty years in the Pemberton Holmes office. A banner on a ten-foot strip of computer paper was taped up across the Fort Street office: "Forty years at the helm! Congratulations, Pip!" Artist Nelson Devry made a drawing of Pip, and the downtown staff papered the office with copies of that, plus various collaborative artworks done by the PH departments. On an office flip-chart, someone artistic drew a very good caricature of him in felt-tip pen, and "Ann, Pat, Lillian, Arvid, Bev and Alex" signed it with their comments.[318] Staff, salespeople and managers of the company offered him their congratulations in a *Times-Colonist* display ad,[319] and they arranged for a bagpiper to greet him as he arrived to join the crowd outside and inside the office.

The well-organized Premier Bennett wrote again. "I know how much you have given of yourself to your community, to your province and to your country," he said, "contributing not only to the real estate industry but to a wide range of community organizations in fields as diverse as education, conservation and understanding between peoples. Your distinctions on behalf of Canada through your military service round out a very impressive roster of accomplishments."[320]

Michael Burr, as president of the Victoria Real Estate Board, sent gracious best wishes: "Certainly during your reign you have brought respect for the extensive efforts you have put forth on behalf of both our board and our city, and we are proud of your association. Many happy returns!"[321]

Lieutenant-Governor Bob Rogers sent a long congratulatory citation, ending: "… you have steered this capital ship of commerce through the shoals of soft, hard and non-existent markets; limited, excessive and no mortgage funds; and various other commercial feasts and famines, with consummate skill. May you—and the firm—enjoy continuing success in the future." Huzza!

Federal Member of Parliament Pat Crofton telexed from Ottawa his heartiest congratulations, and Government House Leader Ray Hnatyshyn sent a telepost from Ottawa as well: "I have been informed by our mutual friend Pat Crofton that you will be celebrating your fortieth anniversary [at] your firm ... From one president to another, I extend sincere congratulations. I would appreciate receiving details of your secret, as I would not mind remaining in my position for forty years ... "[322]

A new tone came into Pip's speeches. Reiterating his father's 1947 theme, he emphasized that experience builds judgement. "Let me come back to my very first point of the practice of our profession," Pip said to one group. "It is the study of the past, the knowledge of the present—but most of all, as a result of knowledge, it is keen judgement of the future."[323]

Pip was applying the principles cited for the sixtieth anniversary of the company to the real estate industry worldwide, considering not just customers but the world's peoples: "To flourish, to keep attracting youthful abilities in order to stay vigorous, [the industry] must have certain capacities and characteristics. It must have the facilities to serve [the world] well. It must have the means and stability to give this good service through good and blighted years. It must put the welfare of those who depend on it above the temptation of temporary advantage."[324]

He didn't at all like the prevalence of technological flash outrunning the gleam of substance: "So much of what is done today in our business, because of technology, is in the hands of amateurs. It deserves to be in the hands of professionals."[325] He repeated that to the members of the Real Estate Institute of B.C. on its twenty-fifth anniversary, though less in the context of technology than as a tirade against politicos and others worldwide who were making uninformed decisions on crucial points of land use: "It is my deep conviction that each and every one of the many specialities encompassed by the vocation of real estate is sadly lacking and desperately needed by the peoples in this world ... We are woefully behind. Knowledge and management of the world's real estate is still in the hands of amateurs and needs to be in those of experts."[326]

Preparation for future action, extrapolated from a long-term perspective, got more emphasis in his public speaking:[327] "History is not an account of the past but a lesson for the future. For God's sake, let's not always think of ourselves but of our future. Be a prophet if you wish, but be also one who preserved history and contributed to history."

Next spring, the flotilla to the Church of the Good Shepherd continued its pattern and set sail again, and the good reverend on South Pender suggested to the group they might enjoy donating something to the chapel they visited every year. They took Reverend Littlejohn's suggestion to heart as a most agreeable idea, since they'd already thought of it.

But first, Taipei. The 1986 FIABCI World Congress was in Taipei, where friends Glyn and Nancy Ing lived. "We loved Taiwan—those hills, the tea growing up the sides of the hills right to the top, and having tea while sitting up there. And the people. Great people."[328] Touring agribusiness facilities where cubical log structures produced fresh mushrooms and others where cucumbers and grapes grown on trellises were being mechanically harvested from below by tractors with automatic cutters, he was astonished at the high level of efficiency in Taiwanese food production. Rigorous efficiencies were also being applied in their aquaculture.

Glyn Ing was busy building schools, colleges, libraries and gymnasiums. Nancy, whose parents were English and Chinese, told Pip and Catherine that when she and Glyn first got to Taipei, they'd found themselves in a world of dirt tracks and bullock carts. Nancy was pregnant with their first child at the time, so as a loving husband, Glyn did the logical thing and built and supplied a first-class hospital.

In the distinct Asian societies he'd experienced personally, Pip found much he admired in the individual and collective determination to be the best and to contribute to the community. "Much of that reminded me of Brentwood," he said. He was amazed how the economic miracle of Taiwan was being created on an island similar to Vancouver Island in many ways, and the differences in their economies hit him four-square. He also recognized that their value systems were very different.

His earnestness about urging others to shake off complacency and reach to become their best sometimes caused him frustration. What was billed as a luncheon speech about current and future real estate markets in Victoria, for example, verged on becoming a tirade about entrepreneurial spirit. "The essence of real estate is its variety of changes," he began.

The essence is being aware of and focusing on the forces exerting themselves in the past, at present and in the future—and being able to judge the net effect of those forces. Population is one of the most profound influences, which is what the FIABCI Congress was studying in Taipei: "The Effect of Population Change on Real Estate." For these reasons, I was particularly keen to attend this year's congress in Taiwan, the "economic miracle" island that reflects the economy of Vancouver Island.

I hope you take it as constructive criticism, but let me comment critically on the sad lack of other members of our vocation at those meetings. We speak glibly about the vast potential of the Pacific Rim, and here's a heaven-sent opportunity to meet hundreds of the Pacific Rim movers and shakers. To meet them otherwise or in more advantageous surroundings would be impossible. Equally impossible is to find an opportunity that would even come close in terms of learning to understand something of the Asian mind, philosophies and business practices and to learn what's happening in the Pacific.

There were three of us there from the west coast—three, from Canada's gate to the Asia Pacific. That's sad, and it's short-sighted."[329]

After the Taiwan trip in 1986, he drafted what he called his "Heart of the Dragon" speech. A study of the uses of power and his observations of changes in natural cycles around the planet, it was a speech adapted for and delivered to a number of groups. He underlined firmly two of the points in his notes, one about studying older lands and another on imagining the brave new world Western Canada could represent. From his speech draft:

• A single species, a monoculture—millions of acres of wheat.

- Another single species, another monoculture—also in cities: *homo sapiens.*
- The whole globe is changing, and we're doing it: millions of tons of refuse a day; waste water into our water bodies; ruining the air that is so precious to elementary life; some 1,800 lakes in Norway that can no longer sustain fish life.
- Catastrophic misjudgements are still being made, mostly as we lack appreciation of whole and inevitable cycles and of the balance necessary to keep the wheel turning; desertification is on the rampage; deforestation is going on throughout the world—SE Asia has only two-thirds left, and an area equal to Switzerland is effectively destroyed each year.
- Man is and has been powerful and is becoming more so; consider a World Environment Society; should we so exploit as to destroy?; do not interfere with the basic processes of the World; preserve the diversity of life.
- This is the only planet in our universe we know of (so far) that sustains life as we know it; must call for research and writing, for objects of our responsibility = put $ toward a REAL purpose.
- *Study older lands without the impossible mental static of emotional involvement.*
- *Imagine a land that was starting all over again from its very start, with the knowledge we have today as to how it might be shaped. This is Canada, certainly Western Canada.*
- The Chinese Dragon is Water and symbol of total supremacy. Too much; too little; enough? But we in Canada have it in abundance.
- The setting of Western Canada is on the edge of half the world's population.
- The family that is governed by example, not force, was seen by the Confucians as harmonious, thoughtful and progressive—e.g., Tang dynasty examples.
- Chinese invented bureaucracy to rule great numbers from a central point, a society built as a perfect pyramid with the leader at the crown; but the Supreme State is at total odds with the individual and the family in which the individual is a part.

He ended by emphasizing the long line of time: that history isn't an account of the past but a lesson for the future.

After five years as Honorary Lieutenant Colonel of 11th Service Battalion, Pip was appointed Honorary Colonel. This group meant a lot to him, and he was deeply pleased to see his efforts having an effect.

The battalion is a Canadian Forces Army Reserve combat service support unit within 39 Canadian Brigade Group, which is the Army Reserve structure in British Columbia. The unit's role was "providing transportation for other Vancouver Island units, both militia and cadets, as well as providing support to summer camps in Wainwright, Vernon, Vancouver, Chilliwack, Work Point Barracks and Albert Head." It included the Canadian Women's Army Corps and training platoons for drivers, clerks, food services and vehicle mechanics.[330]

Pip, when asked, commented on his role in the battalion.[331] He was Air Force,

Catherine was Navy, and the battalion was Army. One of the main reasons he joined the Canadian Army militia, he said, was "because it was one way to help kids. First, it helps develop a raison d'être for them—their *own* raison d'être. Most of them have never been in the service before and know very little about it."

Why would they join up? "A great many of them," Pip said, "have some vestige of service connection, and this connection provides a link to wherever and however they want to serve. It's to make sure they understand themselves as being part of the Canadian Army and part of the armed services. The cadets are young, some of them fifteen or sixteen, and they're just marvellous. They find a sense of responsibility for themselves and are very proud of what they do. I love listening to what's on their minds, love talking with them."

What keeps them in it? "It's esprit de corps, which is very intensive, particularly for the female component. They go into it full bore. It's a volunteer proposition, and though they get some credit for it in their schooling, it's not enough." He was working toward achieving more credit for those who served as cadets. "Their service really should get recognition in terms of schooling."

They turned up faithfully at the armoury regardless what else was going on in school, at home, at work. "They love being talked to and at and about. They *glow*. Some of them go absolutely steaming ahead in terms of rank and so on. First class! And if they want to, they can qualify in terms of skills as well. They make great drivers, vehicle drivers, because of a pretty focused awareness of time and place, and also because they're trained to maintain those vehicles and understand the workings."

And Pip's role as Honorary Colonel? "I look for any plausible role into which I can insert myself. When they parade, the Honorary Colonel and the Honorary Lieutenant Colonel are with them, though we're not parading as regular Army officers. And when they parade off-site at various places, at Albert Head and others of that sort, we hopefully get some time with them. It's actually quite a time commitment."

He delivered an occasional shoulder-straightening blast of a speech to the young cadets:[332] "Much is up to us, to you and me, from the recruit to the Colonel. We have our battalion to uphold. The moment you wear the Queen of Canada's uniform, you are a different person, a person with a purpose and responsibility, a soldier FIRST, without whose expert knowledge and devotion the front cannot fight and the back cannot function."

He told them they each had another responsibility. "We need to make our communities aware that you are now someone different," he said, "aware that there is a need, that there is a cause—and the greatest cause is peacemaking, despite foes within and foes without—and aware that Canada is our sovereign country and that we intend to keep it that way." The end of that particular speech was typical: "Do a great job, as I know you will, and have fun, because that too is part of the army life."

In late summer '86 on a quiet afternoon, friends visiting Victoria noticed that Pip was in some sort of difficulty. In fact, he was having a stroke. "I did regain the use of all the bits," Pip said, "but it took time and some skilled help." His recovery was slow but eventually complete enough that those who didn't know him well might not have noticed the after-effects.

Staffers decorated the office for Pip's fortieth year with Pemberton Holmes Ltd. (right and centre right).

Pemberton's on Government (bottom right).

ARTWORK CREDIT: G.P. COOK

Sketch of Pip with pipe (bottom left).

ARTWORK CREDIT: NELSON DEVEY

Nancy and Glyn Ing of Taiwan (top left). This major developer of Taipei infrastructure was "a dynamo."

Investigating the Taiwanese economic miracle, Pip visited an aquaculture site (top right). Near shore but separate, aerated ponds for shellfish were drained for the harvest by bulldozers. The ponds were then cleaned and fresh seawater pumped in.

On cut logs permeated with spores and stacked up (above), valuable mushrooms grew readily in a moist environment and were easily harvested. Pip knew moss and mushrooms and was interested.

*Summer afternoon guests on the deck of the A-frame (below)
leave the lake swallows undisturbed.*

*With Pip on the dock (right), guest Gérard Vieullermet from Paris
(photo middle) came to swim the same day
Alan Curtiss (photo right) arrived from Australia.*

PHOTO CREDIT: MARGIT VIEULLERMET

*Pip inspects the 11th Service Battalion cadets (bottom) at the annual
Commanding Officers Parade, May 1988. "They're just marvellous…"*

PHOTO CREDIT: CAPT. J.D. BRAUN, RSSO/ADJT, 11 (VIC) SVC BN

CHAPTER EIGHTEEN
THIS PACIFIC ISLAND

AT 1000 GOVERNMENT and all around the town, Pemberton Holmes was celebrating its centenary—a hundred years as of February 1987. Pemberton & Son had been operated at first from J.D.'s home, Gonzales, before he opened an office on property he owned in town. He'd bought the property at Fort and Broad in the late 1850s, he said, because he needed a stable for his horse and there was a stable there.[333]

Pip talked with Daphne Goode on her cable TV show, *Movers and Shakers*, in a wide-ranging interview. An excerpt:

DG: Everybody in your company reports to you, and this is localized autonomy.

PDPH: Well, let's say it's pretty hands-on. The essence of our business, really, is to serve...

DG: That kind of rapport I've seen in your offices. With all your departments, you employ about eighty people? In what kind of departments—real estate, life insurance...?

PDPH: Real estate. All the general and life insurances, automobile insurance. Mortgage, both lending and borrowing. Property management. And industrial and commercial real estate, as well as residential sales.

DG: It is the centennial of Pemberton Holmes in 1987... What things would you look forward to in the future—in your future personally and in the future of the real estate business of Pemberton Holmes?

PDPH: My future in the real estate business is getting shorter and shorter, as you might expect by a look at the top of my head.

DG: I don't think you're going to quit, ever.

PDPH: Ah, I'm not so sure about that. I've got a lot of things to do. But as far as our company is concerned, it's just to be the best. That's really what the hinge of our approach to our centennial is. Keep it local—and when I say local, I'm talking about my Island again—and make it the best. You know, as I mentioned earlier, the education in real estate has just rolled on and on, and it still does roll. The newer, younger people we're getting into the business are continually better and better in real estate, educationally, meaning more and more for the clients we look after.[334]

Just before the public celebrations, *Times-Colonist* business writer William Miller also asked Pip to comment on the past hundred years of the company.[335] Asked to give examples of the company's legacy of involvement in the region, Pip mentioned Cathedral Grove: "My grandfather's efforts in getting that now world-renowned park established symbolizes the activist role that Pemberton Holmes Ltd. has played in community affairs since its inception one hundred years ago."[336]

Other land in the region had been preserved as green space, as well, following family tradition and Pip's professional pursuits: the manicured swath of Victoria Golf Club; the sixty-five acres of estuary and forest paths within Cuthbert Holmes Park; the linear park for walkers along the banks of Colquitz Creek. "It is understood that if you live here," said Pip, "you play a role in the community and contribute what you can."

He cited long-term local involvement as part of the reason the company became the only firm in B.C. to achieve a hundred years of family ownership and said the basis of their longevity was public confidence. "Involvement is essential to our reputation, which itself is essential to our success," he said, adding that this was true throughout the firm. Company directors and staff members had been involved for years in United Way, Kiwanis, Big Brothers, the Chamber of Commerce and Camp Thunderbird.

The interviewer paraphrased the comments on regional growth: "Holmes believes Vancouver Island and especially Victoria are on the threshold of unprecedented growth and expansion. Not only has the influx of retired people resumed, but people are retiring at an earlier age. Add the financial muscle of the Baby Boom generation, and the demand for housing, schools, goods and services can only increase."

The challenge with that was to accommodate development without destroying the area's numerous assets, and Pip is quoted urging that farmland not be gobbled up into subdivisions: "I don't think houses should desecrate everything." He repeats his warning that prevailing logging practices and commercial strip development along highways would undermine tourism. "I see no reason why Vancouver Island couldn't be another Switzerland—a pleasant place but also busy with high employment, good income and green fields—but you've got to farm it right."

The PH centenary celebration party was a social and business must-go. The guest list was a long one, and invitees turned out in force. Murals of Victoria and southern Vancouver Island images had been created by Pemberton Holmes staffers and were arranged around the room above displays of framed photos. Several speakers joined Pip in the formal presentations of the evening, and a video man had been hired to make a tape.

The Oak Bay Marina Restaurant, other than being capable of entertaining a group that size, had been chosen for the party because that spot on Beach Drive was once the northeast corner of the Gonzales property. Pip's mother Philippa was ninety that year, and she was there to celebrate, as emcee Ida Clarkson pointed out,[337] as granddaughter of the first president, daughter of the second president, wife of the third president and mother of the fourth.

Pip was still weak from the stroke months before but knew how to play it down. He welcomed everyone and spoke first, thanking them warmly on behalf of everyone in the company group for honouring them with their friendship and their presence that evening.[338] "A hundred years ago," he said, "they viewed the future with an extraordinarily clear focus. They strove to qualify and quantify the land and sea, to identify and nurture the resources, to achieve a thriving free port in Victoria for the coming Far Eastern markets, to firmly fix Esquimalt as a naval base for defence, to attract capital for enterprise, development, education, medicine, culture and sport; and to establish through Canada a communication link from Britain to the vast Pacific. And how very recently we've achieved it!"

They went on, he said, to stimulate self-sufficiency in agriculture and preserve public spaces. They wanted to plan urban and rural areas so the environment would remain enviable and rewarding. "I wonder if our vision is blurred by contemporary uncertainties and soaring technologies," he continued. "Are we overlooking the fact that in historic terms, this western seaboard of Canada is in its absolute infancy—and that our opportunities span the centuries ahead? Should we not reassess and reconfirm the wondrous and fundamental values lying under our very feet throughout this incredible island and incredible province?"

He ended by repeating his personal and corporate philosophy: "We at Pemberton Holmes look forward to the challenges of the future, continuing to play a conscientious and conscious role, sensitively responding and actively participating, as a local company is perhaps best able to do, through the lives and families that are part of both company and community."

Bob Murphy of Colliers McCauley Nicholls, as it was then, spoke about Pemberton Holmes and mentioned Pip's way of doing business. "I first met Philip in 1971 when I had just returned to Victoria from eastern Canada. I had two small children under the age of four, and I needed a job. Philip brought me into his firm and paid me a much-needed salary while I was taking a real estate course. That sort of largesse was unheard of at the time."

He said that Pip had invited him into his home and introduced him and his wife to Catherine and their friends. "Four and a half years later, when I wanted to venture out on my own, the thought of telling Pip made my legs more rubbery even than earlier this evening. In Philip's unique style, he took me to the Union Club to chat, bought me lunch and wished me the very best. In a startling display of neighbourliness and consideration, he immediately started referring business to my new company." He said he considered meeting Pip and having the opportunity of working for him when he was new to Victoria "to be one of the most fortunate events my family and I ever encountered."

Dermot Murphy, who'd travelled all over B.C. with Pip in the 1950s and was at the Real Estate Council of B.C. until his retirement, was known for "setting an exceptionally high standard of conduct for the profession."[339] Addressing the group, he remarked on the company's reputation: "Pemberton Holmes has long had a reputation for professional competence and integrity, and people associated with the firm have jealously guarded that reputation. In the Real Estate Council of B.C., we have records going back over thirty-five years and, for many of those years, we have maintained a card index on consumer complaints. We do *not* have a card for Pemberton Holmes, which speaks volumes for such an active firm with so many employees involved in so many transactions. I'm serious. That is an amazing record."

The attitudes and philosophies in firms are invariably the fruits of leadership, Dermot continued, "and the leadership in Pemberton Holmes has been outstanding. I met Pip's Dad, but Pip has been the person I've worked with. Pip's distinguished career in organized real estate hasn't been equalled by any other Canadian..."

The Hon. Grace McCarthy, B.C.'s Minister of Economic Development, had been asked by Catherine to address the centenary theme. "The history of this family and this organization in their work for the community has such depth.... In an unselfish way, Pip, who we all know so well, has been a symbol of what has built British Columbia and what British Columbia means to us. Here we have the most remarkable things that kings and queens of yesterday would have envied — such a standard of living in a remarkable province — but in the past few years during the downturn in the economy, how many times have we heard that things are so difficult?"

She asked the guests to think back and reflect what must have met Pip's great-grandfather a hundred years before. "Think what had to be overcome, and yet he overcame it with the greatest dedication, loving the country and loving the province," she said. "With that love, he contributed to build the province. I want to say to you, Pip, that you have inspired us all in your life of service... In reminding us of a century of service and dedication, you remind us of what we all have to do for the future."

The company's centenary year was the fourth Easter the boaties went to church together. Though they'd originally talked about upgrading the bell rope, they went about it first by installing a substantial marine through-hull fitting to smooth the passage from bottom to top. Then they permanently attached a good long sturdy line for hauling on and finished it off with red and green tassels, one each for port and starboard.

But the sound of the bell itself wasn't very good, so they improvised. Pip, who was the leanest, was pushed up through the steeple hatch until he was wedged beside the bell. "Never been closer to God," he deadpanned. He slathered a whole can of Bardol B ("damned fine stuff") over all reachable bell and clapper surfaces, and what had been a clunk became a reverberating clang. They were delighted to hear it pealing far and clear over churchyard, anchorages and island hills — so delighted they rang it and rang it. "You'd better stop," said an islander, "or people will think there's a national emergency."

More and more boaters joined subsequent annual expeditions — painting the window frames, painting the flagstaff — but gradually, the Holmes pair and some of the other originals bowed out and left them to their own devices.

Pip and Catherine attended the 1987 World Congress in Copenhagen and, while overseas, visited European friends. Then Pip had a heart attack, one that affected him in a number of ways. "When he had that attack," Catherine said, "he lost his French. He had been able to deliver quite a good speech in French, but afterward, when we were in France again and having a meal in a small café, he said to me with consternation and disbelief that he didn't understand what the people around us were saying."

With his health giving him serious problems and a strict regimen having been imposed to maintain what strength he had, he knew it was time to institute the retirement and succession sequences. His daughter Diana was at that point in the residential side of the company as relocations coordinator. Pip's nephew Richard Holmes was in charge of the industrial, commercial and investment property division[340] and later branched out with his own development company. Pip's cousin Phil, who was president of Pemberton Holmes Sidney Ltd., and Pip's cousin Warren, "wonderful with figures," were also involved in the business. His own objective, by medical necessity, was to devote less time to the day-to-day work and more to long-term planning, and quiet discussions began within the company and family about how best to proceed.

A Victoria business journalist interviewed Pip on the personal and professional changes underway in his life, and though Pip kept the retirement discussions private, he was otherwise fairly voluble in the long article that came of the G.E. Mortimore interview.[341] He picked up the Switzerland comparison.

"Vancouver Island can become another Switzerland, as long as you farm it right," he said again. His fondness persisted for the original aims of the Associated Chambers of Commerce of Vancouver Island, though much to his dismay, the association had folded. He said he hoped that Island people, preferring long-term self-interest over short-term greed, would work toward common goals of planned development.

His vision was to see Vancouver Island becoming "a rich sub-province inhabited by several million people living in commercial-industrial parks among forests, fields and gardens."[342]

Specifically, he was envisioning "a network of well-designed communities linked by highways through protected countryside of woods and fields, not commercial strip development and unbridled sprawl." The point was to prevent "houses usurping the farmland and bare soil-eroded slopes where the forests used to be," which would mean "farming the forests" and making "full and balanced use of agricultural and recreational lands."[343]

But how? The interviewer listed "some typical Holmes ideas: build houses as much as possible on hills and mountains and conserve flat land; make tourist visits to Vancouver Island more interesting and profitable by constructing paved loop roads to link Victoria and the east coast of Vancouver Island with its west coast beaches and ports; and organize a Vancouver Island planning and development council."[344]

Mortimore notes that Pip's interest in planned development had been strengthened by what he'd seen during his travels and that public service, good planning and efficient private enterprise were guiding themes throughout his family and company history. "His great-grandfather, surveyor to the Hudson's Bay Company, laid out the first Victoria townsite, made the first survey of island agricultural lands and of Oak Bay and sold the land for Victoria Golf Club at much less than market value to preserve it as green space."[345] That Mrs. J.D. nearly revoked the sale when she discovered golfers breaking the Sabbath wasn't mentioned.

In November '87, an item ran in the business pages of the *Times-Colonist* under the headline "Holmes names cousin firm's new manager." The article is short: "Pemberton Holmes Ltd. chairman Pip Holmes has stepped aside as general manager of the hundred-year-old company and appointed his cousin, Philip C.M. Holmes, to the position. [P.D.P.] Holmes said Tuesday he will continue as chairman and retain the presidency of the holding company, Pemberton & Son Ltd … Philip C.M. Holmes, thirty-three, is the son of company director Terrence Holmes of Sidney, who is Pip Holmes' uncle."[346]

In addition to picking up new duties as general manager of Pemberton Holmes, young Phil wanted to keep his previous duties as president of Pemberton Holmes Sidney Ltd., a post he'd had for three years.

Over Christmas '87 and into the new year, Pip and Catherine took themselves away on a boat tour to the Galapagos Islands. He swam with a Galapagos penguin that seemed to enjoy playing in the water around him, and Catherine and her group of women took photos of a giant tortoise near a walking path. The Great Frigatebirds in flight, rows of flightless Galapagos Cormorants and the Blue-footed Boobies on Hood Island were added to the sightings lists. He was fascinated as much by the geography as by the birds and animals.

Though Pip relaxed the pace of his corporate life, however, he didn't entirely relinquish it. He'd sold the operating company, Pemberton Holmes Ltd., but retained the holding company, which owned the buildings. It reverted to the name Pemberton & Son Ltd., its original corporate name when it was started in 1887 as a home-based business at Gonzales.

As the Mortimore article put it, Pip Holmes also "relaxed the pace of the public service career that runs parallel to his professional career … "[347] It wasn't actually all that relaxed, except perhaps in comparison with his earlier pace.

He'd earned and was awarded the Long Service Medal of the Canadian Corps of Commissionaires, even though he wasn't yet sixty-four. He was thoroughly involved with the army cadets at the armoury and was still on the board of governors of Brentwood College School. He delivered at least one rip-roaring speech to Brentwood students that fall: "The world is full of opportunity and challenge... Go meet it head on, have fun—and *contribute*."

He planned to stay active at Government House—as active than ever, in fact, since beyond his duties related to the Lieutenant-Governor's schedules, he had been asked to help set up a new foundation with a mandate that had elements of pragmatism and idealism. His Honour Robert G. Rogers was approaching the end of his five-year term and was thinking about the best way of instituting a foundation structure within Government House in cooperation with the provincial government.

Lawrence Wallace, a man who knew many wise and practical things, was brought in to expedite matters. "He was a great person," said Pip.[348] Lawrie had an stellar record as a long-term public servant, including, though his personal politics differed, a stint as Deputy Provincial Secretary under Premier Dave Barrett.[349]

Lt.-Gov. Rogers selected Holmes to be founding chairman and president of the board of trustees, and though the term for chair of the foundation was technically a year, it was practical during the start-up to have Pip's term extended to two years, thus overlapping the end of one Lieutenant-Governor's residency and the beginning of another's. In 1988, His Honour David See-Chai Lam was appointed British Columbia's twenty-fifth Lieutenant-Governor.[350]

The British Columbia Government House Foundation was set up to accomplish several things: to foster the preservation of Government House and its grounds and enhance its décor, character and maintenance and its historical and cultural values; encourage the use and public display of British Columbia arts, crafts and designs in and around the buildings and ensure that its grounds would reflect the plant life indigenous to the province; to encourage public awareness of Government House, its historical and cultural values, and in particular the need for its ongoing maintenance and preservation; and to receive gifts, bequests and donations that would assist it in carrying out these and other objectives.[351]

With David and Dorothy Lam welcomed and comfortably settled into Government House, the previous residents acknowledged Pip's contribution:[352] "Now that we are in order in the apartment, I have time to tackle the large amount of correspondence," Bob Rogers wrote. "How thoughtful of you to write. Jane and I have been most grateful to the honorary aides-de-camp who assisted us so well in the performance of our official duties over the past five years. Our special thanks to you and Catherine... I was very pleased to have the Government House Foundation in place before my departure and very much appreciate your invaluable advice as its president. I feel sure the foundation will be a great success, thanks to the energies of the knowledgeable and experienced trustees."

That fall Philip and Nancy White returned to British Columbia. Pip remembers the night he welcomed them back, the same night the federal election returns were coming in on 21 Nov 1988.[353] It had been fifteen years since they left Vancouver and thirty since the founding of the Chair of Estate Management at UBC. In the interim, Philip White became Dean of Commerce and Business Administration at UBC, until an appealing position in a financial foundation drew the academic to Europe. After successful experience abroad, Philip and Nancy bought a home in Victoria not far from the Holmes house.

The party at the Union Club that night, from which *Times-Colonist* publisher Colin McCullough kept slipping away to check election returns, had a triple purpose—to toast the new Lieutenant-Governor and Mrs. Lam, to mark the return of Philip and Nancy White and, not incidentally, to discuss election issues candidly and keep an eye on riding results as they came in across the country.

The campaign had been fought on the Canada-U.S. Free Trade Agreement, which was signed the previous January but was not yet in effect. The Progressive Conservatives won 43 percent of the vote, which gave Brian Mulroney a reduced but strong-enough majority government with 169 seats.[354] The FTA and subsequent NAFTA rolled ahead.

When mid-winter rains on the West Coast gave way to slightly warmer rains, a dinner at the Pink Geranium was arranged for Pip's sixty-fifth birthday. The little inn on Galiano Island opened for the occasion during its winter hiatus, and in mid-afternoon, the skies cleared. Guests arrived on their boats at the marina and were driven to the inn, ready to dine well, sing together and wish Pip all the best. Cards and other messages were read out amid affectionate teasing remarks. Because he loved birdwatching and had the eye of a hawk for spotting flutters and hops at considerable distances, one of the gifts, which everyone signed on the back, was a framed print of Steller's jays.

He was looking forward to balancing work with these quieter interests—birdwatching and the wildflowers he and Catherine identified on hikes up into the alpine meadows. "Wildflower destinations" for their treks with friends included Lake O'Hara, where they went at least annually, and many more: Lac Le Jeune, southwest of Kamloops; tiny isolated Rum Island east of Sidney; and the walks near Buttle Lake in Strathcona Provincial Park and Forbidden Plateau of central Vancouver Island. They made regular visits to the San Juan Ridge, high above the open ocean on southern Vancouver Island, and to lofty Hurricane Ridge, across by ferry to the south side of the Strait of Juan de Fuca. In the same tidy notations he'd made in his flight logbook, Pip continued adding to his impromptu botanical life-list. Some entries were just dates and locations ("Lake O'Hara, VII/89") and some were records of plants found ("*Gentiana glauca*, smooth Alpine gentian, distinctively green-blue blossoms"). When he and Catherine headed up into the hills, they carried jewellers' loupes dangling on neck cords so they could crouch and study the plants in detail.

On medical advice, Pip hadn't attended the FIABCI World Congress the year before in Melbourne, Australia, but he was nonetheless following closely the progress of a global shelter proposal being carried forward by Glyn Ing, president of FIABCI worldwide in 1989. During the Melbourne conference, the executive committee approved the proposal to look into the problems of squatters, housing for senior citizens and issues of shelter and environmental preservation.

Questionnaires in FIABCI's four languages had been sent to all member chapters and related organizations requesting information. Based on specialists' research and analysis of the answers received, they finalized preliminary studies and presented them in three booklets. "We fully realize the enormous scope of these three projects," Glyn wrote to Pip, "and we understand that it is absolutely impossible for FIABCI alone even to draw up an action plan. We have therefore limited the scope of our research efforts and objectives to present only the facts and the seriousness of these problems and to explore what the real estate industry can do to help."[355] He sent Pip copies of the preliminary studies to review before the next World Congress "so that you may offer some suggestions of what we should do from here on."

The 1989 World Congress was in Vienna. Cippy Ciputra, who to their mutual amusement always called Pip his godfather, had written that it would be wonderful to have his godfather present to shake his hand as he was inducted as FIABCI world president. Pip wasn't up to participating in the working sessions, but he flew to the congress in Austria to shake Ciputra's hand on the day of the ceremony, then flew home the day after. Pip couldn't attend the Acapulco meeting in 1990 or the one in Singapore in '91, so it would be several years before he was at another of the events.

By 1989, Pip was able to step back another degree from various corporate responsibilities. Phil Holmes, who had been named general manager of Pemberton Holmes Ltd. when Pip stepped aside from that position two years earlier, wanted to concentrate on the insurance part of the Pemberton Holmes business, so he bought Harbord Insurance and merged the insurance activities under the Harbord name, then sold the real estate side of Pemberton Holmes to Pip's nephew Michael Holmes. The two worked amicably together in side-by-side office space.

Phil Holmes wrote Pip a note in early '91 after chatting with one of the Sidney realty people at a real estate function days earlier: "He asked about you, spoke very highly of you and asked me to pass along his regards. That sort of thing happens all the time, but if I wrote a note for every time someone spoke highly of you and/or asked to be remembered to you, I'd have little time for everything else. True!"[356]

In the next decade, the corporate roles within the family would evolve further. Richard Holmes, who had done very well and was a great support to Pip, was president of Pemberton & Son Ltd., and Michael Holmes was chairman. Another of Pip's cousins, Terrence's eldest son Warren, was happily deep into the numbers as chief financial officer.

Jill and Keith Young (below) joined the Holmeses
on the first Easter boat treks to Pender Island.
The Church of the Good Shepherd (drawing, below)
was the annual destination, after a good hike.
ARTWORK CREDIT: R. GILL

Sonomara *at seven knots (right).*

Geoff Hilliard (bottom) with Philip White and Pip.

The outdoor life, Pacific-style. On Vancouver Island's outer coast, an undisturbed forest floor (top left), a boardwalk to keep feet where they belong (centre left) and a series of pools below hot springs at the shore (bottom left).

Pip tracked and listed wildflowers and birds, here on one of the trails at Lake O'Hara (top right) with Cathedral Mountain looming behind him.

On a cruise to the Galapagos Islands (above), he met this stern Blue-footed Booby in its colony.

Pip's nephew Michael Holmes (right), with Tanya and three of their four children bought the real estate side of Pemberton Holmes from Phil Holmes when Phil wanted to concentrate on the insurance side of things. Pip meantime marvelled at the Callanish Stones, Isle of Lewis (below), here with Catherine's friend Joan Owen. The Owens and Holmeses were travelling around Scotland.

The Brentwood rowing regatta (bottom) has become a major annual event on the Pacific seaboard. Everyone involved with it stays on site in the school's facilities.

CHAPTER NINETEEN
NEW SPACES FROM OLD

IMPROVEMENTS IN COMMUNITY amenities always made good sense to Pip, and in the late '80s and early '90s, he joined the McPherson Foundation theatre restoration campaign. Lawrie Wallace was chairman of the lobby-addition committee, and he contacted Pip as one of the honorary committee members of the foundation: " ... writing to thank you for your efforts on behalf of the campaign and to bring you up to date on the status of your contact list."[357]

Committee colleagues knew the rubrics of carrying out such projects smoothly and well. The campaign revved up in late 1990 for an information-soliciting campaign: "Attached are copies of your list of names and ours of 1988 for the Royal Theatre ... I suggest the best time for approaching the people on your list would be in January 1991, although there is some time before the end of this busy year ... "[358]

Familiar with the processes, Pip drafted a cover letter for the foundation to use:[359] "One of our community's great cultural, educational, recreational and economic success stories is that of the McPherson Foundation in its operation of both the McPherson Playhouse and Royal Theatre ... The Foundation is again responding in raising funds to make the grand old Royal Theatre what it should be through Renovation Phase II, the east wing Garden Lobby and Patio. Would you read through what Lawrie Wallace, Chair of the Royal Theatre Restoration, has to say? I enclose an illustrative pamphlet as well. Then may I phone you within a few days to ask you to join me in support of this excellent, exciting and historic civic improvement?"

Which was followed in February by Lawrie Wallace's mailing to all on the lists:[360] "A fine reception was held at the Royal Theatre on Thursday evening, February 7, 1991 ...

On this occasion, the Hon. Mel Couvelier, Minister for Finance, presented Mr. Ron Lou-Poy, President of the McPherson Foundation, a cheque…on behalf of the British Columbia Heritage Trust. This presentation by Mr. Couvelier marked the official opening of the $460,000 Royal Theatre Campaign - Phase II…"

Followed by a mailing at the end of April: "…would like to invite you and a guest to take your place front and centre…for a Royal reception to review the current status of the campaign and to thank you for your outstanding cooperation and assistance in fundraising [for] the very important restoration of the historic Royal Theatre."

Accompanied by a note jotted at the bottom from Lawrie to Pip: "P., many thanks for your and Merv's presentation to the Real Estate Board. I hear you were great! See you both on April 25th."

Honorary Colonel Holmes was also busy on another local front. Moving the 11th Service Battalion out of the Bay Street Armoury into new quarters was getting complicated. A cavernous structure on Vanalman Avenue in Saanich had been purchased in the fall of 1989, and the battalion moved out of the old armoury in the spring of 1991. Redesign work wrapped up in late 1991, but the new space was found to need major renovations and upgrades to meet building code specifications and to install communications connections. Unit stores, equipment and personnel had to be secured in temporary spaces at Albert Head, the Bay Street Armoury, Royal Roads Military College, HMC Dockyard and Work Point Barracks for the duration of construction.[361]

While fundraising and relocation processes carried on in Victoria during 1992, Pip and Catherine went on safari. Near the end of the tour, they separated from the group on an exploration of their own: a search for Dumbletons.

The tour began in Kenya and continued into Tanzania, Zimbabwe and South Africa.[362] Eighteen people, a sympatico group of Americans and Canadians who were used to travelling often and well, were guided through the itinerary by John Wootton, a young Englishman who affably referred to Catherine as "the other Brit." Her father had been in Africa, and she was eager to see something of it. After a look around urban Nairobi, they stayed a night at the famous Tree Tops, then at the Mount Kenya Safari Club, then at Governors Camp beside the River Mara. The noise they heard through the canvas at night, they were told next morning, was the sound of hippopotamus teeth munching damp grasses.

From the Serengeti plain to Kilimanjaro's base, from the edge of the Ngorongoro Crater to Lake Manyara and Victoria Falls, they were carried along in a fantastical journey, delighted by the nearness of the animals, thousands of birds and the sweep of the land. On the Blue Train, which the group agreed should be called "Pampering Unlimited," they travelled in luxury from Johannesburg to Cape Town, celebrating Catherine's birthday en route. "I was glad it was such a special occasion," said Pip, "because she likes to ignore birthdays." They were driven around some of the heritage sites in Johannesburg and, at a smelter in Gold Reef City, watched gold being poured. "Just marvellous," said Catherine.

The two left the tour in Cape Town to search out Dumbleton family members. After a series of phone calls and some enquiries in a lush green area along the eastern coast known as the Garden Route, they located a direct descendant of the earlier Bertram Dumbleton and arranged to meet him. This contemporaneous Bertram had a hotel named Fairey Knowe, in Wilderness, the recreational area for George. A bond of friendship developed as they shared family histories, and he invited them to join them in South Africa again for the Dumbleton reunion four years later.

In 1992, the year after his mother died, Pip walked along mountain valley paths in Switzerland with the maps his father used when he was there as a boy. It was an important visit for Pip. He had long promised himself to visit the spots in and around Montreux that his father knew.

There was another purpose for being in Switzerland. Pip had been tracked down by an envoy sent to find the Holmeses in Belgium while they were travelling there. The president of FIABCI-Switzerland was running its World Congress in Montreux, and he needed Pip to chair the discussion of issues during the closing plenary session of the 1992 events.

Hajime Tsuboi's opening address to the delegates covered the range of discussions expected that week.[363] A series of dramatic changes in the world situation was taking place, he said, the Gulf War being just one of the earlier ones. The unification of the two Germanies, the disintegration of the Soviet Union and the prospective integration of the European Community market, as well as other events, were combining to shake the established world order to its heels at the same time as the world's economy was shifting from a period of high growth in the late 1980s to a worrisome slowdown. In addition, recent economic slumps in Western Europe, the U.S.A. and Japan had been producing adverse effects on real estate markets throughout the world.

"Against this background," Tsuboi said, "the main theme of the Montreux World Congress, 'Security = Real Estate,' is indeed pregnant with implications. A diversity of related topics will be presented and discussed at the subsequent sessions, which, it is hoped, will lead to a better understanding of the concept of security with special reference to real estate." Insights from a forum like theirs that week, he said, "will be of great use to this distinguished representative group of real estate professionals. Here we will be able to join forces to try to promote international economic cooperation; improve legislative, administrative and business conditions in the real estate community; and contribute to regional development in different parts of the world."[364]

A message at their hotel from Mr. Tsuboi and his wife reached Pip and Catherine: "We would like to have the pleasure of your company at the gala dinner on Friday. This is to confirm. Table 36." They were able to discuss all manner of things in confidence there, then again at a dinner in the privately owned Château de Mont-sur-Rolle. Another dinner was held at the publicly owned Château d'Oron, a military fortress built in 1190. "Standing there eight hundred years. Gives you perspective, that does," said Pip.

· Options for delegates during the week included city tours of Vevey or of Chillon, a daytrip to the city of Lausanne or one of the theme tours—a "chocolate day" or a "music box day"—as a diversion from macroeconomics.

One of the best aspects of that congress, said Pip, was simply being able to walk in the most enjoyable circumstances, because Montreux had been careful to retain its human dimension and keep itself a walkable city. Delegates' badges gave them free access to public transit and special conference buses, with the colour of their badges indicating in a gracious way the preferred languages of the delegates—French (blue badges), Spanish (yellow), German (green), Japanese (grey) and/or English (red).

The plenary forum that Pip was handling had simultaneous translations in the usual FIABCI languages, though Japanese was translated only during certain parts. The two-hour session had to establish the synthesis of the week's discussions and present the conclusions of the congress. It covered a wider range of material than usual for the delegates, who generally didn't have access to the intensely concentrated information the board members were used to having. Pip did a stalwart job of it, and as it happened, this was the final FIABCI event he chaired.

After the congress was over, he and Catherine stayed to look around on their own and found much unchanged. Montreux was where Pip's father had his early schooling. Cuthbert's own father was stationed in India, and his mother was having trouble with the heat of the subcontinent. When it came time to choose a good school for him, they chose one in Switzerland,[365] and she moved back and forth between India and Switzerland according to the season and the school year. While still a boy Cuthbert moved to Victoria, finished his junior schooling and carried on into college in Victoria and then at Oxford, but before he left Switzerland, he was already fluent in his several languages learned through classes, reading and immersion in opportunity.

"My father's various languages had fascinated me when I was a boy," Pip said.[366] "French and German were no problem for him, and neither was Hindustani, because he was brought up in India. He was thoroughly acquainted with Hindi and fudged it with Scottish and Irish and a few other things. He had so many interesting sides to him, not the least of which was being able to say things in all these different ways. Just fascinating!" Being around languages, plural, was an ongoing part of Pip's life.

———————————

The house Pip and Catherine lived in for years ranged steeply upward on several levels, with its back against a rock cliff and its windows facing the Strait of Juan de Fuca. This meant dramatic distant views but stairways from roadway to roof. He bought his parents' house from the estate after his mother died and found it needed extensive renovations, but they were able to move in by 1992.

Once they were in situ, along with some of the renovation crew, many small jobs still had to be done, so they contacted one of the men from the crew who'd left them his phone number. They asked him to come put a few things right, and the versatile Gordie Esdon worked for them, putting things right, from then on.

Pip was short of strength during the year of the move, and Catherine had some surgery, so both were at home much more than usual—at home with Georgie, the black and white cat who came with the house. "He made himself part of our family without much ado," said Pip. "Loved that funny old animal."

The property slopes from the road down to the water, and the north windows of the house give a wide view from the front door to the road. Pip was in the kitchen waiting for the kettle to boil when he witnessed an episode of cat theatre: "Georgie was stalking a pheasant up the driveway, and so was another cat. Both cats were very intently focused on the bird."

From the window, Pip could see the scene developing and realized neither cat knew about the other. "During the dash, that explosion forward for the pounce, they saw each other for the first time and did U-turns in the air. Very funny—just *that* quick! The other cat went charging up the driveway, and Georgie came roaring down to the house no-holds-barred. The pheasant missed the whole thing and was still having a great old time out there."

The CMHC's Distinguished Realtor Award was put up just to the left of the doorway into Pip's den. "That's an award that's really, really sought after," Catherine said. "It does have a lot of prestige to it." Twinned with it, and received within a day of it, is his FIABCI Canada honorary life membership. "Certainly that one as well," she added. The walls above his desk and around the room were filled with awards, commemorative plaques, memorabilia.

When two journalists made a stab at explaining the circumstance of two awards within two days in October '92,[367] both still wrongly assumed Pip's daily work was selling houses: "Philip 'Pip' Holmes, a Victoria real estate agent for more than four decades, was honoured for the second time in two days Tuesday as the Canadian Real Estate Association wrapped up its three-day convention at the Victoria Conference Centre. Some 1,500 agents from 117 real estate boards across the country were attending this forty-ninth annual conference. Holmes, 68, was presented with Central Mortgage and Housing Corp.'s sixth annual distinguished realtor award … by CMHC chairman Claude Bennett … for his contributions to the community and profession."[368]

The second award got a brief mention in the article: "On Monday, Holmes was made an honorary life member of the Canadian chapter of the Fédération Internationale des Administrateurs de Bien Conseils Immobiliers, commonly known as the International Real Estate Federation. Holmes was made a life member of the Canadian Real Estate Association in 1966, the year he was president of the group … He retired in 1989 but still holds a real estate licence."[369]

Which he did, but it was one granted to him as a tribute award after years of service to the development of the industry itself. His own role, he once said, had always been to guide and encourage the people who were actually handling the transactions.

Victoria newspaper columnist Gorde Hunter, apparently also thinking Pip worked day-to-day as a real estate agent, tapped out a pleasant-enough comment about the

CMHC award: "Glad to read about the nice award for quite a guy. Pip Holmes has been one of the top real estate agents in this city for decades, and has just received the 1992 Distinguished Realtor Award from the Canada Mortgage and Housing Association…"[370] Hunter in his column five years before had reported Pip's name coming up in talk of possible successors to Bob Rogers as Lieutenant-Governor and thought it was an excellent suggestion. "The powers that be," he wrote," should think seriously about Pip."[371]

New awards arrived. One certificate for Colonel Philip Holmes was designed around the crest of Elizabeth II circled by red maple leaves, positioned just above the crest of the Canadian Governors General. These Golden Jubilee Medals marked fifty years since the February 1952 coronation in London of Queen Elizabeth II. The medals were given as part of her Jubilee year celebrations, organized by the Department of Canadian Heritage, "to those persons who, like you, have made a significant contribution to Canada, to their community or to their fellow Canadians."[372] The framed certificate was propped up still half-swaddled in its protective wrappings, ready to be moved to their new house.

A letter that May, just before they moved, advised Pip he'd been voted Honorary Governor of the Commissionaires for a six-year term, which pleased him greatly.[373] An earlier letter from Michael Ziegler, head of the Canadian Real Estate Association in Ottawa, also pleased him for what it meant: "Everywhere I go people ask about you and remember you fondly. No other Canadian is remembered the way you are remembered. It makes us all proud."[374]

One treasure in the house was a prize Pip claimed and carried home himself. Looking from his chair into the front hall, he waved toward the heavy wood door that was once the front door of Mountjoy, his Grandfather F.B.'s house. "I was there the day Mountjoy was torn down," he said steadily. "Then what was left burned down, and this was the only thing saved from the fire. It's as solid as ever, very old oak, layers and layers fixed this way and that. The woodworking skill in that door has fascinated me since I was a boy."[375]

Another treasure he created himself. When winds blew down another of the old Garry oaks, he had a tall-backed settle bench made from the wood. It diverted the winds from anyone sitting watching the rock shoreline being reshaped every minute by rising or falling tides.

As a founding member of the Government House Foundation and as a friend and colleague, Pip visited Garde Gardom in London in 1992 when Gardom was Agent General for British Columbia. Pip was also in Britain for the fiftieth anniversary reunion of the RCAF members who'd been in Bomber Command.[376]

The reunion began in St. Clement Danes in London, which since 1958 has been the central church of the RAF,[377] and then continued on the train to Yorkshire, where two thousand people filled Yorkminster Cathedral for a service Pip said quietly was "very moving, so very moving." His group travelled together to Skipton-on-Swale, back to the memorial stone in the square and out to where their airfield had been. No more sound, sight or fuel smell of Halifax and Lancaster bombers. It was farmland again, and the farmer welcomed the old RCAF visitors to walk anywhere and stay as long as they wanted to or needed to.

Touring Africa, 1992.

*Pip visits a market kiosk in Tanzania
(top) that has jewellery and painted
shields for sale and boulders to rest on.*

*"From our room at Treetops..." Water
buffalo (above) slowly arrive at the water
hole beside the famous safari lodge.*

*At the Olduvai Gorge cairn (left) in the
Great Rift Valley of northern Tanzania,
a guide from the Department of Cultural
Antiquities discusses with Pip what Mary
D. Leakey found here on 17 July 1959:
a human-group skull identified as 1.75
million years old.*

Pip's photo from a small plane over Victoria Falls (top), a curtain of water nearly two kilometres wide dropping into a split in the earth. The Zambezi River is the border between Zambia and Zimbabwe.

Another trip aloft to see the immense landscape ended in a hard landing (right). Pip discusses the matter with the Australian pilot of the balloon and another guest.

An elephant farewell (bottom). As they continued south on a 1992 Africa trip, this was the last view of Mount Kilimanjaro, taken from the Amboselli border point.

Fruit seller in Johannesburg (left) in an architecturally striking portico market sells his pears and bananas out of the sun.

Treacherous waters lie south of the Cape of Good Hope (below). Catherine climbed the Cape Agulhas lighthouse above the communications station to see where the Atlantic and Indian oceans meet. Reefs and rocks are now charted forty kilometres out to sea, and strong currents and winds add to the dangers.

Aboard the Blue Train (left), a train they called "Pampering Unlimited," Pip and the staff arranged a sixty-ninth birthday dinner party for Catherine and fellow travellers while rolling toward Johannesburg.

Swiss guards in red-and-white striped Renaissance uniforms (below) pleasantly welcome FIABCI World Congress participants as they arrive for a dinner in Montreux, 1992.

Dermot Murphy (below) receives his friend Pip's hearty congratulations in February 1993 on being named an honorary life member of the Real Estate Institute of British Columbia.

The Holmeses often bought postcards (bottom) of the places they went, some to send and some to keep in their photo albums.

POSTCARD CREDIT: BERANN/BRUGGER AG, MEIRINGEN

Sue Puxley (left) had R.H. Thomson and Pip as visitors at Sloane Street.

The HBC recruited in the Orkney Islands (below) for the fur trade.

Before Atlantic crossings, ships drew water from the well in Stromness (bottom left).

Skipton-on-Swale, Yorkshire (bottom right). An RCAF reunion in 1994 began in London and continued at the old airfield and in the annual service at the village's memorial cairn.

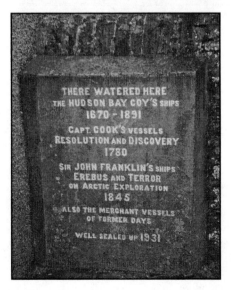

CHAPTER TWENTY
ASIA, AFRICA, EUROPE, HOME

TO TRACK SOME of the places Pip's grandfather had known and just for the pleasure of it, they went travelling to parts of India. Pip was nearly seventy. "We arrived in Bombay in 1993," said Catherine, "and afterward went up to Delhi and took the Raj train around Rajastan. We absolutely *boiled* in Bombay." They'd been advised to shop in the government-approved shops, and they stepped into one to cool off. While Pip was sipping tea offered on a small tray, Catherine took the opportunity to choose a sari to take home. "While you seek some shelter from our sun," the shopkeeper said with a smile, "perhaps you would enjoy to see just a few carpets? No need to buy. No, no. Just to look and enjoy." Pip and Catherine settled down with fresh tea and were shown beautiful carpets flung out expertly one after the other, layer by layer.

The good salesmanship continued, low-key and faultless, and Pip, appreciating the skill of it, decided to buy not one but two: a hall runner and a large carpet, wool and silk. Under a promotion-of-small-entrepreneurs program, the prices were astonishingly reasonable, no haggling was needed and no tax was added. They arranged for the rugs to be shipped to Vancouver Island and carried on with their travels, including a ten-day sailing trip off Thailand. When they got home six weeks later, there was a call from Air Canada to pick up a very large parcel on which there was C$300 payable for storage. The rugs had apparently been shipped by air freight and arrived in Victoria three days after Pip and Catherine left Bombay.[378]

A bareboat charter out of Phuket had been organized by Dr. Mike Penn and his brother and sister-in-law from England, plus Freddy Gardiner and the Holmeses from Victoria. When the first members of the group—Freddy, Pip and Catherine—met in Phuket, the boat wasn't quite ready, so they asked directions to a restaurant within walking distance. The instructions sounded fairly simple, and they headed up the road from the marina.

Reaching a flowered gateway with shaded outdoor tables beyond, they were greeted and motioned to enter, cool off and be comfortable. They joined others already at the large tables and, wanting only a simple meal of some sort, asked for that from a young woman whose English was fairly limited, though not as limited as their Thai.

Others arrived at the tables, and all enjoyed delicious food. When they were ready to leave, they asked their young hostess how much their bill would be and were told hesitantly but very graciously that there would be no bill. This was not a restaurant but the gathering of her family after the funeral of her grandmother.

The area near Phuket in the Andaman Sea was not only hospitable but dramatically beautiful. The islands, rising up sheer from azure water to three hundred feet or more, are limestone outcroppings riddled with sea caves. From sea level, the visitors peered into many of the caves, some full of sunlight and some deep and black where local fishermen in their boats waited out the midday heat in the shadows.

Several islands had ladders zigzagging up the cliffs or up inside cave walls to where the prime ingredients of birds' nest soup were harvested. Anchoring was often impossible because the drop-off went straight down at the shore, so they ran bow and stern lines ashore as they did on the B.C. coast. Catherine and Margaret had regular confrontations with the old galley stove, which needed great amounts of pumping at dawn each day to get the fuel running adequately, "but the men *must* have their bacon and eggs for breakfast."

During one of the first days out, they managed a good sail, but the winds didn't last. When the group planned a shore excursion, Pip found he absolutely wasn't up to it. In flat calm, the sun was searing, and he was increasingly breathless. Dr. Mike asked to see the prescriptions Pip was taking. "It's the blood thinners," he said, and advised Pip to stop taking them until he left the tropics. Pip recovered almost immediately. Mike saved Pip's life, and only a year later when Mike fell victim to cancer, it was shattering for them to attend his funeral.

Roughly seventy years after CJVI's 1923 debut as a five-hundred-watt radio station in the market, Pip withdrew from the CJVI advisory board in Victoria and was thanked for his contribution to the board by Rogers Broadcasting CEO A.P. Viner: "You have served the station and its listeners well and faithfully for more than fifteen years."[379]

Colonel Holmes as honorary aide-de-camp received a note from His Honour David Lam. "Dear Pip," it began. "Many thanks for your letter of 27 September 1993 with which you enclosed such useful information about Lake O'Hara. With your permission, Dorothy and I will keep the pamphlet; however, we are returning your beautiful photographs herewith, with our warmest thanks… It was a special pleasure to present you with your Canada 125 medal last week. You and Catherine have been so supportive during our time in Government House, and we have greatly appreciated your friendship. Sincerely, David C. Lam."[380]

The stepwise saga of the 11th Service Battalion's move to new quarters continued, and its honorary colonel by this time was beginning to wring his hands over it. The battalion did actually move into its new space on Vanalman, but only briefly. Renovation and construction began in August 1992, followed by more than a year of waiting and making do, until both 11 (Victoria) Medical Company and 11 (Victoria) Service Battalion reoccupied the building in December 1993.

To everyone's relief, the convoluted move was complete. Some time after they settled themselves in, they opened officially under the name of a renowned old soldier as the Lieutenant-General E.C. Ashton Armoury.[381] The museum at the armoury was well enough put together to be awarded a fine prize not long afterward, and its collection and exhibits continued to develop. Pip and Deputy Commanding Officer Major Geoff McClelland were photographed there in 1997 beside a first-line field medical exhibit that evoked another Mobile Army Surgical Hospital context, the long-running television series set in Korea about the M*A*S*H 4077 unit. The armoury exhibit was one of a number set up for the annual Victoria area promotion event, "Be a Tourist in Your Own Home Town," and it proved popular with visitors.[382]

He also participated in helping get things going for the Fifteenth Commonwealth Games in Victoria. Public enthusiasm was building fairly slowly at first, so as a member of the board of the Victoria Commonwealth Games Society, he and his colleagues joined forces to prod the momentum a bit. They were old hands at this sort of thing and, in due course, publicity about venues and ticket sales clicked into place. The huge and cheerful volunteer force, well-trained, well-decked-out and proud of their part in the whole effort, helped make the 1994 Games and the nightly roster of free events around the Inner Harbour a happy example of success in how to rally a community.

In 1995, British Columbia had a new Lieutenant-Governor, His Honour Garde Gardom, and Pip continued his service at Government House as honorary aide-de-camp and on the Government House Foundation.

In October 1996, on their second trip to South Africa, Pip and Catherine flew to Johannesburg and on to Nelspruit. Their first destination was the Blue Mountain Lodge in the eastern Transvaal, but the month-long trip took them onward to the tented lodge of Tanda Tula in the Timbavati and other stopping places where they could marvel at the animals and indulge again in the scents and sounds of the African nights.

At the Londolozi Game Reserve, they saw for the second time the fabled Big Five of the African animal kingdom—lion, elephant, rhinoceros, buffalo and the reclusive leopard. At Phinda Resource Reserve, they slept in glass-walled houses built so guests could watch the many birds without interfering with them. Though Pip was a dedicated birder, he knew shore birds best, and these new species intrigued him.

During the South Africa trip, they'd arranged to stay within the four-thousand-acre Fugitives' Drift Game Reserve, because they wanted to visit Rorke's Drift, site of a famous battle. One of the rangers at Londolozi told Catherine that at Fugitives' Drift

Lodge, starting point for battlefield tours, they would be meeting Dave Rattray, host of the lodge and famous raconteur. The ranger added that Rattray would regale them with the battle saga in such detail and with such passion he'd have everyone in tears. Catherine was skeptical, but it turned out to be true.

An article in the *Brentonian* summarized the battle: "Having suffered their worst defeat in history at the Battle of Isandiwana, survivors of the Welsh regiment retreated in 1879 to Rorke's Drift Mission. There, facing an assault of three thousand Zulu warriors, a tiny force of 109 men and 36 hospital patients stood fast… The epic story was retold in the 1964 movie, *Zulu,* with Michael Caine."[383] Eleven Victoria Crosses were awarded after the battle at Rorke's Drift, and the tale has been repeated many a time at many a dinner table around the British Empire.[384] For a specific purpose, Pip carried home two items from there: a shirt and a tall ceremonial staff.

Another purpose of this second African trip was the much-anticipated family reunion. Karen Crowther invited Pip and Catherine to stay with her at Oakhurst Farm, which she was running with her sons Ben and Jake. Her husband Brian, who had died of cancer the year before, was a direct descendant through the maternal line of the original purchaser of the farmland, Bertram Dumbleton. Other people of the seventy-eight at the reunion from all over South Africa were direct descendents of Bertram,[385] but during what they all declared "a joyous occasion," Pip was the sole representative of "the Henry line."

Calling on willing people who'll help you get something special done is a generally pleasant use of power and influence. A number of disparate elements and skills converged, orchestrated by Pip, to produce an evening at the armoury commemorating both sides of a battle. The annual mess dinner at the Ashton Armoury in 1998 was for the tenth time commemorating the events at Rorke's Drift during the Zulu war.[386] The 11th Service Battalion — Pip's cadets — is a sister unit to the Royal Regiment of Wales, which is the successor to the South Wales Borderers involved in that war.[387]

"The military mess dinner may be dying out in some areas," journalist Patrick Murphy wrote,[388] "but in Victoria, the glittery gala of flamboyant uniforms, sparkling medals, brass bands and pipes is celebrated as a chance to train and edify young officers in refined dining… Regiments gear such a formal occasion to something near and dear to the heart of the unit. In the case of the Ashton units, which are the service and support units to the army, … they have tied in their big annual dinner to the nineteenth-century battle of Rorke's Drift in South Africa."

Major Derek Brown, director of the museum at the armory, said Zulu Chief Mangosothu Behelezi had provided a Zulu uniform to commemorate the battle and Lieutenant Colonel Roy Beech had contributed a complete Zulu outfit, which was destined to alternate between the museum collection at the armory and Government House.[389]

But how to display it? Perhaps on a Zulu warrior or best possible substitute. The dinner was fourteen days away when the decision was made. Pip contacted Brentwood's

Head of School, Andrea Pennells, and presented the problem of how to convert a pale thin department store mannekin into a Zulu warrior in full ceremonial battle dress.

Item in the *Brentonian*: "Enter Brentwood's sculpture teacher and professional artist, Geri Leigh, whose three-dimensional work would be familiar to anyone who had attended Expo '86. Exit, two weeks later, with remodelled hair, ears, eyes, nose, bones, muscles and skin, one Zulu warrior ready to preside over dinner at the Mess."[390] The Zulu-solider mannekin stood beside the Welsh-soldier mannekin, both of them accompanied by a backdrop of uniforms from the museum's collection.

Pip brought back from South Africa a grand "staff of authority" to present to Garde Gardom at the dinner. He also brought a cotton shirt with "Rorke's Drift" printed across the front to present to the 11th Service Battalion's Col. Price Carson, who immediately pulled it on over his uniform, to much applause. Pride of place was nonetheless given the fully outfitted and newly made mannekin. "I am so pleased to hear that your fellow members of the Victoria Service Battalion shared your enthusiasm for the sculpted Zulu," Andrea Pennells wrote later. "Geri Leigh did do a marvellous job ... "[391]

Pip was in fine form as master of ceremonies somewhat later at a farewell party for J. Michael Roberts recognizing his years as Secretary to the Lieutenant-Governor and Director of Government House. He'd started there in 1979. The recognition dinner in October 1998, arranged by the corps of the aides-de-camp who'd worked with him, was done up right and thoroughly enjoyed with laughing and applause.

The need to understand and contribute to one's own community and the wider society was a theme that both Pip and John Ralston Saul, each in his own way, had been adamant about for years. "The individual's rights are guaranteed by law," wrote Dr. Saul in *The Unconscious Civilization*, "only to the extent that they are protected by the citizenry's exercise of their obligation to participate in society. Rights are a protection from society. But only by fulfilling their obligations to society can the individual give meaning to that protection."[392]

The two men met in November 1999 at "the Ceremonial Home of All British Columbians," that being Government House, when Col. Philip D.P. Holmes, DFC, CD, received from Governor General Adrienne Clarkson the Vice-Regal Commendation. It was the first year of her term as Governor General, and she and her husband, formally addressed as His Excellency John Ralston Saul, C.C., were in Victoria. Nominations for the honour, recognizing those who serve the Crown in Canada, come at the behest of an incumbent Lieutenant-Governor and are processed by the Chancellery in Ottawa. Pip had certainly compiled a record of service to the Crown in Canada and was proud to receive it.

Pip and Catherine attended the FIABCI World Congress in London, and comparing the London meetings in 1972, 1984 and 2000, they found business communications very much altered by the advent of the Internet. Because it was no longer essential to meet face-to-face annually, as it had been before, attendance numbers declined as electronic contacts proliferated. Though not entirely superseding the value of a shared meal or a well-chaired meeting, or of personally evaluating the character of the person extending the hand, the online handshake had out of necessity been made to work.

When Catherine mentioned that in the year 2000, they went to Churchill, Manitoba, to see polar bears, people tended to ask them if the trip was their millennium celebration.[393] They'd never thought of it that way. They knew there were changes in the habitat for polar bears and decided they should go visit them, so off they went. Pip once replied to a visitor's question about how they celebrated the millennium by turning to his guest and smiling. "Together," he said.

The Gardoms gave a luncheon 2 May 2001 for four Lieutenant-Governors and some of their family members, plus the aides-de-camp and others at Government House. Pip had worked with them all. When prints of photos were ready, they were mailed out with a cheery Gardom note:[394] "Herewith some photographs taken at the luncheon... Quite a 'Rogues' Gallery'—with the exception, of course, of the 'pretty departments'."

The provincial election of May 2001 brought in a new B.C. government under Premier Gordon Campbell. When the Legislative Assembly opened its first post-election session in mid-June, Pip climbed the front steps of the Legislature with the outgoing Lieutenant-Governor and the new Premier.[395] At the start of the second session on a rainy 24 July, Garde Gardom read the Speech from the Throne for the last time in his term and warmly congratulated Her Honour Iona Campagnolo, who would shortly succeed him.[396]

A transition in Lieutenant-Governors meant another transition in Pip's life. He was appointed head of the cadre of aides-de-camp and was continuing to serve on several working committees of the Government House Foundation.

At the annual dinner with all her aides a few years later, Her Honour thanked them and reminded them of all that they'd done since the start of her appointment. By definition, an aide-de-camp acts in confidence as an assistant to a senior officer, and Her Honour's speech at dinner outlined their contemporary roles in B.C.'s parliamentary democracy. "Knowing that numbers of you have served many Lieutenant-Governors," she said, "I am grateful that you continue in the job. For those of you who are new to these ranks, be assured you have joined an extremely professional force... Together with the remarkable staff here, all of you and I are in the business of personifying the strengths of our province and a provincial embodiment of the constitutional monarchy."[397]

Pip also became involved with refurbishing another chapel, but this time he wasn't up in the steeple with a can of Bardol. The alumnae of the Royal Jubilee Hospital School of Nursing had the idea of somehow raising enough funds to restore the Pemberton Memorial Chapel on the hospital grounds. "As you note," they wrote to Pip, "the task of fundraising is a formidable one, especially to those who are unaccustomed to taking on such an effort. However, we are pleased to have found some success...[and are] much heartened by your interest and response."[398] The nurses weren't seasoned fundraisers but they were earnest, and their idea caught on.

The chapel had been gifted to the Victoria community in 1909 by Theresa Jane Pemberton, J.D's wife, and Pip admitted he encouraged the process of restoration with his chequebook and some well-timed convivial urgings to others for donations. His grandmother originally financed the chapel, and two of her daughters, Pip's great aunts, applied their artistic skills—Sophie Pemberton her painting and Susan Sampson her carving. After restoration, the small building became a multi-faith quiet space hemmed in by taller hospital structures. The chapel's basement houses the museum and archives of the RJH School of Nursing Alumnae and serves as a nursing and women's history public learning resource.[399]

The ground around it had been deeply torn up during other construction and the chapel's renovations, but in the City of Gardens, a chapel needs a garden. Pip stayed in touch with this next phase while the concept drawings were developed: a semi-formal Victorian-style garden to complement the era of the chapel, plus a garden nearer the old operating room structure and the Dr. Inazo Nitobe Memorial Garden.[400]

The Pemberton Memorial Operating Room was the next obvious focus. When J.D. Pemberton died in 1893, he left a bequest to the newly built hospital with the hope that the board would commemorate his name in some suitable way. The board received a letter soon after from his widow, saying she would like to make a donation.[401] The medical men debated their options for weeks and finally agreed that the hospital needed scientifically current facilities.

Lord Joseph Lister, professor of surgery in the University of Glasgow, had recognized that postoperative infections were due to invisible germs as previously described by Louis Pasteur, and Jubilee Hospital needed an operating room that could be run antiseptically and where anesthetics could be used. The octagonal brick and stone building containing one operating room was designed by John Teague and opened in 1896. Lord Lister visited a year later and approved of what he saw. Restoring and finding new uses for the Pemberton Memorial Operating Room in Pip's era, and with his support, became a heritage project of the Victoria Medical Society.[402]

Pip was around the hospital more and more not as a benefactor but as a patient. Heading for yet another appointment in his ongoing medical care, he walked several times a week along the window-wall corridor beyond the hospital's main entrance and noted with pleasure through the glass walls the red brick chapel, the small operating-room building and the plants and bushes putting down roots in the gardens around them.

Karen Crowther (right) welcomed her B.C. guests to stay with her for their 1996 visit.

Though her husband Brian had died the year before, Karen and her sons (below) wanted to carry on with the reunion of Dumbletons. Jake on the left and Ben on the right were home helping their mother run the farm.

The main house at Oakhurst Farm (bottom) was decked with flags for the reunion in South Africa. They were descendants of Bertram Dumbleton, the younger brother who stayed who stayed when Henry Dumbleton left for England and Vancouver Island.

Dozens of descendants of Bertram Dumbleton from all over South Africa (top) gathered in October '96. Only Pip (at photo right) was from "the Henry line."

At Balsam Lake near Lac de Seize Iles (left), Pip visits in '97 with his Dupont cousins (l-r): Harriet, Pip, Jean Dupont, Louise.

Hungarian artisan village and open air museum Szentendre (above) was in their 1998 travels.

The Ashton units link their annual military mess dinner (right) to the battle of Rorke's Drift. Beside displays of the Ashton Armoury museum's uniforms, Pip sits with Lt.-Gov. Garde Gardom.

Pip having a grand old time at a tribute dinner (centre) toasting J. Michael Roberts and Sharon Roberts. Their daughter Gillian Roberts sits between them at a table behind.

Presentation of the Vice-Regal Commendation to Pip (bottom) by Governor General Adrienne Clarkson, who visited Victoria with her husband, John Ralston Saul.
PHOTO CREDIT: SGT. JULIEN DUPUIS

B.C. Premier Gordon Campbell and Lt.-Gov. Gardom (left) climb the B.C. Legislature steps with ADC Holmes, 19 June 2001, before the throne speech. The first session was short.

PHOTO CREDIT: TIMES COLONIST

Starting the second session of the 37th Parliament on 24 July (below), ADC Holmes keeps Lt.-Gov. Gardom dry during the review of the troops. They knew Pip well.

At the cenotaph beside Victoria's Inner Harbour (above),
Pip was asked to lay the Battle of Britain memorial wreath for Her Honour Iona Campagnolo in 2003.

PHOTO CREDIT: RUTH SUTHERLAND-BROWN

Photographing polar bears in Churchill (bottom right) was on the itinerary for the millennium, followed the next winter by fishing with Witton Murphy in the Turks and Caicos (right).

The RJH nurses started raising money for a multi-faith quiet space at the Royal Jubilee Hospital (top left) in the chapel Theresa Jane Pemberton had originally funded. The museum and archives of the School of Nursing are in the same structure. The Victoria Medical Society took on the restoration of the freestanding operating room opened in 1896 beside it. Gardens around both were also created, to Pip's great satisfaction.

PHOTO CREDIT: F. BARRET

CHAPTER TWENTY-ONE
DUTY AND AFFECTION

WIDER CIRCLES OF family members evolved and as new babies appeared, Pip encouraged the children on their individual paths. Some thrived and some detoured, some were faithful visitors and some weren't, but he kept close track of family and friends of various ages with steady interest. He said the Brentwood motto he'd learned seven or so decades before, "From hand to hand," was much on his mind.[403]

Though Pip's good mind was zipping along at its usual clip, his body was getting more tired more quickly. He knew he had to reduce the number of events he went to around town but would never give up the essential pleasures of community involvement and seeing the people he enjoyed. He continued writing: memories, anecdotes, overviews, reflections. The long-distance travels continued for a while as he got older, but the trips had to have much tamer schedules than before.

In Bermuda for the 2001 Christmas holiday, they met up with Catherine's niece Penelope and her family, who were staying with friends. Pip and Catherine were lent a house on the condition they would take care of Trixie the resident dog, described as a cross between a standard poodle and "something bigger." She in fact weighed in at more than a hundred pounds. "Dog's unofficial nickname became Slobberchops," Pip said. "Perfect name because of her way of drinking water — some for the dog and the rest of it for the kitchen floor. And she was terrified of thunder. Absolutely turned to jelly during a big storm and ran to Catherine for protection."

That launched his curiosity about the workings of the dog-mind: "Now, what *exactly* is it that dogs fear in the thunder? Can it be just the noise? Might be the electrical charge of the air during the storms. Must find out." He continued to think about it and commented later in the afternoon he suspected it might be that the low-frequency sound in thunder provokes deep fear in many dogs because it's the same deep resonance, though on a much different scale, of aggressive canine attack mode.[404] He decided he'd ask about that when a suitable person came within reach of good conversation.

Their trip to Turkey in 2002 was mainly a land trip, Pip said, not a coastal cruise. He'd promised himself he would one day see several special places: Istanbul, Konya, Cappadochia. Not overtaxed by the itinerary, he arrived home laden with film rolls to be developed and said he found the journey profoundly satisfying. Because he had to start kidney dialysis in 2004, he said "the Konya trip" had been taken just in time.[405]

A home-based dialysis machine was bought, and having the Cycler meant Pip didn't have to keep going three times a week to the kidney dialysis unit at Royal Jubilee Hospital. Every evening, Catherine hooked him up to the machine, which worked all night, and every morning unhooked him so he'd have his days free for other plans.

"All this has meant we kept close to home, and the great benefactor has been the garden," their Christmas 2004 letter says. They had a bridge built over two garden pools on the sea side of the house and, at a late summer garden party the year after, christened it Sai Wai, or Bridge of Happiness. "Pip designed it on a Japanese theme, and by matching our photographs of bridges taken when we were on visits to that country, we were able to get the exact shade of red that denotes Good Luck, Happiness, etc."[406]

It was Pip's eightieth birthday in 2004 and their fortieth anniversary. "We gave thanks for an action-packed fun life together. What happens in the future, who knows? — but hopefully, if all goes according to plan, we shall once again be packing our bags and travelling, with an additional suitcase for the Cycler!"[407]

A dinner for all the aides-de-camp and partners is held at Government House every January, and in 2006, Pip and Catherine as usual planned to go. Someone who was already there greeted Pip as he arrived and asked if "all this" meant he was retiring, which mystified him, but when he and Catherine saw the place settings and menu cards, they realized the dinner had been planned in his honour. Pip said later he was glad the dinner was sprung on him in 2006 and not in '07, because he had still had enough energy in '06 to have fun. The dinner really was sprung on him, because he deliberately hadn't been told.

And such a tribute it was. After greeting the honorary aides with their spouses and partners, and after reviewing the year past and outlining upcoming events, Her Honour spoke about Pip's long service to the Crown and gave an overview of his life.[408]

Tonight in a departure from our regular format, we are celebrating a special honour as we pay tribute to the long service of our warmly respected team-leader, Colonel Philip "Pip" Holmes. Strictly speaking, our records show that Colonel Holmes joined these ranks in 1978, while Lt. Commander David Harris came into the service two years earlier, in 1976, and Major Don Crocker joined us in 1979. But with a tip of the hat to both David and Don for twenty-nine and twenty-six years of service respectively, further research revealed that Pip had earlier served as honorary aide to the Hon. Clarence Wallace between 1950 and '55, bringing his total service to this

House and its succeeding occupants to thirty-two years of dedication—so far!

There are some things to tell you about Philip Despard Pemberton Holmes. First, he knows a very great deal about duty and service. Born in Victoria, a graduate of Brentwood College and the University of Victoria, Colonel Holmes descends from a heritage of aristocratic and adventuresome forebears...

Her Honour explained that on his mother's side, "Pip's great, great, great grandfather was Peter Warren Dease, who was Chief Factor for the Hudson's Bay Company and Surveyor of Canada's North-west and Arctic coastlines." She and Pip had discussed various aspects of Canada's north, whether eastern or western, and he had explained how his boyhood admiration for the superb surveyor and explorer had influenced him. Before continuing her speech, she reminded those present of certain British Columbia place names: "Dease River, Dease Mountain and Dease Lake, British Columbia, are all named for this intrepid explorer, whose Arctic journals are published under the title From Barrow to Boothia." Her Honour continued her address:

Although Pip was eventually destined to follow his father, grandfather and great-grandfather into real estate, where to this point there have been six generations of Pemberton Holmes engaged, first he chose to serve Canada... [by] entering the Air Force, to emerge four years later as a man who had been tempered in the crucible of war, seasoned as a Squadron Leader and Flight Commander, and who was recognized in his citation for the Distinguished Flying Cross as an exemplary leader: with outstanding courage, keenness and initiative in command of his flight, with fearless example and undoubted ability.

This is the man we proudly gather to salute this evening. As author of his life, Philip Holmes speaks out with clarity and vision in a first-hand account of the World War II bombing in which he took part, saying: "We were at war—nation against nation—and there was no mercy in it. I felt utterly convinced that to win the war against Germany, what I and thousands of other Canadians were doing in No. 6 Group was critical to our victory, and I still do. It was either win or have our civilization and its peoples utterly destroyed." That is an ethic that I believe speaks for our Canadian troops in Kandahar, Afghanistan, where our fellow-officer Major Harjit Saajan is serving this country tonight in harm's way.

A civilian again, Philip Holmes soon quickly became the youngest president in the history of the International Real Estate Federation. He worked ceaselessly, rising at dawn, cycling five miles every day before breakfast, working long hours in business, arriving home late at night to write speeches and in general burning the candle at both ends until a higher power reminded him of his mortality and he abruptly changed lifestyles.

Since then, Pip and his soulmate Catherine have traversed the world together. They have adventured through every inviting and some not-so-inviting vistas and continue to journey along the life's highway with customary gusto and charm. [In the] draft of his autobiography, the secrets of Pip Holmes' success as a human being and business person are being generously revealed.

Her Honour paraphrased some of those for her audience: to associate with and join a variety of business and community organizations and assist them through personal and corporate example; provide exceptional education and training opportunities for employees; show by personal and corporate example that representing the client is good business; at suitable occasions and times, to deliver speeches emphasizing the benefits of good support for education and training; and to support Canada's armed services and what the Lieutenant-Governors represent.

On that final point, Philip Holmes is one of the founders of the Government House Foundation. He has uncounted numbers of good works and voluntary "gifts of self" to his credit… Importantly, in my opinion, Colonel Holmes has been a distinguished and continuing presence to succeeding Lieutenant-Governors, to all of whom he has been an admired and valued presence.

We pay tribute to Colonel Holmes for his years of service to Canada, this province and this Office. In particular I wish to thank you, Pip, for acting as Leader of this Cadre, because I know that you treasure and value each and every one gathered here this evening as much as I do. Pip, you are a model of civility, restraint, loyalty, duty and a certain undefined elegance to which all of us aspire. We salute you on behalf of all those you have served, both with our fondest wishes and our abundant thanks.

At the end of this address, Lieutenant-Governor Campagnolo invited the honorary aides-de-camp and her honoured guests to stand and raise their glasses "in a toast to a great partnership: Colonel Philip 'Pip' Holmes and his love, Catherine Holmes, and the Crown of British Columbia."

———————————

To support his school and for his own pleasure, Pip attended as many of Brentwood's big spring regattas and Old Boys Day gatherings as he could. He also decided to help support students attend, so he and Catherine donated two of Emily Carr's paintings to the school, asking that the proceeds from the eventual sale go toward establishing a bursary. The Pip Holmes Bursary Trust has grown steadily with donations since its creation, and Pip said that setting it up was one of the most rewarding things he'd ever done.

When they were making the arrangements, Pip was adamant that he wanted this to be a bursary rather than a scholarship. Being good at your schoolwork is one thing, he said, but innate natural leadership is another kind of quality. When that quality showed itself in a young person, Pip didn't want financial constraints to prevent them from flourishing in the school's salutary environment. He wanted to help those students become the people they had the potential to be and find joy in contributing to the good of the community.

One boy's parents wrote in 2006 after he'd received a bursary: "We would like to thank you both so much for your wonderful generosity in providing assistance to our son to attend Brentwood. He has loved every moment of his first term at the school and has developed personally, academically and athletically in the short time he has been there. Our hope of sending our children to Brentwood seemed, at one time, an impossible dream. Your help has made our dream a reality, and for this our family will always be truly grateful."[409]

An escalator-chair was installed on the stairway of the house so Pip could ride up to the second floor. After supervising its installation and scrutinizing its engineering, he climbed aboard the chair and rode it up the stairs. At the top, he looked for several minutes at the four photo portraits hung there, four ovals in one frame: "the old man," J.D., who he said he would love to have known; his "beloved Grandfather Pem," F.B., who welcomed him "to live at Pemberlea among its patterns and its creatures"; his father Cuthbert, "my life inspiration and a top-notch business mentor"; and then himself, "brought up during part of my early life by my grandfather in that marvellous farm setting," guided "strongly in business ethics and community service by my father," then living and working "in devoted teamwork with Catherine in all life's work from '64 onward."

Being on the job at the Government House levée, New Year's Day 2007, was one of the happier days of Pip's life, he said. It was Her Honour's last levée in office, and he was determined his health wouldn't interfere with him being at his post. He stayed until the day's events were done, which triggered the almost intolerable back pain that followed overexertion. He chaired a Government House committee meeting a while later, a meeting of artists, designers and others concerning installation of shimmering artwork panels in the Great Hall and restoration of certain stained glass windows. "Sense of completion in that," he said. "Beautiful work." He added that it might have been his last committee meeting. "Done enough meetings."

In the late winter and spring of 2007 as he became less and less physically active, he loved people to come visit. One day, after a morning of physio and a few bites of lunch in the dining room, he needed to nap for several hours. The doorbell rang. It was another friend dropping in. From deep sleep, Pip emerged into the front hall toward his unexpected guest, full of hospitality: "A surprise, surprise, surprise! A pleasure, pleasure, pleasure to see you!" People would ask him over and over how he was doing, and his reply would be: "All the better for seeing you!" It was a heartfelt comment and seemed medically accurate.

Pinky, mascot elephant from the bombing missions, had one of his ears mended, and Pip at some points seemed to be on the mend too. On his eighty-third birthday in early February, he discussed with pleasure the stained glass windows, old and newer, of the B.C. Legislature and the Thistle Chapel in Edinburgh's St. Giles' Cathedral. In his chair by the window facing the straits, watching gulls ride the winds, he put down the heavy old binoculars, stretched out his arms angled like gulls' wings and copied their swooping.

One of the drivers who took Pip to and from medical appointments said he didn't always want to be driven straight from home to hospital or vice versa, so he and Pip would take occasional brief impromptu side-tours to familiar places en route and tell each other stories about them. When Pip's back was particularly painful, the driver knew how to take the smoothest roads so his passenger wouldn't be jostled and jarred. "And on Valentine's Day this year," he said, "Pip suggested we ought to make a little stop at his favourite flower shop to choose bouquets for my wife and for Catherine." They made their choices and Pip arranged to have them sent.

Pip asked Catherine to take him to Glen Coxford, his barber for many years, because his hair was curling up against his collar and bothering him. "Better," he said afterward. "Moustache too." When Pip became too weak to go the barbershop in Oak Bay village, Glen briefly closed the shop and went to the Holmes house with Rocky, a dog much-loved by Pip, to do the trim.

Journalist Jim Hume and his son, photographer Nic Hume, visited Pip in early March. Jim and Pip had known each other a very long time, and the Humes' feature on him in the *Times Colonist* drew wide comment.[410] Response to the piece came from afar as well, in a phone call from West Germany from a man who hadn't seen Pip for decades but never forgot him.

One couple new in town had been told that "when you get to Victoria, the one person you must look up is Pip Holmes." They did and were welcomed. Friends came to visit him for tea, to keep in touch and wish him well. His daughters drove southward to see him, and his son and daughter-in-law flew northward to do the same. People from Pemberton Holmes and colleagues from various real estate organizations came to say hello.

Her Honour Iona Campagnolo arrived quietly at the front door to visit with him for a while. When Andrea Pennells and her husband came by, she promptly moved a small chair right next to Pip's, and the two of them put their heads together for a good long chat. Men from the military, long-time sailing companions and close business associates came to the house for short visits. Gordie was everywhere inside the house and out in the garden, putting things right as usual but, more and more, helping Pip. Neighbours dropped by with soup, or flowers and notes, to share short chats. Catherine's two nieces arrived from England, and caregivers came to tend to Pip and let Catherine get the occasional night's sleep.

Many people were welcomed into the house, and for a while he seemed to gain energy each time someone arrived. He wanted to live as before, wanted to enjoy their company, but he was exhausted. "He was so gallant then," Catherine said, "and it was heartbreaking to see him fighting to live." Pip died on 18 May, early on a Friday morning.

Christ Church Cathedral in downtown Victoria filled with nine hundred people for the funeral service on 29 May 2007. The Very Rev. Logan McMenamie was the officiant, and the Rev. Canon Penelope Black was assisting. High up behind people in the pews, the Brentwood College School Choir and organist Michael Gormley filled the space with music.

After the hymn "Onward Christian Soldiers" and Psalm 121—"I will lift up mine eyes unto the hills…"—the first reading was given by Lieutenant-Governor Campagnolo, as she had asked to do. She chose an excerpt from Tennyson's "Crossing the Bar," in part: "For tho' from out our bourne of Time and Place / The flood may bear me far, / I hope to see my Pilot face to face / When I have crossed the bar."[411] The second reading, Ecclesiastes 3:1-8 — "To everything there is a season" — was given by Philip White.[412]

Dermot Murphy began his eulogy with a comment about Pip's "many and multifaceted activities and interests that made him knowledgeable in a wide variety of fields." He added near the end of his remarks an observation frequently made about Pip: "How he had time to do all he did was extraordinary." Andrea Pennells quoted "High Flight" by John Gillespie Magee, Jr., a poem much loved by pilots, and characterized Pip as "a wise mentor, an encouraging friend, an inspiring leader, a wit with a mischievous sense of humour…" She noted how rooted he was in family heritage of knowing the land, "which had come alive through boyhood days canoeing in the harbour at Victoria and fishing in the Fraser and Thompson Rivers. Pip loved this land and helped so many others, through his exemplary leadership of the real estate profession, to make it their home."[413]

The Brentwood College School Choir sang "My Own Dear Land," a sort of personal Canadian anthem to Pip. It suited him: "Ever to thee I'm bound in love and duty / No dearer land to me in all the earth / By all sweet ties of home and love and beauty / To thee I cleave, dear land that gave me birth."[414]

A short description of Pip's life and qualities printed in the order of service conveyed his nature well: "He had a rare zest for living, a compassionate, wise and mischievous buoyancy and quality of leadership that inspired people to broaden their outlooks and become their best."[415] Pipe Major John Mager, who led so many ceremonial entrances with his bagpipes, played "Flowers of the Forest" as the casket was taken down the front steps of the cathedral.

Many of the things Pip did were public and produced obvious social or professional effects, but as Dermot Murphy suggested in 1987 at the Pemberton Holmes centenary events,[416] the public record doesn't tell the full story:

> He never ceased to surprise me by his innovations, his hard work and his respect for people… His courtesy in dealing with people was unfailing, and his distinguished career in organized real estate hasn't been equalled by any other Canadian. Pip went forward from the provincial scene to influence matters first at the national and later at the international levels.

> Philip Holmes has been extremely effective, and those effects will continue far into the future. That ability to contribute effectively appears to have been a family characteristic passed from generation to generation, as each generation has left its mark on British Columbia.

> I'm amazed that so much is known about Pip and his work, because in practice, he tends to perform good works as if he were in the secret service. It's not so much a question of not seeking personal recognition as of actively taking steps to avoid it, so while much is known, I'm convinced there's much more that is unknown.

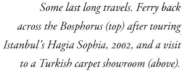

*Some last long travels. Ferry back
across the Bosphorus (top) after touring
Istanbul's Hagia Sophia, 2002, and a visit
to a Turkish carpet showroom (above).*

*The pilot's-eye view was the best way
to see the world, Pip said. A young
pilot (right) who took Pip up to see an
Alaskan glacier (centre right) asked him
if he'd ever flown before.*

The garden evolved substantially after 1992 (top), with the Sai Wai bridge ("our Bridge of Happiness") christened in August 2005. Cox's Orange Pippin trees grow beside the east fence, defying the salt winds, and produce heritage apples in quantity.

Gordie Esdon (above) kept the Holmes house and garden running well for them. Heather Player (left) took care of Pip's nursing care and later did the same for Catherine, helping her with many tasks.

PHOTO CREDITS: CAMILLA TURNER

The Strait of Juan de Fuca from Pip's window chair, in summer (top) and in winter (centre). He watched the tide patterns, weather systems and constant traffic of commercial shipping, research vessels, whale-watching tours and pleasure boats. It was a prime birdwatching spot, especially for oystercatchers on the rocks and gulls in the wind.

Pip in March 2007 (right) with his talisman elephant Pinky and RCAF logbook brought out for the journalist and the photographer. He gathers his thoughts after one of the questions.

PHOTO CREDIT: NIC HUME

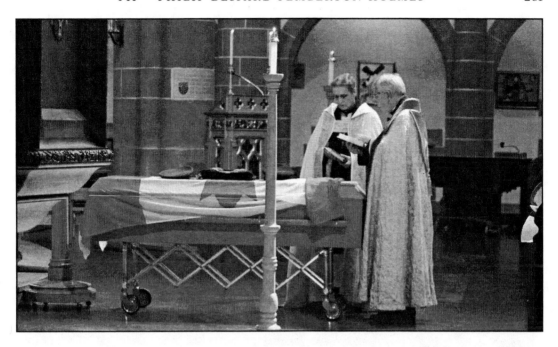

After the eulogies, the Rev. Canon Penelope Black (top) and the Very Rev. Logan McMenamie continue the service at Christ Church Cathedral with prayers and readings.

PHOTO CREDIT: GARY WEBSTER

In front of Carol Sabiston's textile assemblage panels chosen by Pip's last committee (bottom), Her Honour Iona Campagnolo speaks to guests at the Government House reception after the funeral.

PHOTO CREDIT: GARY WEBSTER

TO CATHERINE - WITH FOND MEMORIES OF A REMARKABLE AND GENTLE MAN!
MAY 29, 2007

CHAPTER TWENTY-TWO
FOR LOVE OF THE FUTURE

THE PEOPLE WHO filled the cathedral were invited by the Lieutenant-Governor to gather at Government House after the funeral service, and hundreds of them did. Their entries filled pages in the book of condolences that was set out during the reception.

Some of Pip's family also added affectionate comments on the condolences link to his obituary notice online, and some shared their impressions of him in a tribute document assembled by Pip's nephew Richard Holmes, who himself added something more from family lore. "It is particularly fitting that we gathered at Christ Church Cathedral to remember Pip," he wrote, "as in the north entry wall you will find a small wooden cross hand-carved by a French farmer who buried the remains of Pip's uncle, J. Despard Pemberton, eldest son of F.B. Pemberton and eldest brother of Pip's mother Philippa. Lt. Despard Pemberton was one of the first pilots in World War I. He was shot down over enemy lines in France in 1917 and mortally wounded and crashed in a farmer's field. It was not until a few years after the end of the war that the cross managed to be returned to Victoria."[417] When Pip was leaving to join the Air Force, Pip's parents would have remembered Despard's death and that of his brother Warren, both of them in the Royal Flying Corps during the First World War and both killed in action.

Richard wrote that Pip's survival of those wartime bombing runs was more than luck: "He led an almost charmed life with huge successes, well-deserved accolades and a most admired reputation, but the really important thing to remember about Pip is that it wasn't serendipity but his personal skill, tenacity and leadership that brought him this recognition."[418]

A few of the impressions of Pip mentioned by family members were that he was affable, confident and inspiring, had optimism, innate strength and a rare charismatic magnetism, and that he was definitely dapper. He was, they agreed, always a good dresser. "Pip with his great eyebrows and fine moustache," said one, "was always extremely well-dressed, distinguished and stood out in a crowd." One of his daughers, moving beyond haberdashery, wrote that the Kipling poem "If" is one of the great tests of life and that Pip in every way surpassed the test.[419]

A Salt Spring Island realtor commented: "All I can say is that Pip was extremely honest, friendly and well-loved by all his employees. I loved it when he would come over to the island, and I missed him when he retired..."[420]

Letters of condolence reached Catherine over the next weeks and months, and she replied to each of them. One of the first letters was a note from Pip's nephew in Toronto, R.H. Thomson: "Even though I knew his days were ending, when I got the news, it was a shock... He was a larger-than-life uncle for me and had a large part in my heart. I will be standing in the back [of the cathedral] in spirit on Tuesday because Pip was a man who enriched my life."[421]

A woman who was related to him and knew him well wrote that Pip was one of a kind. "Even as a young girl, I remember him, back in World War II. When we saw him, he was on leave and totally exhausted, but he had the ability to make you feel you were the one person he wanted to see."[422]

One man who knew Pip through Brentwood's board of governors called him "the nearest thing we had on this earth to a perfect gentleman." He remarked on Pip's ability in conversations "to make me feel as though I were the centre of the universe" and added a comment similar to those expressed in a number of letters: "His personality was cast in a mould that has now been lost, it seems, but I know that by his personal efforts he always wanted chivalry and integrity to be part of everyone's life."[423]

In the six months after Pip's death, more than three hundred letters came to the house, with more coming in as people who knew him in various connections in various countries learned he was gone. Lieutenant-Governor Steven Point, reading his first throne speech in the Legislature the following February, mentioned Philip Despard Pemberton Holmes as one of the exemplary British Columbia citizens who had died in the previous parliamentary year.[424]

Michael Roberts, who had been Director of Government House from 1979 to 1998 and Secretary to the Lieutenant-Governor of B.C., wrote a warm letter from himself and his wife Sharon:

> Over the years, I came to admire and deeply respect the many dimensions of his character—his values, his experience in an amazing variety of human activities, his wisdom, his old-world manners and gallantry, his passionate pursuit of causes he believed in, and his ever-present charm. He was loyal to his friends, fair and respectful to those with whom he didn't agree, and comfortable with—and refreshingly outspoken about—his beliefs. Above all, he was a gentleman, and a gentle man.
>
> His was a remarkable life, and one uncommonly well-lived, marked by intellectual curiosity, extraordinary professionalism in all his many endeavours, unswerving

dedication, and always that irrepressible joie de vivre. His contributions and unfailing commitment to his profession, to his community, to his province, to Canada and to the Crown—in both peace and war—exemplify the highest qualities and ideals of citizenship.

We will greatly miss Pip and will carry with us our private thoughts and remembrances of him—his vitality, his warmth, his courtliness, his willingness to help, and the courage and dignity with which he faced his final illness. We will miss his quick response to the question, "How are you?" with "All the better for seeing *you*." In anyone else, it would be a throwaway line, a cliché. With Pip, it was sincerely meant, because he genuinely liked people. He was a man whose company you sought and treasured, simply because it enriched your life.[425]

Catherine developed a cough on the day of Pip's funeral at the end of May and after her near-exhaustion had a hard time in June and July recovering her energies. She arranged thoroughly good care, kept to a schedule of daily walks, resumed some of the projects and activities she'd postponed during Pip's illness and was thinking of taking "a nice restorative little trip along the Turkish coast" in a year or so. She continued her replies to the letters of condolence and visited with her friends but had more and more trouble getting her breath.

For years, including the summer before, she would exercise with a long swim to and back from the base of the cliff at the west shore of the lake. Once the water in the lake warmed up in 2007, she set out for one of her swims and was astonished that she could barely make it back from the nearby raft. The incident thoroughly dismayed her.

"He was my life's breath," she said. "Maybe my breath went with him when he died." Catherine responded to her progressive decrease in strength with an increase in attention to several things she wanted to see done and in place. Then with matters in good order, she died on 13 December 2007,[426] thirty weeks after Pip.

INTO THE FUTURE: PIP'S PHOTO ALBUM

PIP SAID HE worked hard for the sake of the future, and that's reinforced by the pictures he particularly enjoyed in his photo albums and special picture frames.

Grandchildren arrive and grow up.

James Philip Durell Maxwell (top), son of Jennifer and Ian Maxwell, arrives on 28 January 1989. Hannah, Jennifer's eldest child, grins at her grandfather (right) as they leave for a garden party at Government House. Heather and Gillian McDonald (above), daughters of Susan and Shaun McDonald, are buffeted by gusts and giggles.

Christmas holiday at Silver Star ski resort, December 1995.

At dinner in Anne and Michael Tyler's chalet at Silver Star (top, l-r): Catherine Holmes, Pip's son Craig Francis, Anne Tyler, Pip, Craig's wife Cindy Francis.

Everyone into the snow (above). Pip declined the skiing and sat on the sidelines with camera to record their earnest concentration and progress.

Indoors to warm up (left, l-r): Craig Francis, Pip's daughter Jennifer Maxwell, Pip, and Jennifer's son James.

On the cottage porch at Maltby Lake (above), a family gathering after a good meal (l-r): John Thomson, Carmel Thomson, Diana, Catherine, James almost hidden by Harley on his lap, a young friend of James's seated in front of Catherine, Pip seated in front of the window by the post, Hannah, Lary, Ernie almost out of the frame at the right, and Hannah's husband Ian in the foreground. Photo circa 1999.

During Jennifer's birthday celebration at the lake in 1996 (above), she holds James on her lap and reads her father's card. The portrait on the table is a Spanish cavalier painted by Sophie Pemberton. Pip had the painting cleaned and reframed to give Jennifer as a birthday gift.

On the A-frame's dock, a swimming day (top, l-r): Laurie Pederson, Pip, James, Diana, Jennifer, Nicole Pederson, Stephanie Pederson. The green canoe tethered at the end of the dock was the one Pip bought Catherine as a birthday present.

Celebrating Lary's 1996 birthday party (centre left, l-r): Diana, Gill McDonald, Susan, Heather McDonald, Shaun McDonald, Catherine, Jennifer, Pip.

Water lilies thrive on both sides of another dock. On a September day (left, l-r): Ian, Lary, Pip, James on Pip's lap, Jennifer, Diana.

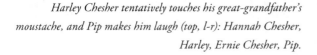

Harley Chesher tentatively touches his great-grandfather's moustache, and Pip makes him laugh (top, l-r): Hannah Chesher, Harley, Ernie Chesher, Pip.

Ernie Chesher (right) with his son Harley, Pip's great-grandson.

Visiting Pip and Catherine and settled comfortably at the top of the stairs (above, l-r): Ian, Jennifer, Harley, Hannah, and leaning at the last second into the picture, James.

Cindy and Craig (top) walk their "property guards" along the shore near their California home. The animals are a malamute-wolf cross and love the resident cats.

On a Tahoe holiday (above), Pip's gift—"one of Maarten Schaddelee's sculptures"—has its unveiling. Craig's choice was "Reunion," this pair of beluga whales.

Pip and Craig (above) after lunch on the deck facing Lake Tahoe, Nevada.

Pip and James enjoying each other's company (top) and Pip happily wedged between Susan's two daughters (right), who had outgrown the giggles but were delighted with a good shoulder hug. The two granddaughters (l-r) are Gillian and Heather McDonald.

NOTES TO THE TEXT

1   Hughenden [Manor] and Wycombe notes, personal papers from Catherine Holmes, 13 June 07.

2   They returned from Swellendam to live at Hall Grove, Windlesham, Bagshot, Surrey.

3   Belcher Street was later renamed Rockland Avenue.

4   Henry Cuthbert Holmes was born 15 December 1890.

5   These dates in Cuthbert Holmes' life were those provided by Pip and discussed with several others. Various dates are given by different sources — e.g., Cuthbert having joined the company in 1920, 1921 or 1922, and becoming third president of it in 1933 or 1938. The change in company name from Pemberton & Son to Pemberton, Holmes Ltd. is reported as both 1938 and 1943. The current name format, without comma, is used in this book. A definitive company history, if and when done, could cite original sources unavailable from Pip's personal files. G.E. Mortimore has this: "He became president in 1933. Through friends, relatives and associates, he mobilized mortgage capital and enough money to buy out the non-family investors. The business was incorporated in 1943 as Pemberton Holmes Ltd. The new name recognized Cuthbert Holmes' part in the firm's revitalization." G.E. Mortimore, "Pemberton Holmes, 100 years later," *Victoria's Business Report*, Vol. 5, No. 10 (October 1987), p. 30.

6   Peter Warren Dease (1788-1863) was born at Michilimackinac on 1 January 1788, and served the North West Company in the Mackenzie River district. From the 15th Report of the Geographic Board of Canada, 31 March 1917, a supplement to the Annual Report of the Department of the Interior, Ottawa, 1917: "Dease entered the fur trade as an employee of the XY Company in 1801. Upon the union of the North West Company and the Hudson's Bay Company in 1821, he became a Chief Trader. Dease was on Franklin's Arctic expedition of 1825-27, and in 1828 became a Chief Factor for the HBC." HBC Governor George Simpson wrote of Dease in 1825: "This gentleman is one of our best voyageurs, of a strong robust habit of body, possessing such firmness of mind joined to a great sauvity of manners, and ... great experience in the country — would be a most valuable acquisition." Akrigg, Helen B. and G.P.V. Akrigg,

British Columbia Place Names (Vancouver: University of British Columbia Press, 1997). From 1830 to 1834, based at Fort St. James, he was HBC superintendent in charge of the New Caledonia District, then was senior officer of the Dease and Simpson Arctic Expedition, 1837-39. He was known for skilled exploration, for which Queen Victoria granted him a Civil List pension of £100 a year, and was adept at company administration. He and Elizabeth had eight children together, and after he retired from the HBC in 1842, they settled in the Montreal area. His Arctic journal has been published, most recently with Arctic historian William Barr as editor, under the title *From Barrow to Boothia: The Arctic Journal of Chief Factor Peter Warren Dease, 1836-1839* (Montreal: McGill-Queen's University Press, 2002).

7   Dease Lake, 58°38'00"N/130°04'00"W; head of Dease River, NE of the community of Telegraph Creek in the Cassiar Land District. Also Dease River, Dease Creek, Dease Plateau, three reserves and the community of Dease Lake. Website of B.C. Integrated Land Management section of the B.C. Geographical Names Information System, http://ilmbwww.gov.bc.ca/bcgn-bin/bcg10?name=15450; accessed Sun 6 May 07, cjt.

8   John Bell, who was born on the Island of Mull, began his career with the North West Company in 1818 and, following the coalition of 1821, became an HBC man. He never did become a chief factor like his father-in-law, but one of his sons (Peter Warren Bell) did achieve that position. John Bell as chief trader had a successful career in the Mackenzie River District and the company's Athabasca District, among other postings, before retiring to a farm in Quebec. Entry at John Bell, *Dictionary of Canadian Biography*,
http://www.biographi.ca/EN/ShowBioPrintable.asp?BioId=38414; accessed 1930 hrs Sat 25 Aug 07, cjt.

9   John Bell's son Peter Warren Bell "was in the employ of the HBC from 1852 to 1895, attaining the rank of chief factor." Entry at John Bell, *Dictionary of Canadian Biography*,
http://www.biographi.ca/EN/ShowBioPrintable.asp?BioId=38414; accessed Sun 9 Sept 07, cjt.

10   Liz Bryan, "Roadtrip: a South Island fling," *Westworld*, Spring 2007, p. 23: "Below [Fort Rodd Hill] is a second historic site—Fisgard Lighthouse, built in 1860 and now housing a museum dedicated to charting the shipwrecks along the West Coast's Graveyard of the Pacific and the intricacies of the Fresnel lens."

11   J.D. Pemberton served from 1856 to 1859, "and though he was not a supporter of British Columbia joining Confederation, he did not favour annexation to the United States." Geoffrey Castle, "Beneath the arches, links with a pioneer family," *Times Colonist*, 9 December 1984, p. 4.

12   Born "Frederic," he later used the spelling "Frederick." Conversation with Catherine Holmes, 27 July 2007.

13   Holmes Hill is not labelled in the 1932 or 1946 editions of Davenport's map, "Southern Districts of Vancouver Island," or on the 1935 or 1939 editions of the Department of National Defence sheet 415g Malahat but was gazetteered 16 January 1950 as Holmes Peak. British Columbia's geographical names listing for Holmes Hill, as of January 2007, carries the note, "Origin/significance not known." Website of the Integrated Land Management Bureau,
http://ilmbwww.gov.bc.ca/bcnames/g2_search_by_name.htm; accessed 22 Jan 2007, cjt.

14   J.D. Pemberton had sold his interest in the Douglas Lake Cattle Co. before he built Gonzales. The house was dismantled in 1952, leaving in place its gateposts and the redwood trees J.D. planted when he moved in.

15   F.B. Pemberton was second president at Pemberton & Son when Fred Maurice was hired. Mr. Maurice continued working there for fifty years and became the company historian. F.B.'s secretary was Thomas Johnson Ross and his stenographer, "an august personage," was Victoria Alexandria Phipps, sister of A.E. Phipps of the Imperial Bank. Excerpt from text layout for a Pemberton Holmes company publication article, "From our Past," in PDPH files.

16   Conversation with Pip, Jubilee Hospital, 10 Jan 07, cjt.

17   "De Dion-Bouton was a French automobile manufacturer operating from 1883 to 1932 ... In 1893, following some experiments, de Dion became convinced that the future lay in the internal combustion engine." http://en.wikipedia.org/wiki/De Dion-Bouton; accessed Sun 6 May 07, cjt.

18   The Douglas Lake Ranch, Canada's largest cattle ranch, was started in 1872 by John Douglas, expanded by new owners in 1884 and incorporated in 1886 as the Douglas Lake Cattle Co. Entry at Douglas Lake Cattle Co., *Encyclopaedia of British Columbia* (Madeira Park, B.C.: Harbour Publishing, 2000), p. 183.

19   "Finnerty Bay" was the name of the Pembertons' summer residence north of Cadboro Bay on the east side of the Saanich Peninsula. The family generally referred to F.B.'s summer residence as Finnerty Bay, or sometimes Finnerty Farm, though the body of water beside the farm is listed as Finnerty Cove in the Victoria Land District, according to the B.C. gazetteer online, BCGNIS, http://ilmbwww.gov.bc.ca/bcnames/g2_search_by_name.htm; accessed Sunday 20 June 07, cjt. The Queen Alexandra Solarium moved from its original location near Mill Bay to the Finnerty Bay property on Arbutus Road in 1958 and is now known as the Queen Alexandra Centre for Children's Health. http://queenalexandra.org/AboutUs/OurHistory.asp; accessed Sun 9 Sept 07, cjt.

20   Conversation with Pip, Mon 13 Feb 07, cjt.

21   F.B.'s only surviving son, Francis John Dupont Pemberton, Pip's Uncle Jake, worked for the family firm after school graduation until he joined the navy in 1940. He remained in the navy after the war, in the diplomatic branch, and became comptroller to the Governor General's household in Ottawa. Excerpt from Pemberton Holmes company publication article, "From our Past," in PDPH personal files.

22   The quotes and descriptions are Pip's.

23   Conversation with Pip about the barn cats, Wed 24 Jan 07. Versions of anecdote are also in other material.

24   "From father to son, and down the line: five generations in local R.E. firm," [no byline], *Daily Colonist*, 24 November 1979, p. 7.

25   G.E. Mortimore, "Pemberton Holmes, 100 Years Later," *Victoria's Business Report*, Vol. 5, No. 10 (October 1987), p. 31.

26   Grant S. Whittkamp, "After Canoe Arrival – Fort Victoria," *Business Examiner*, October 1984, pp. 4-5.

27   Bisley Shooting Ground lies within the National Rifle Association's (NRA) shooting centre at Bisley Camp in Surrey, thirty miles from London, England. It is a well-known shooting ground in Great Britain for rifle shooting, shotgun skeet, and so forth. From the website: "Enjoy the challenge of the highest clay pheasants in the country, of rising teal, bolting rabbits, driven grouse and of bursting partridges followed by the welcome of our comfortable Victorian clubhouse." http://www.bisleyshooting.co.uk/home.htm, accessed Sun 10 June 07, cjt.

28   Carol Huber, in *Gold Panning* (Chugach National Forest, 1997) writes: "Gold has a specific gravity of 19.3, meaning it is more than 19 times heavier than an equal volume of water." Quoted on http://hypertextbook.com/facts/2004/RuwanMeepagala.shtml; accessed Sat 3 November 07, cjt.

29   Sequence confirmed with Catherine Holmes, Wed 31 October 2007. cjt.

30   The boys would have clocked the distances on their bike trips in miles, not kilometres. Distances, with Victoria as base point, are taken from http://www.enorthernbc.com/Distance-Chart.asp?Community=Victoria; accessed Sun 10 June 2007, cjt.

31   Juno Beach website, http://www.junobeach.org/e/2/can-eve-eve-war-e.htm; accessed Thurs 2 August 2007, cjt.

32 The British Commonwealth Air Training Plan to train pilots and air crew in Canada was also inaugurated the same day, 17 December 1939. Veterans Affairs Canada website, http://www.vac-acc.gc.ca/content/history/secondwar/fact_sheets/pdf/wwchronol.pdf; accessed 2 August 2007, cjt.

33 His place and date of enlistment are given as Vancouver, 30 March 1942; http://www.airforce.ca/wwii/ALPHA-HO.HR.html; accessed Sun 3 June 2007, cjt.

34 Link Trainers were devised after 1929 by E.A. Link as a safe way to teach new pilots how to fly by Instrument Flight Rules. The machines were used in the Second World War and for decades afterward in military and civilian contexts. Link, a former organ builder, "used his knowledge of pumps, valves and bellows to create a flight simulator that responded to the pilot's controls and gave an accurate reading on the included instruments." See http://en.wikipedia.org/wiki/Link_Trainer; accessed 17 May 07, cjt.

35 Dates of his training progress are given in online air force records thus: trained at No. 4 ITS (graduated 7 November 1942), No. 5 EFTS (graduated 9 January 1943) and No. 3 SFTS (graduated 14 May 1943). Commissioned April 1943. http://www.airforce.ca/wwii/ALPHA-HO.HR.html; accessed Sun 3 June 2007, cjt.

36 Pip Holmes comments in WWII material from John Eggenberger interviews.

37 Website of the Canadian Aviation Museum, entry at de Havilland D.H.82C Tiger Moth, http://www.aviation.technomuses.ca/collections/artifacts/aircraft/deHavillandDH82CTigerMoth.shtml; accessed Sat 3 Nov 07, cjt.

38 Website of the Powerhouse Museum, Sydney, Australia>Gosport speaking tubes>Statement of significance, online at http://www.powerhousemuseum.com/collection/database/index.php?irn=213509&search=communication&images=&c=&s=1;accessed Sat 3 Nov 07, cjt.

39 Pip Holmes comments in his own WWII retrospective material and from John Eggenberger interviews.

40 Ibid.

41 Ibid.

42 Ibid.

43 The RCAF formed No. 6 Bomber Group on January 1, 1943, and No. 433 "Porcupine" Squadron began in September 1943, one of the last RCAF heavy bomber squadrons to be formed. It was the most northerly of all Bomber Command stations. Fifteen Canadian squadrons were formed within Bomber Command, "located two to a base on seven airfields in Yorkshire ... As the ground stalemate continued, Britain looked more and more, if reluctantly, to Bomber Command for its offensive weapon." J. Douglas Harvey, *Boys, Bombs and Brussels Sprouts: A Knees-Up, Wheels-Up Chronicle of WWII* (Toronto: McClelland and Stewart/ Goodread Biographies, Canadian Lives Series, 1983), p. 13.

44 J. Douglas Harvey, *Boys, Bombs and Brussels Sprouts*, p. 11.

45 "Holmes Ms. Airforce Section," notes from Prof. William Rodney, p. 2.

46 J. Douglas Harvey, *Boys, Bombs and Brussels Sprouts*, pp. 13-14.

47 Aircrew Association, Vancouver Island Branch, *Listen to Us: Aircrew Memories* (Victoria: Victoria Publishing Company/Morriss Printing Co. Ltd., 1997), p. 7.

48 Jim Hume, "Diary of an officer and a gentleman," *Times Colonist*, Sunday 11 March 2007, p. D-5.

49 David Lennam, "The war that should have ended all wars," *Victoria Regional News,* Wednesday 9

November 1994, p. R-5.

50   Tiger Force came into being in April 1945, and Canadian aircrew overseas were canvassed whether they'd be willing to volunteer for it. The war in Europe was ending, as of May 1945, and by June, 21 percent of those approached had agreed to serve against Japan. The idea was that training was to be carried out in Canada using Lancaster 7s and, ultimately, Lincolns, which were few in number and still in final development. Notes from Prof. William Rodney, 16 October 2007.

51   Note to Philip Holmes, Esq., 25 January 1946, from Vincent Massey, Canada House, Trafalgar Square, London. Massey was Canadian High Commissioner to London throughout the war; Flight Lieutenant Hart Massey served at RCAF Overseas Headquarters.

52   The initiating citation in full, forwarded by Tambling on 19 May 1945 when Pip had flown thirty of his thirty-three eventual sorties, is documented on the website of the Air Force Association of Canada, http://www.airforce.ca/wwii/ALPHA-HO.HR.html; accessed Sun 3 June 2007, cjt.

53   Conversation with Pip at home, 22 January 2007, cjt.

54   G.E. Mortimore, "Pemberton Holmes, 100 Years Later," *Victoria's Business Report*, Vol. 5, No. 10 (October 1987), p. 32.

55   "Pin to son," *Daily Colonist*, 8 January 1946, [n.p.]

56   Conversation with Pip, January 2007, cjt: "Funny how short a time it was since we were excited to see a plane! None visible at all, ever, in Victoria when I was a boy."

57   The 1887 office building burned, so a new building was built in 1910-11 on the same property, this time of reinforced concrete. First named the Pemberton Building, it is now called the Yarrow Building and is the home of the old Victoria firm McGill and Orme. PDPH speech, 11 February 1987, at the Pemberton Holmes Ltd. centenary reception, Oak Bay Marina Restaurant, Victoria, B.C.

58   "The First Sixty Years," commemorative pamphlet printed for Pemberton Holmes Ltd., 1947.

59   John Shaw/Historical Committee of the ACCVI, "From Inspiration to Achievement: the First Half-Century of the Associated Chambers of Commerce of Vancouver Island, 1918-1967" (Victoria: ACCVI, 1966), p. 11.

60   Highway 14 is commonly called the West Coast Road, though that extends beyond Sooke as well. "Highway 14 is one of the oldest byways in B.C., the first trail to connect Victoria's fort of 1843 with the pioneer settlements that sprang up along the Pacific coast to Sooke." Liz Bryan, "Roadtrip: a South Island fling," *Westworld*, Spring 2007, p. 23.

61   The square Norman tower and red roof are visible from the water, with a three-hundred-year-old bell installed in the belfry that had been bequeathed from Queenswood House in England. Ornate leaded windows, dormer windows in the vaulted ceiling and a central stained glass window light the dark brown wood interior. The pews, in old English design, face one another across the centre aisle rather than facing forward the altar. From the text accompanying a limited edition print, "Golden Cross"/Brentwood Anglican Chapel, by Aurelia Jacobsen, Aurelia Jacobsen Studio Gallery, Brentwood Bay, B.C.

62   Daphne Goode interview 11 February 1987 with PDPH, broadcast series *Movers and Shakers*, a Rogers Cable TV Victoria Production, director Chris Ash.

63   Grant S. Wittkamp, "After Canoe Arrival – Fort Victoria," *Business Examiner,* October 1984, pp. 4 5.

64   Geoffrey Castle, "Beneath the arches, links with a pioneer family," *Times Colonist*, 9 December 1984, p. 4: "Many Victoria buildings are associated with pioneer families. The substantial brick Pemberton Holmes building at the northwest corner of Government and Broughton streets is a fine example of this

and also of Thomas Hooper's architecture, with his characteristic arched window treatment dominating the upper storey. The different faces on the pier capitals may have been made to identify with the products of the first owner of the building, C.H. Vernon, who owned the British Columbia Pottery Company. After the Government Street building was constructed in 1899, several firms occupied the premises over the years, including Waitt and Company, the piano store that Herbert Kent managed; Erskine, Wall and Company, grocers; and the Victoria Book and Stationery Company. It was in 1947, following the sale of their Fort Street building to Norman Yarrow, that Pemberton's moved to Government Street."

65   John Shaw/Historical Committee of the ACCVI, "From Inspiration to Achievement: the First Half-Century of the Associated Chambers of Commerce of Vancouver Island, 1918-1967" (Victoria: ACCVI, 1966), p. 11.

66   PDPH conversation, John Eggenberger notes, p. 97.

67   PDPH recap of John Eggenberger material, 27 Apr 07, cjt.

68   Canadian Oxford Dictionary, 2001 edition, at "Lieutenant-Governor" (the representative of the Crown in a province; the acting or deputy governor of a state, province, etc., under a governor or Governor General). For edification of the heritage community in particular on a point of Canadian lore: Lieutenant-Governor is a hyphenated term, whereas Governor General (the representative of the Crown in a Commonwealth country that regards the Queen as head of state) is not. Their plurals follow the word "governor" in each case, not the modifier, hence plurals "Lieutenant-Governors" and "Governors General." Abbreviations, if used, are Lt.-Gov. and Gov. Gen.

69   Nootka-Nanaimo aeronautical map, PDPH personal files, 1951 file.

70   Conversation with PDPH, Friday 9 February 2007, cjt.

71   Photo caption, *Victoria Times*, 9 December 1950, [n.p.].

72   Material on coverage of the visit, from the B.C. provincial archives: "On the surface, Royal Visits appear to run seamlessly and with great decorum. Achieving this has always been a challenge, and the whole operation is very much like a complicated dance. All the participants must know their parts. Numerous pamphlets in the B.C. Archives library, and records from the Department of the Provincial Secretary, show how highly choreographed each event must be. For the visit of Princess Elizabeth and the Duke of Edinburgh in 1951, Premier Byron Johnson was issued a 13-page pamphlet (NW 971.V831e) printed by the Provincial Committee of Arrangements that outlined every moment of the three-day visit to Vancouver and Victoria which would require his participation."
http://www.bcarchives.gov.bc.ca/exhibits/jubilee/protocol.htm; accessed 10 Feb 07, cjt.

73   As suggested by the note from W.A.C. Bennett, Premier, Office of the Premier of B.C., 15 October 1952.

74   FIABCI Directory 2005-2006, p. 18. Further details are given on the FIABCI website. 2 June 1951: "Constitution of the International Federation of Property Managers with Germany, Austria, Belgium, France, and the United States ... Second International Congress of the Federation." Canada was part of it early on. "During this period [1951-58] the Netherlands, Switzerland, Spain, Italy, and Canada acceded to the Federation as full-fledged members." Organization's website,
http://www.fiabci.org/about-history.aspx; accessed 10 Feb 07 and 14 Nov 07, cjt.

75   P.D.P. Holmes, Keynote Address, Real Estate and Stock Institute of Australia, Fourth Australian Convention, Canberra, 6 October 1975, p. 1.

76   Excerpt from a letter sent by Alexis Noldé, Secretary General, FIABCI Paris, to Denis Hayes, Worldwatch Institute, Washington, D.C., 2 September 1976.

77   Letter from Cuthbert Holmes to "Darling Pip" from hospital, 17 July 1953.

78   Conversations with Pip, information from family photo albums and Catherine Holmes obituary notice, *Times Colonist*, Sunday 23 December 2007, p. B-9.

79   Speech to members of the Real Estate Institute of B.C., [1985], p. 2. From internal evidence, the speech was delivered in Vancouver, probably in 1985, the year before Expo '86.

80   B.C. Association of Real Estate Boards, First Annual One-Day Conference, Hotel Vancouver, "open to all licensed real estate sales agents in British Columbia." Postage for the conference program mailed from Vancouver to Pemberton Holmes office in Victoria cost two cents.

81   Speech by PDPH to members of the Real Estate Institute of B.C., [1985], p. 3. From internal references, including those on the upcoming Expo '86, it appears the speech was delivered in Vancouver in 1985.

82   PDPH speech to members of the Real Estate Institute of B.C., [1985], p. 4-5.

83   The Real Estate Agents Licensing Board of B.C. was later replaced by the Real Estate Council of B.C. The quoted comment about salesmen's calibre is from Pip's speech to the Real Estate Institute of B.C., [1985].

84   PDPH speech to members of the Real Estate Institute of B.C., [1985], p. 5.

85   Speech by Dermot Murphy to guests at the Pemberton Holmes Ltd. centenary, 11 February 1987.

86   Material from a PDPH retrospective speech delivered at the Union Club the night of the Canadian federal election, 21 Nov 1988, when Pip was welcoming Philip and Nancy White back to Canada after their years in Europe.

87   The 1958 act was superseded by the Real Estate Services Act, assented to 13 May 2004; http://www.qp.gov.bc.ca/statreg/stat/R/04042_01.htm; accessed Sun 14 Jan 07, cjt.

88   The REIBC Hall of Fame includes a number of those involved in this intense period of change; http://www.reibc.org/AboutUs.cfm?template=HallOfFame; accessed 10 Feb 07, cjt. Professor White's mandate at UBC as of 1958 included bringing in suitable undergraduate and graduate courses pertaining to the new legislation enacted that year. To start, he put in place the licensing program for sales agents, which consisted of five courses: (1) Licensing course and examinations for sales agents' licences; (2) Licensing course and examination for agents; (3) Diploma course and examination (three years), in the final year of which the student had to choose real estate as their option; (4) Diploma course and examination (three years), in the final year of which the student could choose appraisals as their option; (5) Diploma course and examination encompassing both real estate and appraisals.

89   From a PDPH retrospective speech delivered at the Union Club, Victoria, B.C., 21 Nov 1988,

90   Segment of a letter from PDPH dated 29 April 1958 to Colonel P.S. Cooper, commandant of Canadian Services College Royal Roads, asking him to address the Capital City Commercial Club at an upcoming lunch meeting in the Pacific Club, 625 Fort Street.

91   Segment of a letter from PDPH dated 8 January 1958 to the commanding officer of #2455 AC&W Squadron.

92   Letter in 1958 file [August 1958], with signature "Taylor."

93   Pip turned thirty-five in 1959. His own retrospective notes phrased it this way: "The fire was laid toward great and lasting change, and the faith of those who had gone before me was getting closer to being justified. This then was the fire which, when lit by the first spark, would provide the flame and guiding light toward the remainder of my professional ambitions—or far more correctly, my ambition for my

chosen vocation."

94   "Realtors Fight Ribbon Growth," [no byline], *Daily Colonist*, Victoria, B.C., 10 April 1959, p. 23.

95   From files and from discussion with Pip and Catherine Holmes at Jubilee Hospital, Royal 1, Tues 10 Jan 07. cjt.

96   Obituary for Sophia Theresa Deane-Drummond, *Daily Colonist*, 1 November 1959, [n.p.]

97   *Little Boy Blue*, Sophie Pemberton's award-winning 1897 portrait of a boy, is on permanent display at the Art Gallery of Greater Victoria, Victoria, B.C. Website of the Art Gallery of Greater Victoria, entry for Sophie Pemberton: http://www.aggv.bc.ca/mansion-madness/artist_s_pemberton.html;accessed Sat 25 Aug 07, cjt.

98   His 5BX plan booklet was still in Pip's files. When asked, he said he knew the regime and worked his way through the levels, then kept it up. http://www.nfb.ca/collection/films/fiche/?id=13996; accessed 21 January 07, cjt. Also, http://archives.cbc.ca/IDC-1-41-615-3304/sports/fitness/clip2; accessed 21 January 07, cjt.

99   Grant S. Wittkamp, "After Canoe Arrival – Fort Victoria," *Business Examiner*, October 1984, p. 5.

100   Phone conversation with Dermot Murphy, Mon 19 February 2007, cjt.

101   "Realtors Given Unique Gavel," *Penticton Herald*, Friday 3 June 1960, p. 1.

102   Item in CAREB delegates' newsletter, 1964 Montreal meeting, Queen Elizabeth Hotel, [n.d.].

103   Theresa Jane Pemberton was part of the congregation that followed Rev. Cridge when he left his post as Dean of Christ Church Cathedral and walked to the site where they would establish the Reformed Episcopal Church of Our Lord in Victoria. The church, now a national historic site, has been given "a thorough and sympathetic renovation" and is "an important component of social and ecclesiastical heritage." See its own website at http://www.churchofourlord.org/history.htm; accessed 26 April 2007, cjt.

104   Eulogy text for Pip, delivered by Dermot Murphy at Christ Church Cathedral, Victoria, B.C., 29 May 2007.

105   William Miller, "Century of Public Service for Pemberton, Holmes," *Times Colonist*, 7 February 1987, B-1.

106   G.E. Mortimore, "Pemberton Holmes, 100 Years Later," *Victoria's Business Report*, Vol. 5, No. 10 (October 1987), p. 32 ff.

107   Newsletter of the Canadian Chapter/International Real Estate Federation, Vol. 2, No. 5 (September/October 1974), p. 1.

108   Note from Cuthbert Holmes to Pip Holmes, 13 April 1965.

109   Speech text, PDPH addressing the FIABCI congress in Tokyo, 1979, paraphrased and quoted.

110   In its earlier years, the name changed slightly several times. FIABCI was founded in Brussels as the Fédération Internationale des Administrateurs de Bien-Conseils Immobiliers and was known after 1964 by a shorter form of the name, the Fédération Internationale de Professions Immobiliers, and in English as the International Real Estate Federation. Through the years, however, it has also been referred to in various languages by its original acronym, FIABCI.

111   Excerpt from a letter from Alexis Noldé, Secretary General, FIABCI Paris, to Denis Hayes of the Worldwatch Institute, Washington, D.C., 2 September 1976. Hayes was going to be delivering a paper at the 1977 Congress, and Noldé was providing background on the organization's founding, history and scope.

112   List adapted from "Who are the members?" section, *FIABCI Directory 2005-06*, p. 18.

113   Item from filed clipping [no headline or byline available], *The Victorian,* Friday 23 May 1975, [n.p.].; in PDPH personal file for 1975.

114   Note from Cuthbert Holmes to Pip Holmes, 7 November 1965.

115   Note from Cuthbert Holmes to Catherine Holmes, November 1965.

116   Text of PDPH speech to members of the Canadian Association of Real Estate Boards (CAREB), 1966 annual meeting, Saskatoon, Saskatchewan.

117   Preamble to the Code of Ethics of the professional division, Real Estate Institute of British Columbia, adopted from NAREB in the U.S.A. Known after 1916 as the National Association of Real Estate Boards and later called the National Association of Realtors, NAREB is the Americans' nationwide real estate association. The quote opens the preamble to their Code of Ethics and Standards of Practice. See http://www.realtor.org/mempolweb.nsf/pages/code?opendocument; accessed 4 August 2007, cjt.

118   PDPH speech to the delegates, 1966 CAREB annual meeting, Saskatoon, Saskatchewan.

119   Letter from Cuthbert Holmes to Philip Holmes, 21 October 1966.

120   The invitation from Lt.-Gov. Pearkes and Mrs. Pearkes specified "Costume of 100 years ago or earlier." The Centennial Ball on 22 April 1966 was "commemorating the Union of the Crown Colonies of Vancouver Island and British Columbia." Text of Government House invitation and dance card, PDPH 1966 file. The "Gonzales" personna he chose had personal and geographical significance for Pip. According Freeman Tovell's extensive research on the life and times of Juan Francisco de la Bodega y Quadra, repeated explorations along the west coast to Alaska, with charting and naming of many coastal features, had been undertaken by the Spanish naval contingent based at San Blas, Mexico, in the late 1700s. The B.C. gazetteer confirms this legacy of Spanish names.

121   Tony Dickason, article on Cuthbert Holmes Park, *The Oak Bay Star,* 5 February 1975, p. 8.

122   Grant S. Whittkamp, "After Canoe Arrival – Fort Victoria," *Business Examiner,* October 1984, pp. 4-5.

123   Entry on Cuthbert Holmes Park, http://www.gov.saanich.bc.ca/resident/parks/pdfs/cuthbertholmes.pdf; accessed 15 June 07, cjt.

124   Speech to the Windsor Real Estate Board, 1968, "Challenge of Change," pp. 3-5.

125   Excerpt from PDPH handwritten notes, 12 January 2006, "My Life in the Vocation of Real Estate."

126   Newsletter of the Canadian Chapter/International Real Estate Federation, Vol. 2, No. 5 (September/October 1974), p. 1.

127   Chamber president, 1945 to 1948.

128   Carla Wilson, "Movers and shakers," *Times Colonist,* Saturday 17 June 2006, p. D-11.

129   "Keys to Success: Education and Training—Chamber of Commerce Week, February 19-23: leadership in action," *Times Colonist,* Monday 19 Feb 2007, pp. B-4, B-5.

130   Carla Wilson, "Movers and shakers," *Times Colonist,* Saturday 17 June 2006, p. D-11.

131   "President Speaks Out," *Impact: Magazine of the Greater Victoria Chamber of Commerce,* June 1970, [n.p.].

132   *Victoria Times,* Monday 19 April 1971, [n.p.]

133   Maury Gwynne column, "The Third Page," *The Victorian,* p. 3.

134   Ibid.

135   Letter dated 14 July 1972 from D.A.L. Tait, President, British Columbia Chamber of Commerce, to Philip Holmes regarding his appointment and responsibilities.

136   Letter dated May 1973 from Pip Holmes to Frank Beinder, in PDPH file for 1973.

137   Year-date confirmed with the Brentwood College School website, http://www.brentwood.bc.ca/about/history.php; accessed Sunday 4 Feb 07, cjt.

138   Al Forrest, "Pip Holmes scales down his territory—but not his enthusiasm," *B.C. Business*, April 1979, [n.p.]

139   Letter dated 28 December 1972, from Victoria Mayor Peter Pollen to Philip Holmes: "It would give me great pleasure to present this certificate to you personally at the Inaugural Meeting of City Council at 2 p.m. on Monday, January 8th, 1973 ... " In December 1996, Victoria city council resolved that Pip be nominated to serve on its newly created Honorary Citizens Committee to develop a process and rationale for selecting and recommending citizens to receive this recognition. Letter to Mr. Holmes from Robert Woodland, Manager, Legislative Services, City of Victoria, dated 8 August 1997.

140   Letter dated 6 February 1973 from Pip Holmes to B.E. Willoughby, Gibson Willoughby Ltd., Toronto.

141   Pip considered Vancouver Island a beautiful natural precinct of its own and privately felt very strongly that the ACCVI was valuable and should have continued in existence. "It was a great shame this association [ACCVI] later folded, because there was much good that could have come from it for Vancouver Island in future years." It lost momentum, however, and other factors drew control of the Island's future into other spheres. Conversation with Pip, 15 December 2006, cjt.

142   Interview with P.D.P. Holmes, *Victoria Times,* Tuesday 20 March 73, p. 16.

143   From Pip's files, the meeting notes for his own comments plus his speech notes, "A Blueprint for Vancouver Island," ACCVI papers, Monday 19 March 1973.

144   Ibid.

145   Newsletter of the Canadian Real Estate Association/CREA, September-October 1974, p. 6.

146   PDPH notes, May 1973, FIABCI World Congress, Sydney, Australia, p. 5.

147   Ibid.

148   Letter dated 20 December 1973 from Pip Holmes to Roderick Fraser, Director of the Department of Travel Industry, British Columbia Government, Regent Street, London, England.

149   *Real Estate Institute of British Columbia Education Report,* January-December 1973, pp. 1-4.

150   Note dated 12 March 1973 from Pip Holmes to Pemberton Holmes staff concerning Michael Page, on company letterhead still citing 1002 Government Street.

151   Minutes of a Meeting of the Directors, FIABCI Canada, Toronto, Wednesday 14 February 1973, p. 10.

152   The organization was formally called the Canadian Chapter/International Real Estate Federation (IREF) until 1974, when in keeping with a request from the FIABCI Executive and with due approvals by Chapter Directors and CREA Directors, the IREF/Canada name was changed to FIABCI Canada. That had commonly been used as an informal title before the formal change. Newsletter of the Canadian Chapter/International Real Estate Federation, Vol. 2, No. 5 (September/October 1974), p. 2.

153   Minutes of a Meeting of the Directors, FIABCI Canada, Toronto, Wednesday 14 February 1973, p. 11.

154   Press release from FIABCI headquarters, Paris, May 1975.

155   Personal conversation 13 February 2007 with Catherine Holmes. cjt.

156   *FIABCI Directory 2005-06* lists the sequence of FIABCI World Presidents, pp. 35-36.

157   Newsletter of the Canadian Chapter/International Real Estate Federation, Vol. 2, No. 5 (September/October 1974), p. 8.

158   Pip "was elected Chairman of the Canadian Chapter/IREF (FIABCI) during the Annual CREA Conference in Halifax in September [1974]. He assumed office November 1, 1974." Newsletter of the Canadian Chapter, International Real Estate Federation, Vol. 2, No. 5 (September/October 1974), p. 1.

159   NWL Financial Inc. is a wholly owned subsidiary of National Western Life Insurance Co.

160   Tony Dickason interview with Pip Holmes, *The Oak Bay Star*, 5 February 1975, p. 3.

161   Ibid., p. 8. He might have added: "And hire someone like Mrs. Larsen." She was the Holmes's excellent housekeeper for twenty-six years.

162   Section quotes are from "Real estate is economic key says leading Canadian realtor," *Business Life in Western Canada*, January-February 1975, p. 21.

163   Ibid.

164   Sven Menne, "Norwegian Real Estate School," research paper and resolutions prepared for the Association of Norwegian Real Estate Brokers, Spring 1975.

165   FIABCI press release, Paris office, 23 May 1975.

166   FIABCI Congress reports, 18-23 May 1975. Excerpts from *FIABCI Reporter*, Vol. 26, No. 3 (July 1975), pp. 22-23.

167   FIABCI press release, Paris office, 23 May 1975.

168   Lorne Nicholson was B.C. Minister of Housing in 1975. UBC library archives, Akrigg collection. cjt.

169   *CREA Reporter*, Vol. 5, No. 7 (July 1975), p. 1.

170   *FIABCI Reporter*, Vol. 26, No. 3 (July 1975), p. 10.

171   "Zambia seizes land, theatres," [no byline], Associated Press wire service, *Daily Colonist*, 1 July 1975, [n.p.].

172   Ibid.

173   Letter dated 3 September 1975 from Catherine Holmes to a friend; letter quoted with permission.

174   Ibid.

175   CAH's blue-notepaper list in the 1975 file gives the outline of their travels for 1975 and 1976, but not for the first half of 1977.

176   Denmark, 10-12 December 1975. Itinerary outlined in sequential brief articles under the headline "World President visits member countries," *FIABCI Reporter*, May 1976, pp. 20-21.

177   Conversation Mon 26 Feb 07 with Pip and Catherine Holmes, cjt.

178   Mark Ricketts, "Governments don't understand us," feature profile, "In Person," *The Financial Post*, 6 September 1975, p. 9.

179   Keynote Address, 6 October 1975, Fourth Australian Convention, Real Estate and Stock Institute of

Australia, Canberra, p. 1.

180   Ibid., p. 2.

181   "FIABCI Exchange Student Reports," [no byline], *Vancouver Realtor*, April 1976, p. 10.

182   Excerpt from transcript of PDPH handwritten notes, 12 January 2006, "My Life in the Vocation of Real
       Estate."

183   A large photo of Señora de Holmes y Philip Holmes appeared in the Mexico City newspaper *El Universal*,
       19 de Marzo de 1976, p. 22.

184   "Hold for arrival in Chicago," 19 March 1976 telex from Jack Pontius reached P.D.P. Holmes evening of
       Sunday 4 April 76.

185   Material quoted and paraphrased from FIABCI press release, American Chapter, Monday 24 May 1975,
       11:50 a.m. release in sequence of press releases issued that day, pp. 1-2.

186   Press release from FIABCI out of Vancouver, B.C., "More co-operation urged to solve world's growing
       housing problems," 1 June 1976, p. 1.

187   The fifteen-page brief from the FIABCI organization for the UN Conference on Human Settlements was
       formally titled "The Essential Role of Real Estate Professionals in the Solution of Human Settlements
       Problems." A copy of it is in PDPH file for 1976 attached to the document of signatures of heads of all
       FIABCI national chapters.

188   FIABCI brief to the UN Conference on Human Settlements, "The Essential Role of Real Estate
       Professionals in the Solution of Human Settlements Problems." Quote appears under the heading "Values
       of Adequate Housing," p. 9.

189   Text of the plaque, transcribed 14 Sept 07, cjt: "American Chapter, International Real Estate
       Federation, an institute of the National Association of Realtors, in grateful appreciation to Philip P.D.
       Holmes, Worldwide President, International Real Estate Federation, and his wife Catherine, for their
       outstanding contributions in serving the real estate professions and the public among the free nations
       of the world ... and for his devoted leadership as Presiding Officer of the XXVII World Congress,
       where the profound knowledge of the representatives from more than thirty-five free nations of the
       world rededicated their support for worldwide freedom through their individual nations and as FIABCI
       members to the United Nations. Presented this day of May 1976, San Francisco, California." It is signed
       (in brass) by W. Douglas Morrison, president, FIABCI/American Chapter; John Cotton, chairman,
       XXVII FIABCI Congress; Philip C. Smaby, president, National Association of Realtors; and H. Jackson
       Pontius, executive vice-president, National Association of Realtors.

190   Memo dated 2 July 1976 from Alexis Noldé to Philip Holmes.

191   FIABCI information on the Global Housing Foundation: "FIABCI enjoys 'Special Consultative' status
       at the United Nations, in several forms ... FIABCI advises the United Nations on various aspects
       regarding property activities. The United Nations and above all ECOSOC, its Economic and Social
       Council, are currently working on a number of property issues. Policy: Fiabci's role is to establish and
       develop policy concerning property matters and pass this information on to the United Nations. This
       has been especially the case with regard to the thorny problem of the homeless or that of the property
       business and the environment. Charity Initiatives: Fiabci and the UN have also instigated a number of
       charity property initiatives. One of these programmes was the creation of the Global Housing Foundation
       and the construction of dozens of houses in Nicaragua, in collaboration with the United Nations. René
       Frank, Fiabci honorary deputy president who started this programme, succeeded in ensuring its future
       development. For that reason, he was awarded the UN-Habitat trophy in 2003. Sustainable Development

is a term that incorporates the following notions: problem of the homeless; property rights; environment; codes of ethics." FIABCI website, www. fiabci.org > FIABCI and International Organizations > FIABCI and the UN > Global Housing Foundation; accessed Sat 17 March 2007, cjt.

192 Note dated 13 Aug 76 from Baïa Noldé to Catherine Holmes at FIABCI offices in Paris: "Noel Taylor has sent us a very big picture of Pip on the horse at the rodeo, and I will have it framed for the office."

193 Letter dated 9 August 76 from Catherine Holmes to Baïa Noldé.

194 Letter dated 2 September 1976 from Alexis Noldé to Denis Hayes, Worldwatch Institute, Washington, D.C.

195 T.F. Molesworth, Information Program, APREF Third Congress, 17-20 October 1976, p. 2.

196 Ibid.

197 Information from *FIABCI Reporter*, May 1976, p. 24.

198 Information Program, APREF Third Congress, 17-20 October 1976, pp. 12-13.

199 Letter dated 8 September 1976 to Eileen Goulet, Secretary to Mr. P.D.P. Holmes, from E.M. Harcourt, Congress Chairman, Third Congress of the Asia Pacific Real Estate Federation.

200 *FIABCI Reporter*, Vol. 28, No. 1 (March 1977), p. 5.

201 This from Catherine Holmes in conversation, 20 March 2007. cjt.

202 The range of activities of Mitsui was then and is still immense. In the 1970s, when Pip was there as head of FIABCI, Mitsui was finding that the natural gas projects it had been promoting before the decade's worldwide oil shocks "increased in importance as alternative energy sources and for the decentralization of supply routes." Website of Mitsui & Co., Ltd., www.mitsui.co.jp/en; accessed 11 Nov 07, cjt.

203 Mr. Watanabe is identified in a May 1975 FIABCI press release as "Mr. Takejiro Watanabe, Japan: Chairman Emeritus, Mitsubishi Estate Co. Ltd.; Chairman, Mitsubishi Development Co. Ltd.; President, Keiyo Land Development Co. Ltd.; President, Tokyo Kotsu Building Co. Ltd.; President, FIABCI-Japan; FIABCI Medal of Honour, 1968."

204 Conversation with Catherine Holmes, March 2007. cjt.

205 Excerpt from a letter from Diana Smith, Wed 6 Oct 1976.

206 Conversation with Catherine Holmes, March 2007. cjt.

207 "Tentative December '76 travel schedule" document set up by Alexis Noldé, secretary-general of FIABCI, Paris office, and relayed to Pip.

208 Executive minutes 30 Nov 76, point (1), from PDPH 1976 file.

209 *FIABCI Reporter*, Vol. 28, No. 2 (June 1977), p. 5. Caption below half-page photo of the pair.

210 Conversation with Pip Holmes, Mon 26 Feb 07. cjt.

211 Various sources, including
http://www.st-lazarus.net/world/history.htm; also,
http://www.st-lazarus.net/world/arms.htm; both sites accessed Mon 26 Feb 07, cjt.

212 Letter from Pip's daughter Diana, Wed 6 Oct 1976. This is another excerpt of the letter that reached him in Thailand with concern about the coup.

213 Letter dated 14 Jan 77 from Pip Holmes, President, to Michael Page, Manager, Pemberton Holmes Ltd.

214   Reply letter dated 21 January 1977 from M.H.E. Page to P.D.P. Holmes; also, conversation with Catherine Holmes, 19 June 2007. cjt.

215   Letter dated Fri 11 March 1977, signed "Philip Holmes, 488 Beach Drive," *Victoria Times*, p. 2. A shorter version of the same letter was carried in *The Victorian,* Wednesday 9 March 1977, as its Letter of the Day.

216   Letter from the office of Hon. James A. Neilsen, B.C. Minister of Environment, 26 April 1977; letter in PDPH 1977 file.

217   *Victoria Real Estate*, 8 April 1977, clipping of photo and ID caption, front page of second section.

218   *Daily Colonist*, 13 April 1977, [n.p.]; clipping in PDPH 1977 file.

219   *Uusi Suomi* (Helsinki), 21 May 1977, p. 21.

220   Briefing notes from file, FIABCI-Finland administrative staff to Pip Holmes, May 1977.

221   Letter from Philip D.P. Holmes to E.M. Harcourt, 18 April 1977.

222   Meeting memo flagged, scarlet subfolder, 23-25 Sept 75, PDPH 1977 file.

223   "Congress Notebook," *Estates Times*, No. 401 (10 June 1977), p. 1 ff.

224   J.T. Blair Jackson,"Retiring FIABCI World President urges partnership of business, government to solve mounting problems," *CREA Reporter*, Vol. 7, No. 7 (July 1977), pp. 1-3.

225   PDPH overview speech to FIABCI World Congress, 1979, Japan.

226   Pip's notes attached to the text of his own FIABCI congress address, PDPH 1977 file.

227   Excerpts from "Congress Notebook," *Estates Times*, No. 401 (10 June 1977), p. 10.

228   Woody Weight's term started 11 June 1977. The next FIABCI World President from Canada would be Albert Fish in 1987.

229   *FIABCI Reporter*, Vol. 28, No. 2 (June 1977), p. 4.

230   Letters on PDPH two-year presidency, including Ciputra note, in subfile within PDPH 1977 year-file.

231   Letter dated 25 July 77 from Pip Holmes to R.W. Frewin, c/o Chambers & Frewin, Hornsby, NSW, Australia.

232   Letter to Philip Holmes from Tadeo Hashiba, Auditor, Mitubishi Estate Company Ltd., Tokyo., and Secretary-General of the FIABCI-Pacific Committee, 13 July 1977.

233   Letter dated 15 August 1977 to Mr. and Mrs. Holmes from Tadeo Hashiba.

234   United Nations Economic Commission for Europe – Seminar on the Impact of Energy Considerations on the Planning and Development of Human Settlements, Ottawa, 3-14 October 1977. The Canadian Secretariat of the Ministry of State Urban Affairs Canada was co-organizer with the Environment and Human Settlement Division of the Economic Commission for Europe in Geneva.

235   Conversation with Pip, Friday 15 December 2006, on the design-language components of architect Christopher Alexander, published in 1975 as *A Pattern Language* and *A Timeless Way of Building*. cjt.

236   Letter from Jean Bailly to Pip Holmes, 30 May 1978.

237   PDPH speech text, delivered at BCREA annual convention, Vancouver, May 1978.

238   Letter dated Friday 2 June 1978 to PDPH from Dennis O'Leary, President, B.C. Real Estate Association.

239 Equipment list from the conference program, FIABCI World Congress, Hamburg, 3-9 June 1978.

240 Letter dated 27 June 1978 to the BCREA, to the attention of Mr. Dennis O'Leary, from Pip Holmes.

241 FIABCI – UECL meeting, Brussels, 24 July 78; translation of memo dated 24 July 1978, titled "FIABCI-UECL Contact Meeting, p. 2.

242 UIPFB congress, Torremolinos, Spain, 25-27 September 1978; the Union Internationale de la Propriété Foncière Batie (International Union for Built Real Estate Property) is currently named Union International de la Propriété Immobilière (U.I.P.I.) or, in English, International Union of Property Owners; name and statutes approved in the Congress of Torremolinos, Spain, 29 September 1978; http://www.confedilizia.eu/UIPIdxEN.htm; accessed 24 June 07, cjt.

243 Information but not wording from article, "Directors royally feted during Victoria meetings," *CREA Reporter*, Vol. 8, No. 9 (September 1978), p. 3.

244 *The Valley Interim*, Vol. 1, No. 1 (March/April 1979), p. 2.

245 *Daily Colonist*, Wed 28 June 1978, p. 29.

246 *Research Report and First-Phase Overview, Victoria Civic Conference Facility,* November 1978 report by Ken Stratford, Stratford Discovery Associates Ltd.

247 Ibid., p. 1.

248 The Edmonton situation: "By the summer of 1978, after seven years' debate and with funding finally in place from mainly municipal sources, plus some provincial money and a 1 percent tax levy on local businesses, Edmonton gave approval in principle to a new downtown convention centre." From "The Convention Centre Controversy," *Business Life*, September 1978, pp. 27-28.

249 Essential financial support was being provided by the business tax of the City of Calgary. "1977 Annual Report of the Affairs of the Calgary Convention Centre," Appendix D, *Research Report and First-Phase Overview, Victoria Civic Conference Facility*, Stratford Discovery Associates, November 1978.

250 The Hon. Grace McCarthy, B.C. Provincial Secretary and responsible for the travel industry at the time, was proposing the location be the pier at the foot of Burrard Street, Vancouver. She also set up a funding formula for federal, provincial and municipal participation in the project. The National Harbours Board had picked the same pier site in an earlier study, and the general manager of the Port of Vancouver was "wholly supportive of the concept," calling it "a crucial element" in the central waterfront. Vancouver mayor Jack Volrich, regarding this as a very high priority, suggested the underlying thinking of ongoing discussions: "Vancouver has a vital role to play as Canada's leading sea port on the Pacific Rim." Papers in PDPH 1979 file.

251 UN Committee on Human Settlements, Nairobi, Kenya, 26 March-8 April 1979.

252 "Minister Sumarlin: Business Entrepreneurs Should Solve Employee Housing Problem," [bylined Our Reporter], *Indonesia Times*, Vol. VI, No. 21 (26 May 1979), p. 1.

253 "The new federation obtained consultative status on the United Nations Economic and Social Council" as of 21 July 1954: FIABCI website, www. fiabci.org > Who We Are > FIABCI history, at 1954; also FIABCI and International Organizations > FIABCI and the UN, p. 5; accessed Sat 17 March 2007, cjt.

254 FIABCI website, www. fiabci.org > FIABCI and International Organizations > FIABCI and the UN > Global Housing Foundation; accessed Sat 17 March 2007, cjt.

255 "Global Housing Foundation was launched in 1999 when its founder, René Frank, took up a challenge from the United Nations Commission on Human Settlements (UNCHS) as to why the private real estate

industry did not do more to help solve housing crises around the world. GHF was established as an independent, U.S.-based not-for-profit organization that leverages the expertise and resources of the private real estate community to build new affordable housing in inner-city slums around the world." Global Housing Foundation website, http://www.globalhousingfoundation.org/about_us_history.html; accessed 20 June 2007, cjt.

256   "René Frank, Fiabci honorary deputy president who started this programme, succeeded in ensuring its future development. For that reason, he was awarded the UN-Habitat trophy in 2003." FIABCI website, www. fiabci.org; accessed Sat 17 March 2007, cjt:

257   FIABCI website, www. fiabci.org, and FIABCI Directory 2005-2006.

258   Excerpt from transcript of PDPH handwritten notes, 12 Jan 2006, "My Life in the Vocation of Real Estate."

259   Conference papers, FIABCI 1979 Congress, Tokyo, in *FIABCI and Myself,* pp. 17-19.

260   "Influential Victorians? Depends on definition," Editor's Notebook/To the Point, *Victoria Times,* 3 March 1979, [n.p.]

261   Al Forrest, "Pip Holmes scales down his territory—but not his enthusiasm," *B.C. Business,* April 1979 [n.p.]

262   "Profile: Pip Holmes is Victoria," *Business Life,* December 1979, p. 36.

263   Ibid.

264   The song from World War One, *How 'Ya Gonna Keep 'Em Down on the Farm? (After They've Seen Paree),* was written by Joe Young and Sam M. Lewis with music by Walter Donaldson. It became a great popular success during and after 1918 and was performed by a large number of artists. The title became a well-known expression.

265   "Reporters Notebook," *Daily Colonist,* 4 August 1980, [n.p.]

266   *Daily Colonist,* 24 November 1979, p. 7.

267   "Profile: Pip Holmes is Victoria," *Business Life,* December 1979, p. 36.

268   General entry online about the *Times Colonist,* http://en.wikipedia.org/wiki/Victoria_Times-Colonist; accessed Sat 27 Jan 07, cjt.

269   "Holmes joins planners," *Daily Colonist,* 20 January 1980, p. 38.

270   General information on the Provincial Capital Commission/PCC from PDPH files and from sections of its website: http://www.bcpcc.com/board/governance.htm; accessed 1 March 2007, cjt.

271   Ibid.

272   Conversation with Catherine Holmes about Pip's involvement in various PCC projects, 1 Mar 07, cjt.

273   Excerpt from PCC funding list, covering 1980-84; at website http://www.bcpcc.com/initiatives/history_80.htm; accessed 1 March 2007, cjt.

274   Conversation with Pip and Catherine Holmes, 13 Feb 07, cjt.

275   Letter dated 25 July 1980 to Pip and Catherine Holmes from Mrs. Yuriko Toike of Tokyo, with regards from her husband and herself.

276   Cantell by 1981 was British Columbia's Assistant Deputy Minister of Consumer and Corporate Affairs. Cantell grew up in New Westminster, a place he loved, enlisted in the RCAF, graduated from UBC's

Law School as a member of its first class and practiced law on the mainland before moving to Victoria in 1951. He was Director of Policy and Planning in the Ministry of Corporate Affairs and then Deputy Superintendent of Brokers, eventually retiring as Superintendent of Insurance and Real Estate. Having served his country and his province, he passed away 20 October 2007. *B.C. Real Estate Association Bulletin*, Vol. 4, No. 2 (July 1981), p. 9; and obituary notice, Edward Thomas Cantell, Q.C., *Times Colonist,* 26 October 2007, p. B-11.

277   MLAs on 23 June 1981 were in second reading debate on the principles of Bill 23.

278   British Columbia *Hansard*, Tuesday 23 June 1981, Morning Sitting, pp. 6341-6343, www.leg.bc.ca/ hansard/32nd3rd/32p_03s_810623a.htm; accessed Sat 17 March 2007, cjt.

279   Ibid., pp. 6345-6346.

280   Ibid.

281   "Philip (Pip) Holmes of Victoria, a CREA past president and immediate past president of the FIABCI organization, has been appointed chairman of the 1982 Toronto Congress." From "CREA board of directors previews new structure, operations program," *CREA Reporter,* Vol. 8, No. 9 (September 1978), p. 3.

282   Website of the Union of British Columbia Municipalities/UBCM, http://www.civicnet.bc.ca/siteengine/activepage.asp?PageID=240&bhcp=1; accessed 2155 hrs Thurs 8 Mar 2007, cjt.

283   G.E. Mortimore, "Pemberton Holmes, 100 Years Later," *Victoria's Business Report*, Vol. 5, No. 10 (October 1987), p. 32.

284   Ibid.

285   The analysis was written in mid-1984. Grant S. Wittkamp, "After canoe arrival – Fort Victoria," *Business Examiner,* October 1984, p. 5.

286   *B.C. Real Estate Association Bulletin*, Vol. 4, No. 2 (July 1981), p. 10.

287   FIABCI Congress, 6-12 June 1982, Toronto. Delegates from forty countries were lodged in the Royal York Hotel and Harbour Castle Hotel. CREA staff and members produced a substantial real estate exhibit and a repeat of the successful international marketplace sessions, sponsored luncheons and delegate gifts and provided publicity, promotion and personal welcomes on pre- and post-conference tours. PDPH notes for speech to CREA chapter members, July 1981.

288   Letter dated 30 April 1982 to Pip Holmes at FIABCI-Canada, from Gustav J. Saedberg, Kristiansand, Sweden.

289   Talking with Pip Holmes Mon 26 Feb 2007, asking him for information from his own perspective. cjt. Also, information from website http://www.commissionaires.ca; accessed 2120 hrs Mon 26 Feb 07, cjt.

290   "Holmes longs to put nature on his canvas," [no byline], *Times-Colonist*, 22 October 1982, p. B-2.

291   Ibid.

292   Ibid.

293   "A more spectacular fire was reported from fire box 23 at 3:10 a.m. on 23 March 1909, when the two-year-old premises of Pemberton & Son, also housing the Pacific Club, was razed to the ground. To dash any renewed hopes of straightening Broad Street, Fred Pemberton promised a bigger and finer building would be built immediately in its place—a building with elevators!" Text of PDPH speech, dated 11 Oct 1983, at event commemorating "90 years' interrelationship of good faith between the public who insure, the insurer who

accepts that risk … and we the agents who represent the interests of both." Sun Insurance was represented by a Mr. Evans at the event, and Pemberton Holmes Ltd. by its insurance manager, Roy Barras.

294   Beaumont Marine Park, not yet created in 1983, is not mentioned; the entry had only "an anchorage." 2 July 07, cjt.

295   Pip's comments in conversation, 8 Feb 07, cjt.

296   Pip's comments in conversation, 8 Feb 07. cjt.

297   See website of the Ciputra Group: www.ciputra.com

298   Pip's coments in conversation, 8 Feb 07. cjt.

299   Conversation with Pip and Catherine; http://whc.unesco.org/en/list/592; PBS Specials, "Borobudur," http://www.pbs.org/treasuresoftheworld/a_nav/boro_nav/main_borofrm.html; Borobudur entry, http://en.wikipedia.org/wiki/Borobudur; accessed 1455 hrs Mon 19 March 2007, cjt.

300   Letter dated 14 July 1983 to Pip and Catherine Holmes from Lennart and Puck Ljungquist.

301   Letter dated 12 Dec 1983 to Pip and Catherine Holmes from Woody and Marg Weight.

302   "Holmes longs to put nature on his canvas," [no byline], *Times-Colonist*, 22 October 1982, p. B-2.

303   Mr. Arvid Chalmers said he believes the Salt Spring office was opened in 1974 with Gus Bolton as manager. Next was Dale Neilson as manager until 1982, when Chalmers took over as manager until buying out the office in 1989. E-mail to Catherine Holmes from Nicole Lee, office manager, Pemberton Holmes Ltd. Cloverdale, Wednesday 31 October 2007; printout to Camilla Turner 2 November 2007.

304   Grant S. Wittkamp, "After canoe arrival – Fort Victoria," *Business Examiner*, October 1984, p. 5.

305   Letter from Pip Holmes to Mr. and Mrs. Nicholas Abkhazi, dated April 5, 1984. The property on Fairfield Road years later became a popular public garden, Abkhazi Gardens, owned in trust by TLC The Land Conservancy.

306   Letter dated 5 June 1984 to Pip Holmes from Ralph Pritchard.

307   Letter dated 28 Sept 84 to Pip Holmes from D.G. Hudson, Parade Coordinator, Royal Canadian Air Force Association, No. 800 (Pacific) Wing, re Battle of Britain Parade, 16 September 1984.

308   Letter dd 12 October 84 to Pip Holmes from Dean Daniels, executive vice-president, Spokane Board of Realtors. The Mr. Wilson he refers to was Lord (Harold) Wilson, British Prime Minister 1964-70 and 1974-76. http://www.number10.gov.uk/output/Page129.asp; accessed 6 August 07, cjt.

309   Pip's speech notes, titled "C of C," handwritten, 24 October 84. PDPH 1984 file.

310   "Holmes resigns posts," *Times-Colonist*, Wed 21 November 1984, [n.p.]

311   Photo and letter in PDPH 1984 file.

312   Letter dated 22 Nov 1984 to Pip Holmes from Howard E. Petch.

313   Letter dated 20 Nov 1984 to Pip Holmes from Dr. Alex McAuley, Department of Chemistry, University of Victoria.

314   Letter [n.d.] to Pip Holmes from Patrick L. McGeer, Minister, Ministry of Universities, Science and Communications, Province of British Columbia.

315   Letter dated 26 November 1984 to Mr. Philip D.P. Holmes from Hon. W.R. Bennett, Premier, British

Columbia.

316   Conversation with Pip and Catherine, 10 January 2007, cjt.

317   Ottawa's Buzz Bourdon, CD, advises there is no such medal as "the Canadian decoration" but that the reference is probably to the Canadian Forces Decoration awarded for twelve years' service. "A common mistake made by many," he adds. Mr. Bourdon read the two wartime chapters in manuscript form. E-mail from Buzz Bourdon to Camilla Turner 1531 hrs Thursday 5 July 2007.

318   Computer printout banner plus flip-chart portrait, PDPH year-file, 1985.

319   Display ad with the headline "Congratulations, Pip!" placed by Pemberton Holmes Ltd., *Times Colonist*, Friday 1 November 1985, p. A-12.

320   Letter to Pip Holmes from B.C. Premier Bill Bennett, 1 November 1985.

321   Letter to PDPH from Michael Burr, President of the Victoria Real Estate Board, 22 October 1985.

322   The Hon. Ray Hnatyshyn, President, Queen's Privy Council for Canada and Government House Leader. Telex, November 1985, PDPH 1985 file.

323   Segment is from the final section of a speech, 26 June 1986, to the Victoria Chapter of the Real Estate Institute of Canada, on the theme "The Effect of Population Change on Real Estate" following the 1986 FIABCI World Congress in Taipei.

324   Adapted from Cuthbert Holmes's text of corporate principles for Pemberton Holmes Ltd., printed in company pamphlet, "The First Sixty Years."

325   Marty Douglas, director and sales manager, Coast Realty Group, Comox Valley, quoting Pip, "What's so bad about part-timers?" *REM/Real Estate Magazine* 1 May 2001. http://remonline.com/rem/news/newspage.aspx?pageid=1064&status=yes&top=75; accessed 2326 hrs 25 Nov 06, cjt.

326   Address by Pip Holmes to members of the Real Estate Institute of B.C. on its twenty-fifth anniversary, from PDPH "1980s speeches" file.

327   Ibid.

328   Conversation with Pip and Catherine Holmes, 24 Jan 07. cjt.

329   Pip Holmes speech to the Victoria Chapter of the Real Estate Institute of Canada, 26 June 1986, Harbour Towers Hotel, Victoria.

330   The 11 Victoria Militia Service Battalion (VMSB) stood to on 1 September 1970, with roots back to 1950. http://www.army.dnd.ca/11SERVICE_BATTALION/history.htm; accessed 12 Mar 07, cjt.

331   Conversation with Pip Holmes, Monday 26 February 2007, cjt.

332   Pip's notes for speech to 11 (Victoria) Service Battalion cadets, 1985 file. cjt.

333   Segment of Pip Holmes speech at the Pemberton Holmes Ltd. centenary celebration, Oak Bay Marina Restaurant, 11 February 1987.

334   Excerpt from transcription of Daphne Goode interview with Pip Holmes from DVD of her Rogers Cable TV program, *Movers and Shakers,* at the start of the 1987 Pemberton Holmes Ltd. centenary celebrations. Transcribed Fri 4 May 07 by Camilla Turner.

335   William Miller, "Century of public service for Pemberton, Holmes," *Times-Colonist,* 7 February 1987, p. B-1.

336   First-growth forest segment west of Cameron Lake on the route to Port Alberni. Letter dated 10 February
      1920 to F.B. Pemberton, c/o Pemberton & Son, Victoria, from "the B.C. Minister of Mines" [William
      Sloan?]: "I have yours of the 5th inst. with reference to the preservation of some part of our Vancouver
      Island standing timber, particularly that lying between Cameron Lake and the foot of the Alberni Hill,
      for scenic purposes. May I say that I appreciate the importance of this and am taking the matter up with
      Hon. T.D. Pattullo, Minister of Lands, within whose department this comes."

337   Emcee for the speeches and presentations was Ida Clarkson, host of *The Noon Show*, a live one-hour
      program seen in Victoria for thirty years, starting 1961. Drew Snider, "TV showed us ourselves," *Times
      Colonist*; information from
      http://www.friends.ca/News/Friends_News/archives/articles03070401.asp; accessed 16 July 2007, cjt.

338   Segment of Pip Holmes' speech at the Pemberton Holmes Ltd. centenary reception, 11 February 1987,
      Oak Bay Marina. Pip's remarks transcribed May 2007 by Camilla Turner from a DVD copy of the
      original tape.

339   Pat Moore, governor of the Real Estate Foundation, discussing the rationale for the Dermot Murphy
      Lecture Series on Applied Ethics, said: "He set an exceptionally high standard of conduct during his many
      years in the profession, and we felt some form of recognition would be appropriate." The seven public
      presentations sponsored by the Real Estate Foundation wrapped up 5 December 1996, having examined
      comprehensively seven questions: "The Doctrine of Public Trust and the Real Estate Professions";
      "Putting Ethics into Planning and Land Use Policies"; "Professional Ethics and Codes for Planners,
      Real Estate Agents, Developers, and Architects"; "Greater Victoria's Land Use Future"; "Developing
      Moral Leadership: Theory and Practice"; "Techniques for Working Through Ethical Quandaries"; and
      "Kelowna and Environments: Growth Management and the Need for Dialogue." Dermot Murphy Lecture
      Series, online at http://www.realestatefoundation.com/publications/newsletter/97_21-3.html; accessed 27
      August 2007, cjt.

340   G.E. Mortimore, "Pemberton Holmes, 100 Years Later," *Victoria's Business Report*, Vol. 5, No. 10
      (October 1987), p. 32.

341   G.E. Mortimore, "Pemberton Holmes, 100 Years Later," *Victoria's Business Report*, Vol. 5, No. 10
      (October 1987), pp. 28-32.

342   Ibid., p. 28.

343   Ibid., pp. 28-29.

344   Ibid., p. 29.

345   Ibid., p. 29.

346   "Holmes names cousin firm's new manager," *Times-Colonist*, Wed 18 Nov 87, p. B-12.

347   G.E. Mortimore, "Pemberton Holmes, 100 Years Later," *Victoria's Business Report*, Vol. 5, No. 10
      (October 1987), pp. 31-32.

348   Conversation with Catherine Holmes, 26 Jan 07, on phone; separate conversation with Pip Holmes, 28
      Jan 07. cjt.

349   Lawrie Wallace had worked with distinguished jurist Mr. Justice Tom Norris and UBC's Prof. Frederick
      Bowers in the late 1950s on electoral boundary reform at the time the province's 1958 real estate act
      was being drafted. Wallace is mentioned at various times through the decades in the online record
      of debates in the B.C. Legislative Assembly, including a 1981 debate on amending the real estate bill.
      See also 1980 reference to Wallace, Wednesday 5 March 1980, night sitting, p. 1282 (http://leg.bc.ca/
      hansard/32nd2nd/32p_02s_800305z.htm); and 1989 budget debate speech by Mr. Mowat, Debates of the

Legislative Assembly of B.C. (*Hansard*), Tuesday 4 April 1989, afternoon sitting, p. 5870, (http://www.leg.bc.ca/hansard/34th3rd/34p_03s_890404p.htm#05870) ; accessed Sat 17 March 2007, cjt.

350   http://www.fccbc.ca/NewsletterArticles/DavidLam.htm; accessed 12 March 07, cjt.

351   British Columbia Government House Foundation website:
       http://www.ltgov.bc.ca/house/foundation.htm; accessed 31 May 07, cjt.

352   Note dated 3 October 1988 to Pip Holmes from Robert G. (Bob) Rogers after the end of his term as Lieutenant-Governor.

353   Material from an undated speech, which from internal evidence was delivered the night of the federal election, 21 Nov 1988, looking back on Philip White's career and welcoming David and Dorothy Lam to Government House.

354   http://en.wikipedia.org/wiki/Canadian_federal_election,_1988; accessed 25 Jan 07, cjt.

355   Letter dated 13 May 1989 to Pip Holmes from FIABCI world president Glyn T.H. Ing.

356   Letter dated 23 March 1991 to Pip Holmes from Phil Holmes (Philip C.M. Holmes of Sidney, B.C.).

357   Letter 25 April 1988 to Pip Holmes from Lawrence J. Wallace, President and Chairman, Royal Theatre Lobby Addition Committee. The McPherson Foundation was later named the McPherson Playhouse Foundation.

358   Letter dated 17 December 1990 to Pip Holmes from Lawrence J. (Lawrie) Wallace, Royal Theatre Restoration project.

359   Draft of a letter handwritten by Pip Holmes in his 1990 file, from its context and position perhaps November 1990.

360   Letter dated 18 February 1991 to Pip Holmes *et al* from Lawrie J. Wallace, Chairman, Royal Theatre Restoration.

361   Website of the 11th (Victoria) Service Battalion,
       http://www.army.dnd.ca/11SERVICE_BATTALION/history.htm; accessed 12 Mar 07, cjt.

362   Selective economic sanctions imposed internationally against South Africa in 1985 were gradually being lifted as the National Party government began dismantling the apartheid system in the early 1990s. The first free general elections were held in 1994, and Nelson Mandela became president. http://www.africanaencyclopedia.com/apartheid/apartheid.html; accessed Tues 3 July 07, cjt.

363   Conference program papers, FIABCI World President Hajime Tsuboi's opening address to the delegates, 25 May 1992, FIABCI 1992 World Congress, Montreux, Switzerland. Mr. Tsuboi was, according to his letterhead, Chairman of the Board, Mitsui Real Estate Development Co. Ltd., Tokyo.

364   Ibid.

365   About his grandmother, Cuthbert's mother, Pip commented: "Can you imagine what it must have been like for her to move from Switzerland to the Caleb Pike homestead? It's a tiny log cabin beside Holmes Peak, a long, long ride on horseback to and from Victoria, which itself was still small. She used to get into town only once a month and said to friends that it was all becoming very difficult. A very strange existence indeed it must have been for her after her gentle, sociable life in India and in Europe." Conversation with Pip and Catherine Holmes in their dining room, 23 Feb 07. cjt.

366   Conversation with Pip Holmes, 14 January 2007, cjt.

367   The FIABCI Canada honorary life membership was awarded to him on Monday 26 October 1992, and

the CMHC Distinguished Realtor Award on Tuesday 27 October 1992.

368   *Times-Colonist*, Wed 28 Oct 1992, p. D-10.

369   Ibid.

370   Gorde Hunter, "One Man's Opinion," *Times-Colonist*, Monday 2 November 1992, [n.p.].

371   Gorde Hunter, "One Man's Opinion," *Times-Colonist*, Monday 14 December 1987, [n.p.]

372   The beginning of Elizabeth II's reign was 6 Feb 1952; her coronation was 2 June 1953. Wording is quoted from text attached to the framed certificate, front and reverse sides, PDPH 1990s file, Box #9.

373   Letter dated 29 May 1992 to Pip Holmes from Alastair C.M. MacIsaac, Colonel Commandant, Victoria and Vancouver Island Corps, Canadian Corps of Commissionaires: "Your nomination was approved formally at the annual general meeting ... 28 May 1992. The term of office for an Honorary Governor is for a period of six years." He had been Chair of their Board of Governors from 1982 to 1984.

374   Letter in December 1991 to Pip Holmes from R.E. Michael Ziegler, President, Canadian Real Estate Association, Ottawa.

375   The front door of Pip's own home came from Mountjoy, home of Grandfather Pem (F.B. Pemberton) on Foul Bay Road. Conversation with Pip 14 January 2007, cjt.

376   Ten years later he attended the sixtieth anniversary events as well.

377   St. Clement Danes. "In 1941 the church was ... badly damaged ... by incendiary bombs. In 1956 work began on restoring it. The Royal Air Force was the main benefactor of the church, and in 1958 it was dedicated as the Central Church of the Royal Air Force. The book of remembrance inside the church lists the names of over 125,000 service men and women who lost their lives in the war."
http://www.virtual-london.com/sightseeing/places-of-worship/st-clement-danes-central-church-for-the-raf.html; accessed 21 Aug 07, cjt.

378   Conversations with Catherine Holmes, Wed 13 June 07 and Friday 27 July 2007. cjt.

379   Letter dated 26 October 1994 to Pip Holmes from A.P. Viner, President and CEO, Rogers Broadcasting, Toronto; the information on CJVI origins is from the website of the Vancouver Radio Museum, http://www3.telus.net/vanradiomuseum/CJVIGallery.html; accessed 22 June 2007, cjt.

380   Letter in October 1993 to Pip Holmes from Lieutenant-Governor David C. Lam, concerning Lake O'Hara information and the Canada 125 Medal.

381   The Lieutenant-General E.C. Ashton Armoury opened officially in Saanich on 5 February 1994. "The Armoury now houses 11 (Victoria) Service Battalion, 11 (Victoria) Medical Company, 12 Military Police Platoon, the Lieutenant-General E.C. Ashton Museum and No. 3005, Royal Canadian Army Cadet Corps (11 (Victoria) Service Battalion)."
http://www.army.dnd.ca/11SERVICE_BATTALION/history.htm; accessed 24 June 2007, cjt.

382   The photo of the two men ran on the front page of *Lookout*, a publication serving Canadian Forces Base Esquimalt. The photo credit published is B.P. Clarke. *Lookout*, Vol. 42, No. 11 (17 March 1997), p. 1.

383   Andrea M. Pennells, "From Buthelezi to Brentwood," *Brentonian*, Fall 1997-Spring 1998, p. 30.

384   Rorke's Drift background from PDPH 1998 file and two websites.
(1) The event was at Rorke's Drift, Wednesday 22 January through Thursday 23 January 1879; http://www.rorkesdriftvc.com; accessed 1045 hrs Fri 16 Feb 07, cjt.
(2) In one account of events, the British were attacked on 22 January by Zulu Chief Cetshwayo, and were shocked by the extent of the Zulu resistance. They lost at least 850 of their own men and 470 black

allies. The Zulus lost approximately a thousand soldiers;
http://www.places.co.za/html/rorkesdrift.html; accessed Fri 16 Feb 07, cjt.

385   Bertram was the younger brother of Henry, genealogical head of "the Henry line" and Pip's forebear. Bertram was the one who bought his older brother's land in South Africa and stayed, whereas Henry returned to England. See Chapter One.

386   The dinner under discussion was held 24 January 1998; the battle was 22-23 January 1879.

387   Andrea M. Pennells, "From Buthelezi to Brentwood," *Brentonian*, Fall 1997-Spring 1998, p. 30.

388   Patrick Murphy, "Formal Feast," The Islander section, *Times-Colonist*, 8 March 1998.

389   Patrick Murphy, "Zulu uniform unveiling celebrates epic battle," *Times-Colonist*, Saturday 24 January 1998, p. A5. Entry at Mangosuthu Buthelezi, http://www.britannica.com/eb/article-9018316/Mangosuthu-G-Buthelezi; acccessed1636 hrs Sun 2 Sept 07, cjt. Mangosuthu Gatsha Buthelezi is described as "Zulu chief, head (1972–94) of the nonindependent black state of KwaZulu, and leader of the Inkatha Freedom Party. Buthelezi was descended from the Zulu royal line through the legendary King Cetshwayo."

390   Andrea M. Pennells, "From Buthelezi to Brentwood," *Brentonian*, Fall 1997-Spring 1998, p. 30.

391   Letter to Pip Holmes from Andrea Pennells, early March 1998.

392   John Ralston Saul, *The Unconscious Civilization* (Toronto: House of Anansi Press, 1996); segment at http://www.mcgill.ca/newsroom/news/?ItemID=9975; accessed 20 July 2007, cjt.

393   Conversation with Catherine Holmes, 13 June 07. cjt.

394   Note to Pip and Catherine Holmes from Garde Gardom, 25 June 2001.

395   Legislative Assembly of British Columbia website, 37th Parliament, first session: http://www.leg.bc.ca/37th1st/index.htm; accessed 20 July 07, cjt.

396   Legislative Assembly of British Columbia website, 37th Parliament, second session: http://www.leg.bc.ca/hansard/37th2nd/h10724p.htm; accessed 20 July 07, cjt.

397   Remarks by Her Honour Iona Campagnolo at the annual meeting of honorary aides-de-camp, Government House, 24 January 2004. Full text on the website, http://www.ltgov.bc.ca/whatsnew/sp/sp_jan24_2004.htm; accessed 25 Nov 06, cjt.

398   Letter dated 4 September 2001 to Pip and Catherine Holmes from Betty Chater, Co-Chair, Pemberton Memorial Chapel Restoration Committee, Alumnae Association of the Royal Jubilee Hospital School of Nursing.

399   Letter dated 12 May 2003 to Mr. Philip D. Pemberton Holmes via Pemberton & Son, 1000 Fort Street, Third Floor, from Sharon Welsh, Development Officer, Greater Victoria Hospitals Foundation.

400   Letter dated 15 January 2005 to Pip Holmes from Barbara Owen, Co-chairperson, Pemberton Chapel Restoration Committee. Construction of the wheelchair-accessible Pemberton Heritage Garden, Royal Jubilee Hospital, started in January 2005. See also article on Barbara Owen and the nine-year project by Jeff Bell, "Retired nurses help create a tranquil retreat at hospital," *Times Colonist*, Mon 30 July 2007, p. C-1. Dr. Nitobe was a distinguished agricultural economist, scholar, philosopher, author, educator and statesman. Born in Morioka in 1862, he became a Quaker in Philadelphia (where he met his future wife). Dr. Nitobe attended the Versailles Peace Conference during 1918, perhaps meeting Cuthbert Holmes there, and stayed in Europe while the League of Nations was being created. He became its Assistant Director General until he returned to Japan in 1926 to chair the Institute of Pacific Relations. A prolific

author, he achieved his aim of being a cultural bridge between Japan and the West. *A Japanese View of Quakers* is one title among his books in English. Dr. Nitobe died in 1933 in Victoria, B.C., after representing Japan at an international peace conference at Banff. A number of gardens and museums have been founded in his memory, and a generous gift from the Japanese father of a young patient at the Royal Jubilee Hospital in Victoria funded the creation of its Inazo Nitobe Memorial Garden. http://www.nitobe.org/inazo_nitobe.php and other print and online sources; accessed 30 Oct 07, cjt.

401   Mrs. Theresa Jane Pemberton was generous, and J.D.'s son F.B. continued the family support for hospital projects. G.E. Mortimore, "Pemberton Holmes, 100 Years Later," *Victoria's Business Report*, Vol. 5, No. 10 (October 1987), p. 28: "the firm funnelled in $13 million in mortgage capital from friends and business connections in Britain to finance the growth of Victoria and Vancouver." F.B. supported projects in both cities.

402   "Pemberton Memorial Operating Room," project documentation package, PDPH file, 1990s-2005.

403   The Brentwood College School motto is *De Manu in Manum*, "From hand to hand." The hand in the school crest holds and passes a torch, a symbol of learning and civilization. BSC website, www.brentwood.bc.ca

404   Conversations at lunch and again at tea with Pip, Wed 3 Jan 07. cjt.

405   Annual Christmas letter dated 11 December 2004 to friends and family from Pip and Catherine Holmes, concerning events of August 2004 and onward; plus conversation with Pip at home, 22 January 2007, cjt.

406   Ibid.

407   Ibid.

408   Text and photos of the Honorary Aides-de-camp Dinner in honour of Colonel Philip 'Pip' Holmes, Government House, Victoria, BC, 06/01/21, are on the website of the Office of the Lieutenant-Governor > Speeches > Archive > 21 January 2006: http://www.ltgov.bc.ca/whatsnew/sp/sp_jan21_1_2006.htm

409   Letter to Mr. and Mrs. Pip Holmes from the parents of one boy receiving bursary funding, 8 December 2006. Pip set up a trust at Brentwood College School to continue this funding for students.

410   Jim and Nic Hume, "Diary of an officer and a gentleman," Hume & Hume interview series, Monitor section, *Times Colonist*, 11 March 2007, p. D-5.

411   Alfred Lord Tennyson's 1889 poem, "Crossing the Bar"; http://www.bartleby.com/42/650.html; accessed Sun 29 July 07, cjt.

412   In the King James' version, "To everything there is a season, and a time to every purpose under the heaven ... " www.biblenotes.net/ecclesiastes.html; accessed 20 June 2007, cjt.

413   Andrea Pennells, "Remembering Pip: A Tribute," *Brentonian*, Summer 2007, p. 3.

414   "My Own Dear Land," written by author and lyricist William A. Dunkerley (1852-1941) under pseudonym John Oxenham, and set to the familiar tune of "Londonderry Air"; lyrics online, www.cyberhymnal.org/htm/m/o/modearla.htm; also Remembrance Day website, http://www.mimico-by-the-lake.com/NOV1105.HTM; accessed Tues 28 Aug 07, cjt.

415   The brief text put into the order of service contained contributions from a number of people: "Pip, the name by which he was universally known, was a distinguished leader in the real estate profession locally, provincially, nationally and internationally. With vision and foresight he served and contributed tremendously to the community and was deeply committed to the furtherance of education. Also of paramount importance in his life was his dedication in his service to the Crown. Pip had many hobbies. He loved to ride his bicycle, was a keen sailor, hiker, photographer, birdwatcher and, latterly, a golfer.

All his pursuits were entered into with enthusiasm and an ever-present wit, and with his sense of humour and twinkling eyes, he believed in creating the most enjoyment possible in and around the serious events of daily life. He had a rare zest for living, a compassionate, wise and mischievous buoyancy and quality of leadership that inspired people to broaden their outlooks and become their best. He graced our lives through his life and remains a gift to be treasured always."

416   Dermot Murphy's remarks at the Pemberton Holmes centenary celebration, Oak Bay Marina Restaurant, 11 February 1987. Transcribed from the DVD record of the event, 21 May 07, by Camilla Turner.

417   Richard Holmes, "A Tribute to Pip, 2nd February 1924 – 18th May 2007," a collection of thoughts and comments from himself and family members, printout given to Catherine Holmes, May 2007, p. 1.

418   Ibid., pp. 1-2.

419   Ibid., p. 3.

420   Arvid Chalmers, when asked by Nicole Lee of Pemberton Holmes Ltd. Cloverdale. E-mail to Catherine Holmes from Nicole Lee, office manager, Pemberton Holmes Ltd. Cloverdale, Wednesday 31 October 2007.

421   Letter dated 25 May 2007 to Catherine Holmes from R.H. (Bob) Thomson, Toronto.

422   Note dated 22 May 2007 to Catherine Holmes from Ms. Penelope Hett, Dana Point, California. Pip and Penelope's mother were cousins.

423   Note dated 28 May 2007 to Andrea Pennells for Catherine Holmes, from Norman Redcliffe of Redcliffe Investments Ltd., North Vancouver, B.C.

424   Debates of the Legislative Assembly of B.C. (Hansard), Speech from the Throne, fourth session of the 38th parliament, Tuesday 12 February 2008, p. 9621, http://www.leg.bc.ca/hansard/38th4th/H80212p.htm; accessed Wed 20 Feb 08, cjt.

425   Letter in June 2007 to Catherine Holmes from Mr. J. Michael Roberts and Mrs. Sharon Roberts.

426   Despite Catherine's much-repeated admonition—"The book is Pip's story, not mine"—her own obituary is of interest in the context of their shared lives and is therefore included here. http://www.legacy.com/can-victoria/Obituaries.asp?Page=SearchResults; accessed Sun 23 December 2007, cjt.

Catherine's obituary appeared in the Victoria *Times Colonist* Saturday 22 December and Sunday 23 December 2007 and online at the *Times Colonist* website (433403) on the same dates.

"HOLMES, Catherine. Catherine Cecily Anne Holmes passed away very peacefully at home in Oak Bay in the early hours of Thursday 13th December, 2007. She was predeceased by her loving husband, Philip Despard Pemberton Holmes ("Pip"), who died on 18 May 2007. She is survived by her nieces Penelope and Caroline, her stepson Craig, stepdaughters Diana, Susan and Jenny and their families, the extended Holmes clan and other close family friends. Catherine was born on 8 February 1923. She was the younger daughter of Commander and Mrs. Cecil Webb of Wayside, Bursledon, Hampshire, England. Her father was an excellent and very keen yachtsman and both his daughters were brought up to sail. Catherine and her elder sister Joan were educated at a Quaker School in Saffron Waldron. Catherine joined the Wrens in 1941 and until the end of the war spent her time ferrying people between their ships and landing craft. After the war, she sailed with Uffa Fox, who was a sailing companion of Prince Philip, The Duke of Edinburgh, and worked for Adlard Coles, the well-known author and sailor. In 1949, Catherine married John Mead and soon after they emigrated to Canada, arriving by ship into Montreal and travelling by train across Canada to Vancouver and by boat to Victoria. There, Catherine worked as an executive secretary at the Hudson Bay Company. When John became ill, she cared for him and still found time to obtain her pilots licence. In 1960, Catherine was widowed when John Mead died of a heart attack. She then decided to visit friends in Montana and stayed on to work for a time on a ranch there. Looking for greater challenges, she returned to Canada and joined the Canadian External Affairs Department. After intense training, she was posted to Moscow in 1962 at the heart of the "cold war," an experience that gave her many stories to tell. During home leave in 1964, Catherine reconnected with Pip, who with his wife Joan had been good friends of John and Catherine in earlier days but whose marriage had been dissolved during Catherine's time in Moscow. Pip and Catherine were married on 22 August 1964 at the Church of Our Lord and lived happily together in Oak Bay until Pip's sad death. While not travelling with Pip's work, they spent many happy times sailing on their 35-foot sloop, taking to the skies with Catherine at the controls and graciously hosting their many relatives and friends at their home and at Maltby Lake, all of whom they made most welcome. Catherine will be sadly missed by the many people from near and far whom she touched over the years with her warmth and humour, and whom she inspired with her tireless energy and leadership. There will be a memorial service for Catherine at the Church of Our Lord, 626 Blanshard Street, Victoria, B.C., on 9 February 2008 at 11:30 a.m."

IDENTIFICATIONS AND CORRECTIONS

THE MAIN SOURCES for photographs were Pip and Catherine, though several other people were very kind in providing specific photos. If a reader can add identifications to the photos used in the manuscript, a letter or an annotated photocopy of the image with the additional information would be welcome.

Releasing misinformation into the public record is to be avoided, if at all possible. Care was taken to keep track of sources while researching the outline from Pip's files and during the writing, and various parts of the manuscript were read at the fact-checking stage by people with specific expertise. The intent was to catch obvious mistakes and minimize errors, but precautions may not have prevented them. The interpretation of events in the manuscript, as drawn from Pip's files and interviews with him, is my own, but if a reader has additional information that sheds more light on Pip's life, it would be welcome. Correspondence will reach the author if sent via Trafford Publishing Ltd., 2657 Wilfert Road, Victoria, B.C. Canada V9B 5Z3.

ON THE COVER

THE PHOTO THAT wraps front and back covers is one of Pip's own. His shot of the British Columbia coast was taken from a plane window while he was flying back from Europe in 1998. He has caught the sharp peaks of the Cascades inland and the Coast Range along the Pacific, the profile of Washington State's Mount Baker on the horizon and the peaks, valleys and mists of Vancouver Island in the foreground.

The five smaller photos on the back cover include the FIABCI medallion worn while in office by the International Real Estate Federation's world president; wildflowers and ferns of the rainforest floor, photographed by Pip from the boardwalk near Hot Springs Cove, Vancouver Island; Pip and Catherine visiting on good terms with a smallish elephant in Bangkok; Pip in uniform with his Distinguished Flying Cross and other medals, as photographed by B.C. Government House Aide-de-Camp Dave Harris; and Pemberton Holmes staff in costume during the Victorian Days community festival in Victoria, B.C.

ISBN 1425140068-8